The social history of Canada

MICHAEL BLISS, EDITOR

A STUDY OF WORK AND PAY IN THE

CAMPS OF CANADA 1903-1914

The bunkhouse man

EDMUND W. BRADWIN

WITH AN INTRODUCTION BY JEAN BURNET

UNIVERSITY OF TORONTO PRESS

© University of Toronto Press 1972

Toronto and Buffalo

All rights reserved

ISBN (casebound) 0-8020-1848-3

ISBN (paperback) 0-8020-6135-4

Microfiche ISBN 0-8020-0166-1

LC 79-163834

Printed in the United States of America

An introduction

BY JEAN BURNET

The Bunkhouse Man, based on a doctoral dissertation submitted to Columbia University in 1922, was published in 1928 in the university's series of 'Studies in History, Economics, and Public Law,' along with many outstanding works of scholarship, including several by Canadians.[1] Written at a time when sociology was young in the United States and in its infancy at universities in English-speaking Canada, it was probably not classified as sociology by its author. As an attempt to understand an aspect of social life, it would be so classified today. Since it examines that aspect of social life in a particular time and place, even though many of its themes are of continuing or recurrent interest, it is also a contribution to social history.

The story of the building of Canada's railroads is an important part of its history as a nation, and has attracted the attention of its economic and political historians, its journalists, and its poets. But most accounts of railway building have almost nothing to say of the labourers who did the actual work, and the life they led in the construction camps. Dr Bradwin offered a graphic picture of the bunkhouse men and the conditions they endured during the period 1903-14. He paid particular attention to the railway construction camps (giving us, in passing, the best account of how railways were built in Canada), but indicated that much of what he said applied as well to other kinds of camps and works.

The period Bradwin dealt with was one of prosperity and growth. The government had responded to the depression of the nineties with vigorous policies of railway construction and immigration, and the policies, in combination with other factors, were succeeding. The population was expanding at a rate unprecedented until then and not exceeded since. Of the two and three-quarter million immigrants who flowed into the country, many participated in the land rush to the prairie west that began late in the nineteenth century: the population of the three prairie provinces more than trebled between the 1901 and 1911 censuses. An equal number took part in the development of industry in the cities and towns of central Canada: the population of Montreal increased by 50 per cent, and that of Toronto by 75 per cent, between 1901 and 1911. Somewhat fewer went to British Columbia, where many types of enterprise were booming. Still others joined, for shorter or longer periods, the migratory work force associated with railway, road-building, logging, mining, and hydro development camps.

Although the growth of the urban centres was overshadowed by the even more spectacular growth of cities in the United States, social scientists and historians have seized upon prairie settlement in the early part of the twentieth century as a feature of Canadian society of special interest. They have studied the setting up of communities, particularly ethnic communities, the problems of the wheat economy, the rise of co-operatives, the development of the Progressives, the CCF, and Social Credit, and the growth of religious movements in the west. They have been aided by the westerners themselves, many of whom have written poignant accounts of their homesteading and life on the prairies.

The camps, like the settling of the prairies, have been a characteristic Canadian phenomenon, but they have not drawn comparable attention. Dr Bradwin's study is the only one devoted to them.[2] Perhaps it is because social scientists have found it easier to deal with communities on the one hand and migration on the other than with something in between: a social form that has in many of its characteristics been widespread and persistent but that has no fixed location. Perhaps it is because the campmen themselves, often illiterate and always on the move, have not told their story. Perhaps it is because the camps have been in the north – the mid-north rather than the Arctic – and only recently have most Canadians begun to recognize what Bradwin saw clearly, the importance for Canada of the social and economic development of the north.

The camps were numerous: Bradwin estimated that as many as three thousand large camps were in operation in some years. They employed 200,000 men in the course of a year, upwards of 5 per cent of the total male labour force. They were also durable: they existed from early days of settlement down to the 1920s, and, as Bradwin foresaw, still exist in the 1970s and will probably continue to do so for a long time. Though individual camps are often short-lived, collectively they are by no means an ephemeral phenomenon.

The camps were also important. In the decade Bradwin examined, the bunkhouse men doubled the railway mileage of Canada, building the nation's second and third transcontinental railway lines, the Canadian Northern and the National Transcontinental, across the vast empty spaces of the country. It was soon evident, especially with the dislocations caused by the First World War, that the lines were not economically viable, and they were merged into the

Canadian National Railways. Meanwhile the railway construction camps, and the road construction, logging, mining, and hydro camps as well, had made a large contribution to the development of agriculture in the west and industry in central Canada. They had also helped to shape the lives of the thousands upon thousands of men who had been part of them.

Bradwin noted that it was because of the government's involvement in the construction of the National Transcontinental that he had been free to study the camps along that line. The Eastern Division of the National Transcontinental, from Moncton to Winnipeg, was being constructed by the government, and on completion would be the publicly owned section of the railway. In theory this policy was a significant change from the previous system of granting large amounts of cash and land to encourage private capitalists to construct railways. But, as Bradwin makes clear, the system of awarding contracts to private companies, which engaged sub-contractors, some of whom engaged still other sub-contractors, meant that the camps on this government project were no different from those on any private enterprise. Government inspectors exerted little control over the conditions of work of the rank-and-file labourers; the only difference between private and public construction seems to have been that there were more waste and corruption under the latter system.

As Bradwin showed, the campmen's rewards for their labour were meagre at best. They were provided with good and abundant food, but their living conditions were uncomfortable and unsanitary, their wages were low, and the prices they were charged for supplies were exorbitant. Although some managed to get the stake they sought in order to establish themselves in farming, and some to gain skill or responsibility enough to rise from bunkhouse to residency, many of them left the camps after weeks or months penniless as they had arrived. Fifteen years later Bradwin could confidently state that matters had improved. The publication of his book led to further improvements, and in recent years there have been even more, as standards have changed and technology has developed. Whereas Bradwin could compare the camps unfavourably to nearby towns, today the camps frequently have better facilities than towns of single industry in the north. However, to a large extent conditions were an inevitable result of the transient and isolated nature of the camps and the vulnerability of a foreign-born labour force, and reports from construction camps today indicate that bunkhouse men are still among the disadvantaged, sometimes economically and more often socially and culturally.[3]

The camps did not face all of the problems of settled communities. Their population was almost entirely male and included neither the very young nor the very old. Further, many men stayed in the camps for only a short time, and even those for whom construction provided a career went outside when the job in one particular location was finished or when conditions in a camp were intolerable. Families and schools and some kinds of health and recreation services were unnecessary; religious, political, and legal institutions were rudimentary. Trade unions might have pressed for higher wages and better working conditions, but not only were the unions of the time fully occupied with industrial workers in the cities and larger towns but also it was hard for them to win support among unskilled, transient, and largely immigrant workers.[4]

Outside of economic problems, Bradwin discussed problems concerning medical services at greatest length. The population, composed of fairly young males, was a basically healthy one – 'splendidly endowed [with] rugged strength and native hardihood' – but the lack of sanitary facilities and the hazards of the job made such services essential. The problem of securing and maintaining medical care in isolated camps had led to a contract or prepayment system that was continued in some of the company towns that developed out of the camps, and seems to have been a near ancestor of medicare. As Bradwin indicated, the system was costly to the workers, who paid regularly but rarely had access to medical services and still more rarely to the services of fully qualified doctors; it was, however, profitable to the sub-contractors. It has been easier to improve sanitation, introduce safety measures, and provide emergency care than to remedy the shortage of medical personnel, still acute in northern camps and communities in spite of the efforts of companies, community leaders, and government.[5]

The camps represented the introduction of many of the workers to Canadian life. Labour on construction has always been an immigrant occupation in Canada: many of the jobs require little skill, make few linguistic demands, and offer conditions of work and wages unappealing to the native-born. In the mid-nineteenth century Irish immigrants built the canals and railways; later Chinese contract labourers undertook some of the hardest and most hazardous work on the Canadian Pacific Railway; today, in postwar Toronto and Montreal, Italians are putting up houses and apartment buildings and digging subways. Bradwin was dealing with a period in which immigrants were entering Canada from many lands. Virtually every ethnic group was represented in the bunkhouses, or, in the case of the Syrians, Armenians, and Jews, among the peddlers and traders who also formed part of the camp or among the proprietors of employment offices supplying the camps and works. An exception was that the Chinese were excluded from work on the Grand Trunk Pacific (the Western Division of the National Transcontinental) by its charter, and only admitted to alleviate a shortage of labour. Bradwin presented a detailed analysis of the ethnic division of labour, and although he was not concerned with the speed with which various groups surmounted their entrance status, his analysis offers clues to this.

In the light of recent studies of the occupational and income distribution of Canadians, Bradwin's description of the major division among the ethnic groups into 'white men' – the Canadian born, the American and British immigrants, and such other immigrants as won acceptance from them – and 'foreigners' has considerable interest. The white men, who in the camps held most of the jobs that carried responsibility or required skill, had greater opportunities outside the camps also, and consequently were a smaller proportion of the bunkhouse men than of the Canadian population as a whole. They were more numerous in the residencies, where many more amenities were available. They correspond closely to the groups that now have easy access to the middle and upper socio-economic levels and to élite positions, except that they then apparently included French-speaking Canadians. This adds to the evidence already available that with industrialization the status of French Canadians declined.

Bradwin consistently wrote of French-speaking Canadians and English-speaking Canadians rather than French Canadians and English Canadians. Unfortunately he did not discuss his reasons for this. It would be interesting to know to what extent he, writing more than forty years ago, felt as did the Royal Commission on Bilingualism and Biculturalism, that it was morally preferable to define groups within Canadian society in terms of language rather than ethnic identity or origin.[6]

The thinking of even liberal and compassionate men of the 1920s was characterized by a racism that John Porter holds to have been important in building the Canadian class system.[7] Bradwin's discussion of ethnic differences among the campmen, though occasionally phrased in outmoded terms and often influenced by stereotypes, seems to be almost entirely free of this. His description of the various groups, except, possibly, the Indians, shows insight into the environmental circumstances that helped to shape their attitudes and develop their abilities. He preferred to speak of attainments rather than capacity. He even recorded the discriminatory attitude – 'racial instinct' – of Canadians towards Asians without indicating that he himself shared it. It would be remarkable if he did not: he was writing at a time when opposition to Chinese immigration in particular was extremely bitter, and was about to find expression in the Chinese Immigration (Exclusion) Act of 1923.

Bradwin showed a rare ability to describe with detachment the behaviour of ethnic groupings and of individuals for whom he had deep compassion and concern. It would have been easy for him to depict the bunkhouse men as paragons of strength and virtue, or conversely to stress their failings – brawling, for example, or squandering their earnings on alcohol and gambling in the towns in the off-periods – in making his case for changes in the camp system. His detached look at the situation, revealing as it did the kinship of the bunkhouse men to the rest of mankind, is much more effective than either glorification or denigration would have been.

It is notable also that he exposed the evils of the camp system without blaming a personal villain for them. To have done so would have been to oversimplify. Bradwin was keenly aware of the differences among camps, and preferred to describe a series of cases and to account for variations among them rather than to give a single generalized picture. He also understood the context of the camps – their relation to the many-levelled system of railway building; to employment bureaux; to various types of community; to religious, political, and educational institutions; to public opinion; and to other job opportunities open to the workers. In conveying that understanding to his readers, he prevented them from assuaging their consciences by making a scapegoat of some group of 'bosses.' Instead he tried to goad them to a more difficult course of action, the exertion of pressure for change through a variety of channels – churches, political structures, trade unions, the media, and the universities among them. He was successful. His book created a furore, and as a result some of the reforms he advocated were achieved.

Bradwin was not concerned with general sociological theory, nor did he use elaborate techniques of research and analysis. But his work is in several respects worthy of the attention of Canadian sociologists today. He chose as his object of study a social phenomenon of practical as well as theoretical importance, which was highlighted in Canada; he explained it in social terms, without recourse to biological factors or to moral judgments; he had due regard for the varying forms of the phenomenon and for its several contexts. Finally, he combined the detachment and balance of a scholar with warm human concern and vigorous action. He was not a radical – he is said to have studied Marxian economics in order to confute agitators in the camps, and his references to such agitators are distinctly unsympathetic – but he did practise the sociology of engagement that is being advocated by those who consider themselves radical sociologists today. He was no outsider, unconcerned with finding solutions to the social problems he observed. He played a vigorous role in the camps, attempting both directly and indirectly to improve the lot of the men with whom he worked.

Bradwin's chief sphere of action was education, and, though his one book is a significant contribution to scholarship, it was as a teacher and an educational administrator that he made his career and won renown. As a young man he taught school for a number of years, and became deeply committed to education as a means of improving the quality of life of individuals and of society. Throughout *The Bunkhouse Man* his concern for the education of the campmen, and for the development of strong ties between them and Canadian universities, is evident. One of the characteristics of the ethnic groupings in the camps that he regularly commented upon was their average level of education and their degree of interest in adult education.

As he stated in the 'somewhat personal' introduction to his book, Bradwin went into the camps in 1904 as an instructor for Frontier College.[8] He was a supervisor for the college when he wrote the book. Later he became principal, and remained in that post until his death in 1954 at the age of seventy-seven.

Frontier College is a unique institution, founded in 1899 by a young Presbyterian minister from Nova Scotia, Rev. Alfred Fitzpatrick, to take adult education and recreation into isolated camps and works through the agency of university students. Recently it has also begun to foster community education in isolated and depressed communities. It is a private organization, efficient and successful, deriving its funds from government grants, corporation and individual donations, trade unions, and the student councils of universities. The principle was adopted in 1901 and has been steadfastly maintained that its instructors should be labourer-teachers, working during the day alongside of their students and being paid for their work at prevailing rates, and conducting classes at night for a modest additional stipend. Through the college, hundreds of thousands of workers have become literate, learned English or French, and followed courses in citizenship. For a time, from 1922 to 1931, some were able to obtain university credits, and a few even to complete degrees. In addition, thousands of university students serving as labourer-teachers have acquired experience and funds. The excellence of the college's selection policies and the value of the experience it affords in work and teaching are indicated by the fact that many have achieved high eminence in their later careers.

The college pioneered in the early years of the century in the use of visual aids, in the form of magic-lantern slides, and in the preparation of a basic primer for teaching English as a second language.

Fitzpatrick conceived the college and framed many of its distinctive policies, but Bradwin worked with him for thirty years and then continued to guide the college for twenty more years. He appears to have been an excellent administrator and a gifted publicist. When he died his name was almost synonymous with Frontier College. His book, then, is of interest not only as a contribution to Canadian studies but also as an expression of the views of one of the builders of an important educational institution.

It is fitting that *The Bunkhouse Man* should be reprinted almost half a century after it was written, as Canadians are beginning to repair their neglect of their country's history and outstanding men and to explore the distinctive features of Canada's social structure. It should be of value to social scientists and historians, and of keen interest to many others, including the sons and daughters of the bunkhouse men. That the costs of the book's original publication were borne by the author himself, who took six years to raise the money, is an indication of the advance that has taken place in the financial support of scholarship since the 1920s. That it was first published in the United States, and would not have been written if its author had not had the opportunity of studying at one of that country's great universities, should be a prophylactic against chauvinism.

NOTES

1 Two of the earliest of these were Walter A. Riddell, *The Rise of Ecclesiastical Control in Quebec* (1917), and Samuel Henry Prince, *Catastrophe and Social Change* (1920).
2 A briefer treatment is given in a book by an associate of Bradwin: Alfred Fitzpatrick, *The University in Overalls: A Plea for Part-time Study* (Toronto, 1923).
3 Cf. Trevor Jones, 'Great Slave Lake Railway: They couldn't have picked a better name,' *The Last Post*, I, no 1, Dec. 1968, pp. 32-8.
4 Bradwin did not discuss prostitution in the camps. A. R. M. Lower described the arrival near a construction camp in northern Ontario in 1910 of a convoy of canoes bringing 'Boxcar Rosie' and her retinue, who set up a 'tent of ill-fame.' He noted that the authorities condoned the visits because they kept the men contented. *My First Seventy-five Years* (Toronto, 1967), p. 65.
5 Cf. Rex A. Lucas and Alexander Himelfarb, 'Some Social Aspects of Medical Care in Small Communities,' *Canadian Journal of Public Health,* LXII, Jan./Feb. 1971, pp. 6-16.

6 *Report of the Royal Commission on Bilingualism and Biculturalism,* General Introduction, paragraphs 7-10.
7 John Porter, *The Vertical Mosaic: An Analysis of Social Class and Power in Canada* (Toronto, 1965), p. 66.
8 I wish to thank Dr Eric Robinson, principal of Frontier College, for supplying information concerning the development of the college.

The bunkhouse man

EDMUND W. BRADWIN

To the memory of my parents Joseph and Annie Bradwin

Contents

Preface

The most valuable of all capital is that invested in human beings.
Marshall, *Principles of Economics,* Bk. VI, Chap. 4.

FOR TWELVE YEARS following closely on the beginning of the century, the Dominion of Canada passed for the third time through a period of railway expansion. This activity in railway building culminated ultimately in the completion of a second and yet a third transcontinental extending across the Canadian provinces.

Material progress gives pride to any people. The country heard with much satisfaction of achievements, which, overcoming natural difficulties, bridged great rivers, gridironed the prairies, tunneled mountains and welded the far-sundered portions of the Dominion. But even prosperity may soothe – meanwhile other relationships, equally vital for the welfare of the country, had seemingly been overlooked: these pertained to the labour and housing of men employed on works throughout these various undertakings.

Occasional press reports, which multiplied toward the close of the period, told of discontent among the men at work in camps. Complaints were lodged by the workers themselves with the Federal authorities at Ottawa, resulting at times in official investigations being made locally into the nature and practical operation of wage agreements commonly existing between railway contractors and campmen during that particular period. All of which bespoke unsettled conditions of hire in frontier places across Canada, and a lack of accord in the commoner relationships of master and man.

This uneasiness pervading different camps was not confined to any particular work. Wage agreements during the period were very similar wherever the contract system prevailed. Protests came from bunkhouse men in widely different parts of the Dominion – from camps on the Grand Trunk Pacific west of the Rocky Mountains, from works out on the prairie sections, but most often from men on the National Transcontinental, which was hewed in course for eighteen hundred miles across the lands whose many-pronged rivers drain toward Hudson Bay.

What were some of the causes that lay behind this unrest? In answer to this query the present writer has undertaken to show at first hand something of the conditions of work and pay in Canadian camps commonly encountered in the first two decades of the present century. In pursuance of this no attempt is made to study all the various forms of frontier works; a brochure, however, is presented showing somewhat in detail the work of the navvy during the construction of the National Transcontinental.

This particular undertaking, extending in operation halfway across the continent, and having always, during its ten-year period of construction, a great number of large camps, gives the needed perspective for studying the navvy. The fact, also, that the National Transcontinental was sponsored directly by the Canadian people, being under the control of a Railway Commission specially selected by the Dominion government, affords further freedom to examine some of the camps thereon, as seen in practical operation.

An insight into the methods and conditions of employment on the National Transcontinental will give, to those who desire it, an intelligent cross-section of frontier camps of whatever kind. It affords, also, the further opportunity to survey some of the problems that still confront the campman, and those who hire for work in the isolated places of the Dominion.

For, Canada is still a land of camps! Physical conditions compel it so. Great natural resources, combined with a climate that varies much, and often with suddenness, throughout its wide extent, give rise to seasonal works of diverse kinds.

There are years when three thousand large camps are in operation throughout the Dominion. Among other undertakings these activities are usually associated with lumbering, logging on the Pacific coast, and the cutting of pulp; railway work both for maintenance and along new construction; mining, in its earlier stages, and, in recent years, increasing numbers of hydro development camps. The number of men actually engaged on such enterprises is never constant, but in average years it may be safely inferred that fully two hundred thousand men in Canada, at different periods of the year, follow in some form or other the life of the camps.

Canada as a country owes much to its campmen. Down through whole generations the camps have played an important part in shaping the lives of all frontier workers; qualities incidental to such environments have characterized their ways. Yet, even in Canada, few of us seem to realize just all that this means. We overlook the debt which the country owes the workers in these important fields of labour. With the strides made by the Dominion since Confederation, in trade, in increasing wealth, and in education, there has been correspondingly a strange lack of recognition for the place and the needs of the bunkhouse man.

And here at the outset, one should be first to acknowledge that already there is noticeable a marked betterment in the material comforts provided for men in camps. Many large employing firms, in recent years, have made definite steps in advance in the matter of housing for seasonal workers. In places, whole townsites, on the frontier, have been planned and builded with care, displaying a vital consideration for the physical well-being of employees. Such company towns are a credit and a practical indication of what may be expected when greater concern is shown for those who dwell in the bunkhouse.

But such improvements apply chiefly to the large central camps. Employers may make of their mill-site a place of beauty, while, at the same time the bunkhouse constructed at a distant point remains ignored. In tributary camps of whatever kind, whether they be jobbing in the woods for pulp, or sub-contracting on a piece of railway construction, there is still the invariable herding of men. Even the presence of women occasionally in jobbing camps does little to counteract unseemly methods of housing long established.

Camp customs, too, in matters pertaining to pay are deeply rooted. They are a legacy from the days of the camboose and the shanty in the preceding century when even less concern was evinced for the place of the worker in camps. There are still companies operating on frontier works who through their local officials would have their men make bricks without straw. There is in wage-accounting a trend toward petty exactions, if not at times undue coercion. Definite tendencies still lurk unmolested in the camps of Canada which, in their ultimate effects on the individual labourer, are tantamount to lesser forms of serfdom.

The present writer is not unaware of the complexities that beset all employers who have to deal with seasonal and migratory workers. Various bunkmates of all grades and degrees in the coming and going for years among men in camps will rapidly apprize one of the human factor in all of us, and for which due allowance should be made. But even that need not condone the discrepancies too apparent in the handling of bunkhouse men: the clueless labyrinth is to be avoided, one must have some thread in hand or be lost in the maze.

Nor is it sought, in writing of camps, simply to hurl a spear against men who must necessarily tackle the bigger undertakings.

Undue cynicism but retards. Canada more than other lands must needs encourage individual success. Where is more necessary than in the wider spaces of the Dominion the man of enterprize and constructive capacity? Should we begrudge ample recompense for genuine initiative when the gains accruing are the result of character and ability? Whatever fruits be plucked in person, much greater benefits will enrich the country tardy in development. Rewards in place make thrift the patrimony of a people.

In view of this any invidious feeling toward large companies employing workers in camps is disclaimed. Antipathy toward railway contractors is not intended. As regards the individual sub-contractors the writer knows neither Greek nor Trojan, he is discussing camp methods in work and pay, not companies and their officials. In particular chapters the system of contracting and sub-letting so generally adopted on new railway construction, both in Canada and in the United States, is discussed in the matter of its direct bearing on the wage of the man in the bunkhouse. The question that is uppermost is not whether the employer shall receive ample profits, but whether the worker in camps, under various pretexts, shall be deprived of his pay.

For it is to be noted at the outset that the matter herein contained is presented always from the point of view of the worker himself. The whole question is considered from the standpoint of one who, throughout many years, was himself an occupant of the bunkhouse and the shack rather than of the office and the residency; wage conditions are viewed from the ground up, rather than from the top down. This in itself has great demerits: one may gaze too wanly about, and the pendulum swing too far. With this in mind an effort has been made to obey that hoary and wholesome injunction not to take oneself too seriously. If at times a note of asperity has escaped it is not welcomed; pessimism is eschewed, and the contents are presented suggestively.

While the material used has been procured entirely in Canadian camps, the writer, with but a limited experience along American roads, has much reason to believe that some of the conditions as herein outlined applied as well to similar undertakings in the United States. During the whole period under discussion there was a constant interchange of men employed on camp works, between the

Canadian provinces and several of the bordering States. There is little reason to consider the work conditions of the navvy, in either country, to have been other than uniform.

Several American firms, also, were interested, whether as contractors or as sub-contractors, on the later transcontinentals in Canada. Graduates, too, of leading American universities were not uncommonly in evidence on railway works in various parts of the Dominion, whether as higher officials, with residency staffs, or as company clerks and keepers of warehouse supplies. But while the leading features of the contract system as here discussed, were the continuance of practices long common on new construction in the Republic, yet the full effect when in operation, on the work and pay of the navvy, was most apparent in the building of the National Transcontinental Railway in Canada.

And here it may be asked: What good can come now from making public some of the material herein presented? The camps of the National Transcontinental Railway are happenings of a decade since, and more: the roads are completed and the navvies long departed, their sod huts rotted and the poled shacks ashened by the frequent forest fires; even the larger company camps, formerly the centres of activities of hundreds of men, show desolate now to those who search from passing train, their big-log walls in disorder, with roof and ridge-pole tumbled about: Is the Now the time to remedy the Yesterdays?

Nevertheless, there are various reasons: Two may be mentioned. Notwithstanding the fact that a score of books have been written in recent years that pertain, directly or indirectly, to the building of the Canadian Pacific Railway, there remains to-day too little information, in accessible form, showing the conditions under which men wrought, some forty years since, as navvies on the construction of Canada's first transcontinental. This of itself is sufficient reason for making public those details of life and work in camps during the active construction of the third great through line across the Dominion. They bring to light material which can be utilized later by any one who would construct anew those places which have been cast down.

But, more immediate, while the matter herein presented relates almost wholly to one particular period of camp activity, it is not without direct concern toward the placements and pay of men in the proximate future. While it is true the navvy, as such, as finished his tasks for a time, other bunkhouse men still crowd the works on the frontier, and given the opportunity, conditions in isolated camps, such as marked employment along the National Transcontinental, will surely emerge. The work and pay of men in the frontier places of Canada, even to-day, is not wholly removed from tendencies that commonly confronted the bunkhouse man during the initial decade of the present century.

With this in mind the following chapters are assembled. The writer would seek to chart more clearly certain shoals, that under any circumstances imperil the hire of men on isolated works. Data are now used that were long withheld in the continued hope of improved conditions. But even the discretion of added years may be at the expense of singleness of purpose.

Let there be no mistake, however. This monograph makes no pretense to settle things; it is not a destroyer of that which is, without indicating by finger-posts that which might be. It is an attempt to obtain for the migratory worker employed in camps of whatever kind more security in the matter of his work and pay.

Appreciation is gratefully expressed for the invaluable help in graduate reading received at Columbia University. When, in more mature years, one left at different times the poled floors of the camps for the tiled halls and the class rooms of a metropolitan centre, and listened there from a quiet angle to men at their best, trained by a frequent contact with the world and its needs, there were hours when theory as such seemed not in alignment with human facts, at least as gleaned from camps still fresh in the background. Yet there is always the remembrance of earnestness and purpose, and of words which come only when life has been tested, and decisions are weighted by careful judgments.

Among the men in Kent Hall, who have been of assistance to the writer in giving final form to this monograph, mention should be made particularly of Henry R. Seager. His intimate knowledge of Labour in its various aspects, and his considerateness at all times, have placed me under much obligation.

For their time and help in reading the manuscript acknowledgment is gladly made in this place to Professor R. C. Dearle, University of Western Ontario; to J. R. Mutchmor, B.D., of the Robertson

Memorial Institute, Winnipeg; to Dr. G. O. MacMillan, Provincial Normal School, Hamilton; to W. C. Clark, Ph.D., with S. W. Straus Co., Chicago, formerly of Queen's University, and also to A. J. Wilson, B.D., of St. Andrew's Manse, Napanee.

Introduction

Somewhat personal; close-up with the man in camps

FOR twenty-four years the writer of this brochure has had practical experience with the work and pay of men in frontier places across Canada. In 1904 he first went to the camps as a bushman on the North Shore. He was one of the earliest instructors of the Frontier College, then shortly started by Alfred Fitzpatrick, B.A., and slowly taking shape. With different phases of this work, particularly with those pertaining to bunkhouse men, he has since been closely associated.

Previous to 1904 the writer had never seen the inside of a sleep camp. After five years' experience as a teacher in a school in Culross Township, Bruce County, Ontario, supplemented by a broken course of two years in University studies, he undertook manual labour in camps combined with educational work among the men. His motive, if he had any particular incentive at the time for acting as an instructor, was the bald appeal of a new endeavour and the further challenge to any innate patriotism to serve in this way as a preceptor among the men of the bunkhouse rather than as a teacher following the more regular routine of the class room.

To be an instructor involves bringing opportunities of education in a practical way to the man at his work. During the day the instructor is engaged in manual labour, whether as a lumberjack, a miner or a navvy, in some isolated camp; in the evenings he conducts classes or is otherwise occupied as a leader among the men of his work group. He becomes in this way a pivot of healthy opinion through close association in the daily tasks of the men who compose the polyglot groups so often congregated in the frontier camps of the Dominion. For the instructor himself it is a call for measuring up as a man when tested by the actual contact of the whole day's work.

After two seasons as a local instructor the writer was engaged during the next nine years as a supervisor locating and sustaining other instructors in northern Ontario, and northern Quebec. Owing to the rapid developments, both in mining and railway building, in those parts during that period, his work involved much packing of outfits with tump and line to isolated camps. Supervision itself had to be combined always with a practical knowledge of work in camps, and the readiness to undertake it as occasion required.

Between 1907 and 1914 the writer, as supervisor of the Frontier College, had built two dozen log buildings in bush camps north of Georgian Bay to serve as centres of instruction. At other times, ground was stumped and many tents erected for similar purposes at important camps along railway construction. Box cars, also, at opportunity, were rigged with benches and tables, to help provide adult education to men on railway extra gangs, employed on maintenance work in the Canadian hinterland. In this way he personally assisted in locating many scores of university men as instructors in distant camps.

To plant these labourer-instructors at their respective points frequently required several days of packing by trail away from the steel, or nearest rail supply. But whether following with loaded pack along the broken path of a right of way, crossing undrained muskegs, rafting rivers or along with others pulling an oar in the loaded pointer on the lake, it has meant experience with the different works that confront the various groups engaged in frontier camps.

Tasks of this nature, consistently performed, required also an intimate acquaintance with living conditions in camps. For the first eleven years with the Frontier College, the writer spent two-thirds of each year continuously in camps, for the greater part as an occupant of the bunkhouse. With a passing knowledge of several hundred camps, he has also slept in more than five-score bunkhouses for periods ranging from a few nights to several weeks and months. And let it be added, he, as one, should feel kindly toward these places. As an itinerant in camps, throughout those years that count for much in the life of any man, the bunkhouse was his home. Nor is the memory of such wholly unpleasant.

There was, too, in the pursuance of his work, the further opportunity to know at first hand that particular form of employment common along railway construction known as station-work. Perhaps more than any other class of campmen, these workers experienced at first hand the full effect which local conditions have over circumstances pertaining to work and pay. Frequent contact with the men of such groups meant intimate acquaintance; a rest from the tump line in passing, a drink at the water hole just off the grade, varied occasionally with a chat and a wholesome meal of bread and tea and pork, or at times, an improvised 'flop' for the night on the floor of a shack with both English-speaking or foreign-born workers brought one, year after year, in touch with actual wage conditions, such at least as pertain to the men of the shacks.

Nor has the knowledge acquired of frontier works been limited to any one phase. Following 1905, the writer has known camps on the construction of the Temiskaming road up through the silver area; along the National Transcontinental in later years as it gradually extended east and west from Cochrane and Superior Junction; in the several mining fields of northern Ontario — Cobalt, Montreal River, Larder Lake and Porcupine — on the construction of the main line of the Canadian Northern across Ontario north of Lake Superior; and on portions of the double-tracking of the Canadian Pacific. More extended observations, particularly since the war years, as Director of Instructors for the Frontier College, have given the further opportunity of knowing the migratory workers who crowd the railway extra-gangs of the prairie provinces, the miners of the Drumheller valley and the Crow's Nest, and the loggers on the Pacific coast. This has meant at times in a year an itinerary of 22,000 miles by rail, and trail, or water routes. One would be somewhat less than a campman if out of these experiences he had failed to learn about the place and needs of the bunkhouse.

In view of the foregoing the writer may fairly claim to have gone to camps with no preconceived ideas about the conditions there of work and pay. He was not an investigator. There were in his case no principles of economics to be trued up, nor theory of wages to be tested. In fact the matter herein contained is presented from the human side rather than the theoretical. It is the result of a not unfriendly observation of men on frontier works and made under favourable opportunity. Nor are the uglier features concomitant to such forms of life wholly unknown. Experience has been had during the passing years with vermin, bush fires, rapids, fever and months of hospital.

In 1907 the writer, then approaching 30 years of age, had started an honour course, extramurally, in History and Economics, at Queen's University, Kingston, Canada. These studies were pursued at intervals during eight years as opportunity permitted between lengthy periods of work in camps; the purpose being, not simply the desire for a degree in itself, but to bring to men of the bunkhouse a modicum even of privileges in education too long denied.

Gradually it became apparent that the practices and conditions of labour in frontier places both in Canada and in some of the neighbouring States did not always conform to the best thought and teachings of the universities. Some phases of hire and pay on isolated works were, in effect, but the sowing again of the dragon's teeth.

When the time came, in 1912, to submit a thesis for the Master's degree, then it was that the idea first took shape: 'Why not write on what has slowly become uppermost in your thoughts – Camp Conditions on Frontier Works?' This is mentioned in this place because previous to that time there had been no thought of noting the wage and housing conditions of workers in camps, but the substratum necessary for forming conclusions had already been shaped gradually by the experiences on frontier works during the preceding eight years.

Opportunity came later, in 1919, to resume work already undertaken at Columbia University, reading in the fields of Industrial History, Sociology and Economics. This course was carried on during five different terms. One result has been a fuller study of the bunkhouse man and his environment. It is here presented as a contribution to a clearer understanding of the practical conditions which determine work and pay in the camps of Canada.

Chapter 1

The background of the navvy

Historical outlines of the development of Canada's transportation systems

IN VIEW of the frequent mention that is made throughout this book
of campmen and workers on railway construction, a brief survey will
be given in this place, showing in retrospect the development of
transportation throughout the lands that now comprise the
provinces of the Dominion.

Transportation has always been a problem in Canada. Since the
earliest days of the French Régime the commerce of the northern
part of the continent had followed the Great Lakes, the St.
Lawrence, and the several large rivers that flow into the North
Atlantic. This was a great advantage to Canada. Nature had endowed
her with magnificent facilities for transportation in the great water
system largely within her borders and extending halfway across the
continent. From the mouth of the St. Lawrence to the farther points
at the head of the Lakes stretches a water route of two thousand
miles: To hold the trade of the continent in this natural channel was
the ideal of the valiant French traders, as it was equally the purpose
of their intrepid British successors.

Trade communications for any distance in the provinces, as
indeed elsewhere in North America, until well into the nineteenth
century, were solely by water. Happily in this the country was well
endowed. There were many handicaps, however, frequent stretches
of rapids disrupted transport with many grievous delays, while the
presence of great waterfalls, often in places most vital for trade,
restricted any extended intercourse. All of which served to localize
the interests of the respective provinces and at times engendered
petty prejudices of place and race.

It was the coming, in successive waves, of the Loyalists, during
those years following the American Revolution that first gave a
common purpose to the life of the scattered British provinces. The
arrival of these patriot families meant the infusion of some of the
best blood of the Republic into the activities of the struggling
settlements. Early, they became the warp in the political fabric of
the disjointed communities scattered broadcast between the Detroit
River and the coast line of Nova Scotia.

Displaying quite commonly alertness in trade, these newcomers
became a direct incentive for an increased intercourse among peoples
of the several British colonies. Their efforts, in this direction,
coincided, also, with the more aggressive procedure of the Northwest
Fur Company, who, in those same years, from their headquarters in

Montreal were bidding successfully for the commerce and exchange of the Upper Lakes, and the vaster regions of the interior. All of which made foremost the problem of transportation.

All avenues of trade at that time necessarily implied waterways. Roads, so called, were for the greater part almost impassable, for only those constructed for military purposes at strategic points were graded or improved. Coaches plied but irregularly over the scant stage routes. Land communications between Quebec City and the country at the head of Lake Ontario were so crude that official letters for the Lieutenant-Governor in Upper Canada, as late as 1810, were frequently transmitted through the United States via Albany.

A start had been made with small canals in 1780. These were constructed to overcome the obstacles on the St. Lawrence River just above Montreal. The locks first built were narrow and very shallow, but for many years they were an immense help, sufficient at least to allow the passing of the batteaux and other small craft then employed. For, in spite of handicaps, water-borne traffic was rapidly increasing, by way of the St. Lawrence. Before the turn of the century a lock completed near Sault Ste Marie, circumvented St. Mary's rapids, giving readier access to the western areas.

Then came those years of strife (1812-14) and the attendant dislocations caused by a protracted border war. Frequent invasions ensued with the constant menace of defeat and disruption; all of which showed the people of the provinces the essential need of better transportation if they were to be in a position to defend their land.

Already in the period, immediately following the close of the war, a start was made toward enlarging the St. Lawrence canals. But, while water-borne traffic was thus increased between points on Lake Ontario and Montreal, the falls at Niagara still presented a barrier to through traffic with the Upper Lakes.

Meanwhile surprising development in the regions adjoining the Great Lakes focussed attention in the Republic on the necessity of holding this trade within all-American channels. Finally, in 1825, New York State completed the Erie Canal, thus providing a barge route from Lake Erie via the Hudson River to the Atlantic, more direct in course and independent of the St. Lawrence.

This was a commercial challenge to the superiority of the Canadian route, handicapped as it already was with its four months and more of frozen waterway. In answer, however, the provinces of Canada constructed, during the next eight years, the Welland Canal, less than thirty miles in length, but overcoming at Niagara the great obstacle to direct intercourse between the Lakes. They hoped, in this way, again to divert to the St. Lawrence much of the export trade of the fast-growing states south of the Lakes.

These were big accomplishments under the then existing conditions of trade throughout the provinces. But there were giants in the land in those days: early in the thirties a definite start was made to connect Georgian Bay with Lake Ontario by the Trent waterway; there were, also, as early as this, visions of looping the Ottawa with the Upper Lakes, across Lake Nipissing and down the French River; while Chatham and other towns in the western part of Upper Canada were erstwhile insistent upon the draining of the St. Clair Flats in the interests of navigation. All of which had in purpose the enhancing of the commercial value of the St. Lawrence system as the great outlet from the interior of the continent.

There was promise, too, of big results. The large expenditures for the development of the Erie and the Welland Canals seem to have been justified. Both these canals had been constructed at a time when the region about the Great Lakes showed wonderful development. Secure in the possession of the natural route, the people of the provinces could look forward to attracting a considerable portion of the total tonnage. Trade conditions in the Canadas seemed satisfactory in the first half of the forties. A cursory survey (see Appendix B) of the freight carried through the Erie Canal and through the Welland Canal for a five-year period (1840-45) reflects in a broad way the general trend of the traffic and shows the Canadian waterways to have carried more than a proportionate share.

But important political happenings were at hand. Until the late forties the Canadian provinces had benefited by the Navigation Acts of the Mother Country, which gave a preference in the British Isles to goods shipped from a Canadian port. Much wheat and other produce from the American States had indirectly swelled the ocean shipments from the ports of Montreal and Quebec. The Repeal of the Corn Laws in 1846 however cost Canada the advantages she had hitherto enjoyed in the markets of Britain. Grain from Boston, Philadelphia and Portland could now enter Britain on precisely the same terms as products from Canada, while Atlantic shipment from American ports was further favoured because the risks incurred in the navigation of the St. Lawrence and the Gulf involved higher charges.

This was a blow to the advantages hitherto enjoyed by the Canadian waterways. The reaction was marked. While the tonnage through the Erie Canal progressed in bounds the percentage passing via the Welland rapidly decreased. A further reference to Appendix B discloses the disparity between the tonnage of the respective canals in the closing years, as compared with the first half of the ten-year period. This discrepancy was greatly increased in the following two decades.

Meanwhile a more remarkable change had been wrought in the industrial world. The advent of the steam railways had gradually transformed the methods of transportation. In less than two decades the advantages of the rail haul had been fully demonstrated, and heavy freight was no longer so dependent upon the water systems of communication.

We are apt to think of the steam locomotive as something which peculiarly belongs to our own age, but on the contrary it has an antiquity reaching back beyond a century: Before Austerlitz was fought Richard Trevithick had his steam vehicles operating in the streets of London. When the Duke of Brunswick gave the historic ball in Brussels on the eve of Waterloo the 'Puffing Billy' had been hauling coals from Wylam colliery near Newcastle for more than a year. What potential power the mighty Emperor had overlooked!

The commercial possibilities of the locomotive however were not fully demonstrated until 1825. The success of Stephenson with his 'travelling-engine' on the Stockton Railway in that year encouraged the building of the Liverpool-Manchester line. This was completed four years later, and the feats of the Rocket established clearly for all peoples the place and utility of steam roads.

When these early railways were constructed they were regarded merely as special roads and Parliament made provision that all carriers upon the payment of a toll should have the right to use them. It was soon found impracticable to operate a railway in this fashion and railway companies became not only builders and maintainers of roads but common carriers as well.

It was the memorable administration of Sir Robert Peel in the beginning of the forties in the last century which among its other far-reaching accomplishments really established the railway system in England. Redundant capital in the kingdom was then employed in railway building instead of running risks that made foreign investments so disastrous. Already centres of population in the Mother Country had been looped up by systems of steel lines which were rapidly grid-ironing the whole island. In 1845 there had been invested in railways in the British Isles nearly half a billion dollars, twenty-five years later this had increased to two thousand six hundred and fifty million.

Meanwhile the United States had also been alert to the possibilities of steam railways. Experiments had early been made with steam engines of various patterns and diverse construction, but it was not until 1831 that an actual start was made with locomotive-drawn passenger trains on regular runs. Within ten years some two thousand miles of railways were built, and this mileage by the mid-century had increased again four-fold.

Even with a sparser population and with greater distances intervening in America, between the inland parts and the ports of shipment, the steam roads proved particularly adaptable. Direct lines from the seaboard were hastily constructed into the rapidly growing areas of the middle western states. This great mileage was operated unimpaired throughout every month of the year. It diverted by rail through new channels to the Atlantic a great portion of that immense trade in natural products which had formerly been shipped through the Erie and Welland Canals. Both these had been constructed before the railways were an active factor for the commercial conveyance of goods in heavy bulk. Under the new order the hope long nurtured in the provinces of controlling the grain trade via the St. Lawrence was doomed a second time to disappointment.

Nor had railway building north of the Great Lakes been correspondingly as active. The great stretches of unoccupied lands were big handicaps to the completion of profitable lines. The first railway in Canada, finished in 1836, ran between St. John's, Quebec, and LaPrairie. The length did not exceed fifteen miles and it was but crudely constructed; the wooden rails with flat bars of iron spiked to the top being similar to those used in North Carolina since 1830.

While maps of Upper Canada, published at this time period, show a railway projected from Hamilton on Burlington Bay across the country to the Thames River near London, nevertheless, the only semblance of a railway in Upper Canada, for many years, was a horse tramway, opened in 1839 between Queenston and Chippawa along the old portage road around the falls of Niagara. As late as 1852 the total railway mileage in both Upper and Lower Canada did not exceed one hundred and fifty-nine miles and much of this was in the district surrounding Montreal. Whatever roads were constructed at this time were used chiefly at portages or in order to supplement the existing waterways.

It was soon apparent to the commercial leaders of Canada that if the trade was to be held in its former channels the provinces must combine an effective railway system with their splendid routes of inland navigation. In pursuance of this the Government of Canada proposed in 1849 to assist in the building of any new railways over seventy-five miles in length by a guarantee of the bonds up to half the cost of the road. It was under this incentive that Canada in the early fifties made its first real start toward adequate railway building.

Two projects for railway construction at this time confronted the people of the provinces. One was the scheme for a trunk line extending along the St. Lawrence from Quebec City westward to Montreal and thence through Ontario to the international border. This was intended primarily to supplement the canals already constructed by the people at such great cost. The other plan had in view the union of all the British provinces by one great railway. This had been suggested some years previously by Lord Durham in his Report. Each plan had its friends and its opponents. There were latent in both of them some of the political ideas which then dominated the people: the desire for a closer union of the maritime provinces with the two provinces of Canada and the determination of the Canadian people to share as far as possible in the transportation to the seaboard of grains and other products from the lands being newly opened about the Great Lakes.

These mooted railways were expected to be a boon to the country generally. Capital, however, seemed to take more kindly to the building of lines about the St. Lawrence and the Lakes. In 1852 a decided impetus was given to the building of new roads in the upper province, and within a year some forty miles of steam railways were in operation out of Toronto. Before 1856, close on nine hundred miles of new construction had been completed in the British provinces; New Brunswick and Nova Scotia having obtained during these years their first short lines. Meanwhile, about the head of Lake Ontario the Great Western continued to project new roads, while the through line of the Grand Trunk Railway, in 1859, extended from below the city of Quebec to Montreal and Toronto, and thence across Western Ontario to Point Edward at the foot of Lake Huron, a distance of nearly eight hundred miles.

The first decade of activity in railway construction throughout the British provinces ended in 1862. There were then two thousand and sixty miles of road in operation. In the next ten-year period, however, only five hundred and fifty-two miles of new lines were constructed.

The large amounts expended during several years in railway building had meant the expenditure locally of very considerable sums. For a time boom conditions existed throughout the new towns and districts where construction was in progress. Then followed a period of reaction due not a little to extravagance and mismanagement among the railway builders themselves. These were years that seemed to spell disaster to the investors.

The trunk line too, from which enterprise so much was expected, instead of supplementing the canal system, proved to be a rival. There was not sufficient traffic coming through Canada for both; one robbed the other. In the unequal contest the railway lagged behind. In an effort to secure the needed through-traffic the Grand Trunk was ultimately extended to Chicago, and later, Portland, Maine, was made the winter port of the system.

Meanwhile the project for the building of a railway as a link between the different provinces had hung in abeyance for twenty years. But complications with the United States, which was then passing through the throes of its great Civil War, had shown clearly the necessity for such a road. The friction arising from the Trent affair and the Fenian invasions following the close of the American struggle, accompanied as they were by a period of political deadlock in the Canadian Parliament, were either one of them, sufficient inducement for a stronger political union between all the British provinces. Confederation, in 1867, was the natural outcome, and the

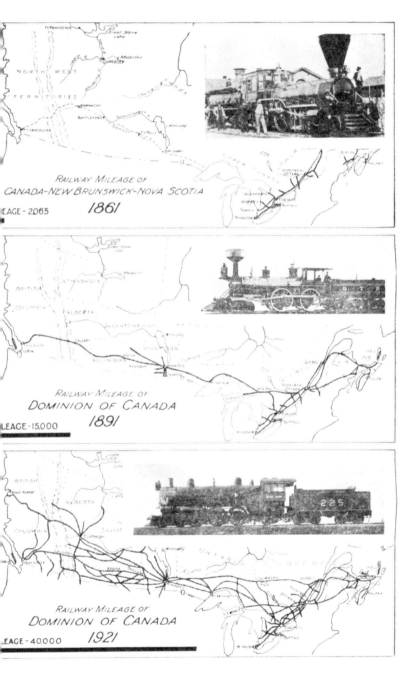

RAILWAY MILEAGE OF
CANADA-NEW BRUNSWICK-NOVA SCOTIA
1861
EAGE - 2065

RAILWAY MILEAGE OF
DOMINION OF CANADA
1891
LEAGE - 15,000

RAILWAY MILEAGE OF
DOMINION OF CANADA
1921
EAGE - 40,000

Three periods of railway expansion: approximate mileage at the close of each period of active construction building of the Intercolonial through all-Canadian territory, long discussed, was finally started in 1870 and the main line completed during the next six years.

The Intercolonial extended from Halifax to Quebec City, a distance of eight hundred and thirty-seven miles, with a branch line from Moncton to St. John, and later from Truro to Sydney. The young Dominion was thus assured of winter ports on the Atlantic at St. John and Halifax, as well as farther north in Cape Breton. This road until 1918 was operated under the Canadian Government, through its Department of Railways.

In 1870, but shortly following Confederation, Canada acquired the immense territories in the North and the West, administered until then by officials of the Hudson's Bay Company. The entry of British Columbia into the new union was now possible. This was conditioned, however, upon the understanding that a railway be built westward through the new territories to the Pacific, thus giving that province direct connection with the eastern parts of the Dominion.

Prior even to Confederation different travellers and reputable engineers had canvassed the possibility of such a highway. As early as 1851 Joseph Howe, the tribune of the Maritime Provinces, predicted the time near at hand when a railway would be built across the western prairies through to British Columbia. Scarcely twenty years later the Pacific province had become a component part of the country, and Canada, in fulfillment of its pledge, prepared to construct its first transcontinental.

The planning of a line through to the Pacific was an enormous task in new construction, and one that had no precedent in railway history. When we consider that the great Republic, capable of such amazing accomplishments, had a population approaching forty million when it attempted its first transcontinental, this, for a people of less than four millions was an undertaking venturesome even to daring.

An effort was made to build the Canadian Pacific road as a great public work, and from the first the railway was a political issue. Between 1876-80 over eight hundred miles were put under contract west of Lake Superior, in Manitoba and in British Columbia. Contracts also were under construction in Ontario. No portion of the work, however, was finished by the close of the decade.

In 1881 the Government turned the whole task over to a group of Canadian capitalists. Arrangements were made, also, to complete the unfinished sections of the road. Enormous difficulties were met and overcome, and the road was completed through the mountains to the Pacific coast in five years.

Canada had now a service extending from ocean to ocean. Regular trains plied between Montreal and Vancouver. There was great activity, too, in new construction of branch roads; southern Nova Scotia, western Ontario, and portions of the prairies were busy with the building of numerous cross lines. This activity, extending into the early nineties, constitutes the second period of railway development in Canada. At its close there were 15,000 miles of steam roads under operation in the Dominion.

A slow but healthy development of the Canadian West followed the completion of this pioneer railway. Meanwhile, before the close of the century, a start had already been made in further railway building by another group of men, which ultimately, in its various enlargements, was to prove a second transcontinental for the Dominion. In 1896-98 the firm of MacKenzie, Mann & Company, contractors, built a hundred-mile railway known as the Lake Manitoba Railway. Other short lines were leased, subsequently, and the nucleus was thus formed of the new system which continued actively to construct lines through the wheat lands of the prairies. From this beginning there gradually developed the Canadian Northern Railway. In 1902 these intrepid builders had obtained Federal permission to build eastward toward Ottawa and Montreal, and westward via Edmonton and the Skeena River to the Pacific coast. Before the close of 1905 they had a line in operation extending from Port Arthur through Winnipeg to Edmonton, a distance of thirteen hundred miles.

Directed by able men, Canadian Northern construction throughout the West was marked by feverish activity during the next ten years. Its lines were pushed up through the Yellowhead Pass and southward for eight hundred miles to Vancouver. By 1915, after many financial vicissitudes, the Canadian Northern had a system which comprised some ten thousand miles in the different provinces; its main line extending from Quebec City to Vancouver.

In view of the steady increase of immigration to the Dominion and the attendant industrial activity that marked the beginning of the present century, the interests behind the Grand Trunk Railway, under the guidance of Charles M. Hays, desiring to participate in the material expansion of Western Canada, conceived the project of a third transcontinental. In fact, ever since the completion of the Canadian Pacific, the Grand Trunk Railway had realized the need of a direct feeder from the prairies.

A plan was submitted to the Dominion Parliament by which the Grand Trunk Railway through its subsidiary, the Grand Trunk Pacific, undertook to build a railway westward from Winnipeg across the wheat provinces to the Pacific, provided the Canadian Government would build a line in Eastern Canada from Moncton and across northern Quebec and Ontario to Winnipeg.

The whole project encountered considerable opposition when before the country. It was suggested, that, in the face of so much needless overlapping of new lines in unproductive territory, both the Canadian Northern and the Grand Trunk Pacific should co-operate wherever possible. Failure to do this led to needless duplication and much loss, particularly in the sparsely-settled portions of the country.

Finally in 1903 an Act was passed by the Canadian parliament providing for the construction of the National Transcontinental Railway. This was followed by an Act, one year later, to incorporate the Grand Trunk Pacific Railway Company. Thus according to their Dominion charters, Canada's latest transcontinental was composed of two divisions, the Eastern and the Western, and both were separate entities.

The Eastern Division, known as the National Transcontinental Railway (N.T.R.), was to be built by the Dominion Government. It extended westerly from Moncton through New Brunswick, northern Quebec and northern Ontario to the city of Winnipeg, a distance of one thousand eight hundred and two miles. On the completion of the National Transcontinental it was to be leased by the Dominion to the Grand Trunk Pacific Company and operated by them. This lease of the Eastern Division was for a period of fifty years at a rental of three per cent per annum of the total cost of construction. For the first seven years no rent was to be charged.

The Western Division, known as the Grand Trunk Pacific (G.T.P.), was to be built by the Grand Trunk Pacific Company. It included that portion of the line extending from Winnipeg, northerly and

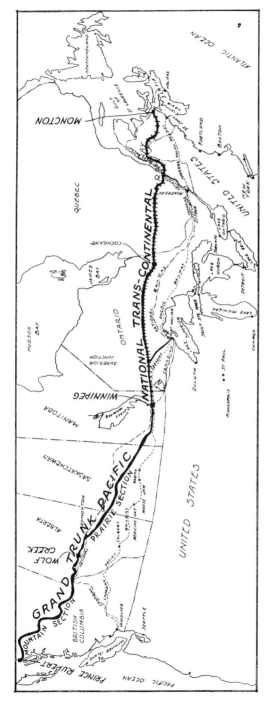

The course of Canada's third transcontinental
National Transcontinental, Moncton to Winnipeg; Grand Trunk Pacific, Winnipeg
to Prince Rupert. Wolf Creek and Cochrane are also shown as mid points.

westerly, via Edmonton, through the Yellowhead Pass of the
Rockies, on to Prince Rupert on the Pacific Coast, a distance of one
thousand, seven hundred and forty-five miles. This Western Division
was divided in turn into the Prairie Section of over nine hundred
miles, passing for the most part through a fertile and producing
country, and the Mountain Section, running westward from Wolf
Creek, in Alberta, for eight hundred miles through a rough,
mountainous and non-producing country.

On the whole Western Division the Dominion Government
guaranteed the bonds issued by the Grand Trunk Pacific Company
up to seventy-five per cent of the cost of construction. These
advances were made only on the approved certificates of government
engineers, and, in the case of the prairie section, were not to exceed
thirteen thousand dollars per mile. The construction per mile in the
heavy mountain section, however, cost many times that amount.

By 1915 the Dominion of Canada had thus brought to
completion three great transcontinentals. But she had overbuilded.
To sustain such a mileage extended over an immense country, much
of it as yet unproductive, would require a population of twenty
million. Unfortunately the outbreak of the World War in 1914
brought further dislocations. The Canadian Northern, whatever had
been its hopes, whose bonds in many instances had been guaranteed
by the Dominion government, continued under most straitened
circumstances. Meanwhile the Grand Trunk Pacific and the National
Transcontinental had also proved unremunerative. To bolster these
roads was costing the Federal government huge sums annually.

There ensued a period of disquietude and political readjustments.
Finally, in 1917, an Act was passed at Ottawa, providing for the
acquisition of the Canadian Northern Railway by the Canadian
government. This system incorporated with all other mileage
controlled by the Dominion was placed under a commission and is
known as the Canadian National.

In 1919 further provision was made to include the Grand Trunk
Railway in the Canadian National lines. The whole system,
embracing in control over 20,000 miles, was placed under a
non-political board of directors. Meanwhile railways in the
Dominion are still in a period of transition. Whether the ultimate
solution will be a continuance of the two great groups, one privately
owned, and the other under government control, or eventually

further consolidation, remains for the years to disclose.

Canada has been fostered by her railways. Steam roads are essential to any new country of great distances, but they are vital to Canadian progress. How otherwise can be welded a scanty population located diversely in disjointed areas – whether long distanced toward the east, pierced at the centre by the great Laurentian barrier, or walled in turn by mighty mountains westward at the Pacific?

These physical handicaps, so inimical to material progress, have long been recognized. Hence the railway building that has harassed the succeeding governments at Ottawa: first girding with branches the rich lands along the St. Lawrence and about the Lakes, then the joining of hands with the Maritimes, to be followed in time with the great trunk lines opening up the rich agricultural lands of the prairies and extending beyond the mountains to the coast. For sectional accord as a continuing people will depend increasingly upon avenues of trade that benefit commonly the life of the whole Dominion.

Interior view of a bunkhouse
This type of building, used for housing campmen, was common on all frontier works in
Canada, particularly from 1890 to 1925.

Camp of a sub-contractor ahead of the steel
Left to right, men's bunkhouse, cookery, foremen's bunkhouse, office, warehouse

Sleeping quarters for the man of the bunkhouse, as late as 1925
Upper and lower bunks, with hewed bench and stags showing at bottom

An improvement in camps
A logging village at the coast; each bunkhouse accommodates 6 to 10 men.

Nationals
employed
on frontier
works

Group of
Spaniards —
noon-hour
siesta

English-speaking
men with
improvised
blanket-tents

Group of
Croations
(Jugo-Slavs)

On their good behavior
A momentary pose by a group of 'Russian' workers

The cook for a group of station-men
Oven at right being fired hot for bread

Shacks used by station-men
An interior and an exterior view

The shanty of the 60's and 70's, showing the framed chimney, the chinked walls, and common mode of roofing
This one was specially constructed in 1900 for demonstration purposes and is consequently superior to the average formerly built on isolated works.

Bunkhouse men at a winter camp
These large central bunkhouses succeeded the shanty in the bush camps of Canada about 1890.

The smaller sized bunkhouse, used in 1924
This building 20' x 32' housed 28 men; the others being at work, only half are shown here: 9 Finlanders, 1 Bulgarian, 1 Belgian, 1 Russian, as well as an English-speaking and a French-speaking Canadian.

Passing on the tote road
Men going-in and men coming-out — the daily procession of foreign-born men to a distant work

Days may be lost in reaching camp

The brighter type among the foreign-born campmen

Chapter 2

The contract system on railway construction

The sphere of the head-contractor and the practice of sub-letting

THE PEOPLE of Canada have paid dearly for their efforts to facilitate transportation. Increasing amounts since Confederation have been expended, particularly on steam communications. During one ten-year period of railway activity, which necessarily has a direct relation to the present study, namely that following 1905, considerably more than one billion dollars (ten hundred and forty-four million), was expended in the Canadian provinces, on the improvement of lines already existing, and the construction of new roads.

In accordance with the methods so commonly pursued in all railway building, a considerable proportion of this entire amount passed through the medium of the railway contractors. It is the purpose of the writer, as has been mentioned, to trace throughout one portion of the field in which these outlays were made some of the conditions of work and pay: a more or less intimate recital of the relations frequently existing between the head-contractor and his sub-contractors, and the effect of this upon the workers in the camps.

The contract system seems inherent in all railway building. As already indicated, we can look for its genesis back in England during the inauguration of railway construction. In those years the ultimate worth of steam roads had yet to be proved, and only able men, undaunted by ridicule, would undertake to construct the first short stretches of steel.

One name looms large throughout that incipient period – Thomas Brassey, the pioneer among railway contractors. He participated in much of the activity pertaining to the advent of steam transportation in England. With four thousand English navvies, assisted by a greater number of French workmen, he constructed, also, for France in 1841 her first real railway extending from Paris to Rouen. Later in the fifties agents of his company sought contracts, also, for the construction of railways in the different provinces of British America.

Brassey, also, may be considered the progenitor of some of the destructive features that marked for a long period the methods of the railway contractor. Early he encouraged sub-letting. He looked upon day-work as a losing game for the employer, and, as far as possible, his work was done by sub-contracting or by other forms of piece work.

It was however in the United States that the railroad contractor came into his own. There the building of new lines over immense distances proceeded in rapid strides. The four decades following 1850 were years of marvelous railway development in the American Union. Other countries were far outdistanced, the eastern states were interlaced, lines of railway reached the Mississippi, and the whole country was criss-crossed by roads of commerce which extended ultimately to the Pacific. This period of expansion was broken only by the years of the Civil War; it culminated in the eighties when in one decade seventy thousand miles of new lines were built, principally in the central and western states. The many railroads of the American republic welded it politically and economicaly.

In the opening up of these vast territories the railroad builders played an increasingly important part. True, times were abnormal and undue haste in places meant inevitable reaction with accompanying years of depression, yet from it all the contractor emerged with his power and influence enhanced.

The first era of railway building in the Canadian provinces was financed largely by English money. In the construction of the numerous short branches, about the St. Lawrence and toward the Great Lakes, methods in building were adopted which had already been proven successful in England and in the neighboring States. The railway contractor was given every encouragement, and wide powers were latent in the charter granted him for construction.

The chief promoters of the first transcontinental across the Dominion, built during the second period of railway expansion, and completed in the middle eighties, were men who had a considerable knowledge of conditions in building, such as pertained to railway construction in the Western States. There the contract system dominated, and large portions of the new Canadian line were constructed under a similar system.

These same methods continued during the active years of building which mark a third period of railway expansion in Canada. There was this apparent difference, however: instead of curbing the sphere of the railway contractor, this latest period expanded his powers unduly. On no previous railway construction was the contractor allowed such latitude. Following the beginning of the century the contract system deteriorated into nothing better at times than a skilful form of sub-letting.

Nor need exception be taken to this method under normal conditions. But the outcroppings of such a system culminate down near the lowest rung in the power exercised by the sub-contractor over the conditions of hire and service among the men on his piece of work. It becomes at times absurd, and, if not wasteful, a direct detriment to the pay of the navvy.

The letting of a railway contract for the building of several hundred miles of grade on a new transcontinental is a matter of some import. In the case of the National Transcontinental Railway such matters were handled from Ottawa, the several contracts being let by the National Transcontinental Commission, representing the Dominion Government. As each section of the new road was ready for a start on construction, a call for tenders was published broadcast throughout the country, and the contract, ostensibly, was let in open competition. That, however, may often be a mere formality. It is obvious that only certain firms will engage in railway construction and the competition lies wholly within well-known groups. Between the dates of calling for tenders and the final letting of the work there is much struggle and stress, or plain wire-pulling, on the part of the men contending for the contract. The co-operation of interested firms is sought — steel plants, bridge works, and machinery outfitters of different kinds — for each of these have usually a favourite in the matter of the contract. Business directorates not uncommonly interlock in such allied industries. Every influence, political and otherwise, is used to secure the contract for a favourite commercial protegé.

The successful bidder, the company receiving the contract, is known on the line as the 'head-contractor.' It may represent a group of men, but usually such companies imply the dominant purpose of one man, and the contract throughout its length is designated locally by the name of the head-contractor.

Once obtained, a railway contract is, in many ways, a sinecure. There are big chances of very material profits during the probable six years of tenure. Indeed, when the contract thus secured extends for hundreds of miles through the hinterland, away from regularly organized districts, the head-contractor has in his new field something of the power of a satrap. He exercises much influence and authority in his demesne. In fact the letting of one of the larger contracts on the National Transcontinental Railway may not unreasonably have been compared to the appointment of a governor, in the historic days, to one of the lesser provinces of Imperial Rome. Some phases of tax farming when the Empire laid tribute, whether in the cities of Numidia or in the villages of Pannonia, were not wholly dissociated from the exactions in pay that foreign-born workers encountered, in a later time, on isolated railway contracts in Canada.

There is an idea prevalent among nine lay persons out of ten that the large railway contractor is at an immense outlay; that the immediate plant which he puts on a work costs huge amounts; that there are always attendant risks of grave losses, and that in the face of all these, he should be amply rewarded for his pluck and business enterprise. This supposition is sometimes right, but it may, also, be far astray. While a contractor has often started work with a valuable plant, yet quite as frequently he has begun work with a very indifferent outfit. It is not uncommon on railway construction for the contract to make the man and his plant too.

Most railway contractors have the faculty of getting loyal service from their immediate assistants. The right men are well paid. From the juniors, among the well-housed clerical staff, to the capable managers and superintendents, the head-contractor has, at his service, a splendid body of trained men. Many of these have followed his fortunes for years, and their ability insures the efficient conduct of his affairs during his continued absence from the line.

The head-contractor, once the contract is secured, hastens to sub-let the different works on the first eighty or one hundred miles, which, so far, only stretches on paper along the location-line already run by the engineers. The cutting of the right-of-way is first sub-let. This means cutting, clearing, and sometimes burning a swath sixty-six feet wide through the woods following the staked centre posts of the engineers. The pile-driving, the trestle work, and some rock cuts will then be let, and a few large buildings erected which later serve as the warehouses and offices of the headquarters camp.

There are numerous contracts let for particular works; one man contracts to do the concrete work called for in the specifications; another will take the contract of cutting railway ties; the medical system and the mail route will, also, be allotted. Finally, ten or more sub-contractors will receive sections of the road which they undertake to complete up to grade level. All these different works are sub-let on a good margin from the price originally granted the head-contractor, whose skill in sub-letting should net him substantial gains on his contract.

The secondary stage of construction includes the laying of steel, ballasting with lifts of gravel and bringing the grade to a finished condition. This is a slow and expensive process, calling for considerable capital expenditure to provide the necessary machine equipment and rolling stock. Work in this stage of construction is not sub-let, being usually performed by the head-contractor himself.

The awarding of a railway contract presupposes, of course, that the preliminary work has already been completed by the engineers. These men, working in groups, and often under primitive conditions, run the try-lines and procure the needed information that determines the final location of the road. It is from the blueprints, supplied originally from engineers in the field, that a work is divided into sections, and then publicly let for contract.

Along the Transcontinental the engineers were the outposts of the Railway Commission. Scattered in residencies at ten-mile intervals, they checked up the contractors, according to required specifications, as the work progressed. They were the local observers for the Government, as well as technical advisers to the Commission, and communications pertaining to the conduct of the work passed weekly between the district engineers and the authorities at Ottawa.

How does the sub-contractor form a basis for the minimum price he will accept for his services? The sub-contractor has access, at the office of the head-contractor, to blueprints of the line which have been supplied in duplicate by the engineers. These show in detail the profile of the road, the mud cuts, the fills, the trestles, the rock work, the ditching, and all other extras required on the whole contract. From these he selects the ten-mile section which appeals most to one of his experience, taking into consideration as well the equipment he has at his disposal. The sub-contractor is further required to sign contracts for the work he undertakes; his plant and equipment, as well as his supplies, are all under lien to the head-contractor for the due performance of the work. He undertakes, also, to finish his contract in a specified time.

From the details supplied at the office of the head-contractor the sub-contractor has a good idea of the number of yards of work to be done on this ten-mile stretch — the extent of the clay excavation and the fills and the total amount of rock to be moved. From these figures he can estimate fairly well the number of men he will need, and he knows, too, quite accurately what supplies to store in his warehouse sufficient to complete his work.

All supplies for each of the sub-contractors are furnished at the headquarters camp. Thus, when outfitted, the sub-contractor is often under obligations to the head-contractor for many thousands of dollars; his van goods, his cookery supplies, his feed, his machine parts, have all been advanced him from the huge stores at headquarters camp. Even the freighting may be handled by the head-contractor and a further indebtedness be thus incurred.

Having arranged for a piece of new work the sub-contractor proceeds at once to erect camp buildings at a suitable point on his location somewhere ahead of the steel. The winter months are largely spent in preparation of the work on his contract which will commence in the spring break-up. The sub-contractor will usually have a small plant, including steel rails of light weight, a donkey engine or two, several horses, some carts, a blacksmith outfit, and considerable lesser equipment, probably, from a former work.

To tote supplies is a serious task. If the camp of the sub-contractor is thirty miles ahead of the steel it will mean sometimes a two or three-day trip, for rough roads have to be hastily constructed, the hills avoided and the swamps and muskegs edged with corduroy. The frequent detours and the many sudden twists add greatly to the length of the haul, for mud at times half envelopes the heavy wheels. Not five hundred pounds can be toted under such conditions, even with a four-horse team. What wonder that sharp frosts, with plenty of snow and ice, are welcomed? With sleigh and team a two-ton load may be taken fifteen miles in a day, but once the break-up is at hand trouble again besets the teamster on every side.

Few scenes in camps surpass in interest the busy hauling of supplies necessary for construction. Various kinds are forwarded — pork, smoked meats, flour, canned goods of all descriptions, dried fruits, raisins, prunes, apricots, and beans for the cookery; hay in bales and oats for the stables; dynamite for the powder cellar; mackinaws, boots, rubbers, socks, shirts, shoepacks, stationery, painkiller, mosquito-oil, snuff and tobacco for the van or office

store. The blacksmith shop, too, will early be requisitioned for
service, so it is rigged with anvil, sledges, big link chains, steel rods
for drills, dump carts in parts, and spares of many kinds. Stores of
whatever sort are the sinews for the construction season, and their
due selection is a matter of deep concern to any sub-contractor.

Transport must usually be performed during weeks in the depths
of winter, and weather then in northern parts must be wooed in its
variable moods. Distance, too, and the uncertainty of the roads tend
toward irregularity that disrupts the best-laid plans. So, while the
sleighing is good, the tote-teams are hustled. The shouts of the
teamsters are heard late and early throughout the short winter days,
and the frosted snow crunches with the heavy hoof as loaded teams
on the sleigh-haul travel with an early start, while yet Arcturus hangs
big in the eastern sky.

True, these be but routine tasks, yet in them lies the tinge of
romance. We are prone in Canada to ignore the heroism of men such
as these in obscure places. The youth of the Dominion know more
of the storied march of Hannibal or the Crossing of the Alps than of
the accomplishments of men on frontier works.

The written pages of textbooks much in use cease not to depict
how men of another land and in a former time, upon conquest bent,
encountered in their onward march the ice of the steeps and snows
of the mountain passes. Combated by inclement weather, they are
urged ever into sustained effort by the vision of fertile valleys
beyond, and loot in recompence from opulent towns on the rich
plains of Piedmont. But during long weeks of the winter months
amid scenes of rocks and wooded isolation, where temperatures are
lower than soldiers would endure, men of the camps in lightsome
mood go daily forth in the performance of their wonted tasks,
turning out often long before daylight with the thermometer
registering 40° below zero.

Here in passing let me acknowledge the tangible accomplishments
of the railway contractor himself. Plans and schemes first visualized
by engineers, have been made real by his practical force and genius.
In a land such as Canada, with its great natural obstacles, and in
many portions still a wilderness but scantily peopled, these men of
action, undaunted by barriers, have tackled undertakings the
performance of which in an earlier age would have been deemed
heroic. Canada can well honour the vision and daring of her railway

builders. Their acts and deeds, often pursued with audacity and purpose and in the face of great difficulties, would not demean the campaign of a marshal.

It is well to indicate, also, before closing this section, something of the nature of the written agreements entered into between the sub-contractor and the officials of the head-office. These will vary in each particular case — according as the work undertaken pertains to clearing right-of-way, building trestles or to the actual construction of the grade. There are, nevertheless, certain stipulations well understood by the men in the bunkhouse which seem to be an essential part of all agreements for sub-letting. Five of them at least may be mentioned here:

1 Agreement is entered into to complete the portion of road between mileage, say 220 and 231, up to grade level, as called for in the specifications supplied by the engineers.
2 The prices are stated which will be allowed the sub-contractor for rock, clay and muskeg excavation. Classification, too, is generally promised, for example, if a piece of work changes (clay develops where muskeg is listed on blueprint, or if an unexpected showing of rock deters the sub-contractor in his work) new and proportionate rates will be allowed, upon the approval of the engineers.
3 A clause provides a time limit for the completion of the work.
4 The head-contractor reserves to himself the right to cancel the sub-contract or to put extra men on portions of it, if he deems it necessary in order to hasten the work.
5 It is also agreed that all needed supplies must be purchased only through the head-contractor.

Doubtless all these precautions are essential. There is need, too, at times, to spur on some of the sub-contractors. For a delinquent on any one sub-contract to hold back the steel when, in the course of months, it creeps up the line, would impose serious loss, not only upon the head-company but upon the other sub-contractors on the same piece of work. Hence the necessity for a more or less stringent agreement between the head-contractor and his sub-contractors.

One thing is favourable to the sub-contractor; he need make no big initial outlay. He starts, however, with a big debit charged against him for supplies. But the sub-contractor counts much on his experience. His credit stands good at the head office so long as he does enough work on his contract to wipe off all advances. The fulfilment of the sub-contract, if he handles himself right, should not only obliterate the accounts at the head office, but leave him a handsome profit as well.

The relation existing between the head-contractor and the sub-contractor, however, seems but to whet the appetite for more sub-letting. At any rate the sub-contractors invariably proceed where possible to sub-let in another form, which final form is in fact the most acute. From the experience gained in his relations with the head-contractor he hastens to let out his work again to small work-groups in 'stations' of one hundred feet each. Some groups will take five, eight, or eleven stations, and they in turn undertake to build their portion of the road up to grade level. In the system of sub-letting, station-work is about the fourth circle out from the head-contractor.

The agreement which the station-men enter into is a replica in substance of that which the sub-contractor has already signed with the head-contractor, with the exception of the rates paid for yardage and the prices charged for goods. The sub-contractor sees to it that his margin on both is sufficient to help defray his debt at the headquarters camp and to insure a safe return on the work he has already undertaken.

The peak of the contract system in railway building was reached on Canada's last transcontinental. There, too, was its weakness most in evidence: sub-letting became an art. Men and officials in the possession of large contracts traded on their holdings, and intermediaries sought profits from transferring their various interests. How did such relations affect wages? The following sections show the contract system in actual operation along railway construction in the James Bay country. The details enumerated are characteristic of similar employments on other works during these ten busy years of construction across the Dominion.

Chapter 3

Work and pay in isolated camps

HIRING THE CAMPMAN: THE PRIVATE EMPLOYMENT
BUREAU IN OPERATION

In the chapters immediately preceding, an attempt has been made to
sketch the background of the navvy. It is intended in the three
sections of this present chapter to enter, with more detail, into the
actual facts of daily life as they pertained to the hire, the housing,
and the pay of men in camps during the last period of railway
expansion in Canada.

The present section will touch briefly on the system of hiring
frontier workers through private employment agencies. This method,
previous to 1916, was commonly pursued throughout all parts of the
Dominion in placing workers on the job, particularly men employed
in bushwork, at mines, and other camp activities. The following
pages show something of the system in operation, particularly in the
five-year period following 1910.

Even until very recent years the private employment agency was
always conspicuous in the various towns adjacent to camp-works.
Indeed it was also much in evidence in the larger Canadian centres,
such as Ottawa, Edmonton, Montreal, Winnipeg, as well as Fort
William, Sudbury, North Bay and other large towns that commonly
served as feeders for all kinds of camp labour, required on the
various frontier works.

Even the legislative enactments of the past few years have not
wholly eliminated the private agencies. Perhaps a score may still be
found in the Province of Ontario alone. They are closely observed,
however, and many of the distinctive practices that were formerly
associated with this business have disappeared in the proximity of
official bureaux efficiently controlled.

The old 'shipping-office' is still remembered: unpretentious and
modestly located, perhaps at a corner adjacent to the station or in a
nearby lane, these places were the rendezvous for unplaced men.
Such an office had always an enticing display of ad-heads plastering
the walls and windows. Notices were paraded to advantage on
bulletins announcing: 'Men Wanted'; 'Good Wages Paid Teamsters';
'Labourers for Construction'; 'Bushmen Wanted, $40. a month';
'Railway Contractor needs 100 men, $2. per day'; 'Men for
Station-work,' etc., etc. A blackboard tilted at an angle for the
advantage of the unemployed conveyed further detailed information
of work to be had, while many items already erased showed the

danger of delay. Even the sidewalk cement in the front of the stand, chalked in colours, would indicate particularly some tit-bit in the way of employment.

To the man who is down and out, and who has eagerly scanned the boards of the different shipping offices, the natural thing to do is to inquire within. Occasionally, but not always, a fee is charged before imparting information as to the details of the work. That will depend on the arrangements already made by the employment agent with the employing company. It is always impressed as an inducement to the men seeking work that the wage offered is considerably higher – perhaps twenty-five cents or fifty cents per day – than that paid locally for a similar class of work.

A common objection raised by men looking for work under such circumstances is the distance to the camp and the railway fare incurred. This, also, is usually coupled with the fact that they have not a cent in their pockets. This predicament, however, while serious, may easily be overcome; the employment agent, because of his relations with the employing firms, can advance the fare. Meals and sleeping places for the whole time en route to the camp – often over a week is consumed in such trips – will be provided for the men, and the whole amount can then be deducted from wages accruing later, once they are located. Sometimes even tobacco is supplied and other inducements are made for the campman to sign up.

Who are the usual applicants at such places? The casuals, some tired of doing nothing, others sore after a big drunk, just the flotsam and jetsam who go to make up the migratory classes in frontier towns. There are others, too, men, foreign-born, newly arrived in the country, and glad of just such an offer to get immediate work with accompanying transportation to their tasks.

Most men 'hooking-up' for work camps of whatever kind, under the old conditions of hire, were asked by the employment agent to sign a contract. These wage agreements were usually worded similarly even for different forms of employment. The rate of pay was definitely stipulated, whether by the hour or the day, and the price to be charged for board was also stated. Further promises were often made for overtime, and Sunday work to be had, if desired, with extra remuneration. Invariably, too, there was the provision that those who remained three to six months on the job would be refunded all the extra charges incurred for their transportation and meals en route to camp.

The whole proposition seems fair. Few applicants but have resolved, under the existing circumstances, to stay at least six months, if not a year, on the next job they undertake. Resolution looms large in such cases, and the refund for transportation looks to be almost in the hand. Indeed it may be said that the employment agent finds this provision in hiring to be the big inducement even when others fail. At any rate it means to the seasonal worker definite opportunity for employment and in new fields; even this, to one of such temperament, is not to be overlooked.

During the period of railway expansion in Canada which had not terminated previous to the beginning of the World War, most large employers of camp workers kept in touch with these small employment agencies – the large railway contracting firms particularly. Nor did any self-respecting agency disdain such arrangements. It meant in effect that at certain seasons all the men booked by it would be readily placed.

The more men shipped the bigger the profits, for the employment agent got from $1. to $2. for each of the men he could sign up. This was not collected from the men, but came from the head office of the contractor, for whom they were signed. This required, however, that the men be landed on the contract; consequently they were taken in bunches, twenty-five to two hundred at a time. The planting of men in this way on distant works often consumed a week or ten days for the scouts who accompanied these gangs.

Such employment agencies commonly co-operated with similar ones in other cities; various offices in North Bay, Sudbury, Sault Ste Marie, Fort William, Toronto and Montreal were connected indirectly, or at least worked through one another. Between 1900 and 1915, before an effort was made at official regulation of the privately-owned bureaux, the employment agent did a lucrative business in the north. A lawyer has been known to divert his efforts for a time to this remunerative trade.

With the continued influx of men from the continent to the camps of Canada, in those years immediately preceding the World War, many of the employment agencies paid particular attention to the foreign-born workers. Quite often such private offices were conducted by men who themselves were not naturalized citizens in the Dominion. Offices thus operated appeared to work in chains.

The methods of all private agencies, which catered particularly to the illiterate foreign-born, varied but little. The main thing was to get the newcomers from Central Europe, blessed as they are with strong arms and broad backs, hastily signed-up and forwarded. Duly informed of the prospective arrival of an immigrant ship, a representative of these agencies would meet the Atlantic boat, crowded with new arrivals, at the docks. Some agents more enterprising than the others would, when permitted, come up the river from Quebec City with the men in the steerage.

Such labour recruits were, of course, pleased to learn so soon of profitable employment awaiting them. Upon landing at Montreal they were herded directly to the agency; there they were patted and stroked the right way until signed up. Then they were soon hustled to a railway camp hundreds of miles distant somewhere in the hinterland. Not infrequently these newcomers from beyond the Atlantic were landed at a frontier work with little more real knowledge of the settled parts of Canada than was already surmised before leaving their native village somewhere in central Europe. Their first impressions of the new land, now that they had arrived, were gleaned intermittently from a car window, as the woods and rocks and lakes of the unsettled northland sped past in ever-widening circles.

Not uncommonly such workers were enticed by the smooth-tongued individuals, rich in dialects, who, while a countryman of theirs, was already experienced in methods of hire common through the Dominion. Such a man was indeed invaluable toward making for the success of any privately-conducted agency. To observe his tactics among his group of nationals, when, for days at a time, a construction train slowly makes its way out from the end of the steel, is to note his callous attitude toward the real interests of his fellow-countrymen. In doing work of this nature he is not unlike the trained steer of the stockyards which decoys into chosen channels its kindred brutes, yet always to its own advantage.

It has already been mentioned that due care was exercised by private agencies in hiring men, to have an applicant looking for work sign an agreement. Regular and in place as this may seem, it gave in turn too little protection to the worker himself. The formal signing of papers may give confidence to the more ignorant but it proves doubly beneficial to the agents themselves.

Many such agreements used by private employment agencies in Canada were emphatically one-sided. The rate of pay and the charges for board were alone expressly stated, but the dozen and one discrepancies and minor losses usually incurred in camps were not fully anticipated by newcomers to forms of frontier works. Too commonly things were skilfully misrepresented if not deliberately falsified and men engaging thus were hastily bundled off to find out for themselves the conditions of work and pay at isolated camps.

There is inserted here a form of hire typical of the work agreements signed by men at private employment agencies for labour during this period of railway construction. Different American offices, as has already been indicated, co-operated in turn with similar branches in Canada. The contract is vague enough except that it articles a man for work at a set wage per day to some employer, and states clearly the advances so far made. Such a form however has little to indicate what will be the real wages when actual conditions are later encountered at camp.

There was another phase of the work of the private employment bureau during those years which deserves to be mentioned. The hiring of men for work as navvies north of the height of land was hampered throughout several years by the peculiar labour conditions which existed in the Cobalt country. The one railway which fed construction on the National Transcontinental passed for sixty miles through the silver area. The many new mining centres, pulsing with the hopes of new-found gains, attracted and held many of the unskilled workers; higher wages, more congenial surroundings, less bossing and a contact with men and enterprises which gave promise of bigger results attracted the more solid type of English and French-speaking men who, ordinarily, would have gravitated as navvies to the railway construction father north.

The continual loss of these better-class workers caused many a heart-burn to the employment agents. From their office at Sudbury, North Bay or Sault Ste Marie they would sign men for work somewhere in the Abitibi country. To land them on the job meant a journey of days, and necessitated passing by train through the mining country. It was their misfortune and constant worry that whole groups of workers thus engaged to go to camps on construction did not hesitate to jump their agreements at the first

S. GREENBERG'S EMPLOYMENT AGENCY
162 EAST 4TH STREET, NEW YORK

STATEMENT of LABOR CONTRACT
in accordance with Chapter 700 of the Laws of 1910.

Name of Employer Name des Stellungsgebenden Alkalmazást ado neve Pracu dajuceho meno Nome del padrone Nama af arbetsgifvaren Imie pracydajacego	
Address of Employer Adresse des Stellungsgebenden Alkalmazást ado czime Pracu dajuceho adressa Direzione del padrone Adress af arbetsgifvaren Adres pracydajacego	*Cochran Ont*
Name of Employee Name des Angestellten Alkalmazott czime Robotnikow meno Nome del Lavorante Namn af arbetstagaren Imie robotnika	*Irony Kuntz*
Address of Employee Adresse des Angestellten Alkalmazott neve Robotnikow adressa Direzione del Lavorante Adress af arbetstagaren Adres robotnika	
Nature of work to be performed Art der auszuführenden Arbeit A munka minősége Jaka robota Specie di Lavoro Det arbete som skall utföras Jaka praca	*Lifting & Ballasting on R. R.*
Hours of Labor Anzahl der Arbeitsstunden Munka orák száma Kelo hodini robit Ore di Lavoro Arbets-timmarne Ilosc godzin roboczych	*10 hours*
Wages offered Angebotener Lohn Felajánlott munkabér Kelo placu Paga offerta Den lön som erbjudes Jaka placa	*$2 00 per day*
Destination of the persons employed Bestimmungsort der Angestellten Az alkalmazottak küldetési helye Dze jo poselanim Destinazione delle persone impiegate Destinationen af de anställda personerna Miejsce przyznaczone do roboty	*Cochran Ont*
Terms of Transportation Transport-Bedingungen Szállitási feltételek Jak budu poslane Condizione di viaggio Villkoren för deras transportering Warunki jazdy	*$24. advanced & deducted*
Remarks Anmerkungen Megjegyzések Posnaoska Osservazioni Anmärkning Uwaga	*Board $60 per day*

If more than one person is engaged, list of names and addresses will be found attached

New York,......*Sept 6th*......1911   *fare after 6 months free*

ENGLISH   GERMAN   HUNGARIAN, SLOVAK   ITALIAN, SWEDISH   POLISH

Typical form of agreement signed at private employment agencies, 1905-14 opportunity when in the Cobalt country. For, with ruthless regularity, in spite of precautions, there soon trickled to the ears of men thus articled, forbidden tales of work and pay in the railway camps; and second thoughts with men so circumstanced prompted quick action.

To protect themselves, the employment agents would sometimes dispatch the men who had signed up with them for railway work in car lots, with two guards in charge. Separate coaches filled with navvies thus scouted were sometimes attached to the regular trains on the Temiskaming Railway. The doors of the coaches bearing the labourers were locked for some hours while passing through the towns of the mining district. But such precautions were often futile, for quite frequently men under agreement to serve as navvies eluded the guards and quietly escaped from the coach windows or other unwatched exits. During those particular years cases were not infrequent of men being handcuffed and thus manacled conveyed under guard to a camp, there to fulfil the terms of agreement for work for which they had engaged at an employment office. No defence is here intended of men who, even under the conditions, violated their wage bargain. Some, doubtless, were culpable in using the transportation provided by an employment agent to reach the Cobalt field. But why the mistrust so general of conditions of work in camps along the National Transcontinental?

One class of workers did not seek eagerly to escape. They were the foreign-born labourers routed north as navvies to some sub-contractor. All things were new to them and strange; Cobalt meant no more to them than McDougall's Chutes or Moonbeam Creek. They sat stolid, passive, rolling their hand-made smokes, taking their orders from a leader, who had often a monetary interest in landing them on the works.

During the greater portion of the period which marks the construction of the two latest transcontinentals the placing of labour of any kind in camps, as already mentioned, continued largely in the hands of private agents. This system, whatever be its merits, soon begat many questionable practices. Responsible men who at one time may have engaged in this occupation were gradually eliminated, their places being taken by another type who placed mercenary objects to the fore. Foreign-born men, often but recently arrived in Canada, were largely in control of the private employment agencies. There was lack of uniformity in the handling of the applicants for work. Charges varied with the individual agent and the brunt of the whole disorder in hiring was borne by the men in camps and bunkhouses.

Changed conditions since 1916
Since 1916 a change has taken place throughout the Dominion in the matter of employment agencies. The private agent, as already mentioned, has been greatly curtailed, and the Federal Government in co-operation with the provinces has substituted a system of bureaux country-wide. They have in view the placement of men according to the need existing for any particular class of workers.

While the purpose of this monograph is, primarily, to provide an estimate of work and pay in camps previous to 1915, the writer desires here to pay due tribute to the men of the employment bureaux both Federal and provincial throughout Canada. Their ability and personal sincerity, invariably, have proven a wholesome factor in recent years toward bettering conditions of hire and pay for men on seasonal works.

Since the employment office superintendent's remuneration does not depend upon the number of placements he makes, he has nothing to gain by misrepresentation of employment conditions. The result is that the information which he furnishes to applicants is dependable. Information is given as to the nature of the work, its location, the rate of wages and the probable cost of board and lodging. Other factors that may bear upon the situation are also indicated, such as the probable duration of employment and possible requirements as to membership in a union.

The public employment office now in vogue provides, further, a channel for the worker to register his complaints and air his grievances. Sometimes the mere expression of his opinion is all that is necessary to 'get the load off his mind,' but if there is a real basis for his complaint it will be taken up by the superintendent in an effort to remedy the conditions which are causing complaint.

For the worker who uses the government service to assist him in finding employment soon learns to regard each local superintendent as a friend. The official, in turn, protects the interests of his applicants, particularly in matters pertaining to wage adjustment.

The government employment service has, without a doubt, checked certain abuses formerly practised by unscrupulous employers. They evidently realize that any question pertaining to the hiring of workers may now be brought to the attention of a department of the government whose primary interest is employment. They realize, too, that consequences may be more serious than in the olden days when employment was nobody's particular business.

Then, too, the establishment of a public bureau has obviated the necessity of a 'wild goose chase' from place to place, to follow up rumours of possible employment. With the public employment office, providing as it does accurate and ready information relating to employment conditions from coast to coast, it is no longer necessary for any worker to travel long distances on the odd chance of securing employment.

When employment is available at a distance, workers securing their positions or jobs through any branch of the government employment service can obtain a reduced transportation rate which saves them ¼c. a mile for any distance where the minimum fare is over $4.00. Thus, under the private employment agency system charges for fares were often padded, but under the government system the cost is less than the standard rate.

But probably the outstanding direction in which the public employment service has improved conditions for the workers has been through the virtual elimination of the private employment agent. While it is true that private employment agencies still exist, their numbers are limited, their personnel has been improved in type and their activities have been supervised to a greater extent than was the case prior to 1916. The element of competition which has now entered into their business has in itself been a factor in reducing exploitation and the other abuses incidental to the operation of the old-style private employment agency.

The Labour Bureaux in Canada have a distinct advantage over the corresponding machinery in the United States, in that there is entire co-operation between the Federal and provincial branches. In the Republic, on the other hand, there is occasionally a lack of accord between a state organization and the central body at Washington. The Dominion Government, too, supplements the work of the different provincial bureaux by a grant proportionate to the amount expended annually.

THE CAMPMAN AT WORK: WAGE CONDITIONS FOR MEN IN A
GRADE CAMP ON RAILWAY CONSTRUCTION

In order to understand more clearly certain aspects of work which in themselves have a direct bearing on the wage of all campmen, it is here proposed to consider the various problems due to peculiar adjustments of place and locality which confront workers in isolated camps. For this purpose the grade camp on railway construction has been selected as being a replica of conditions of actual employment frequently existing in frontier places.

The navvy has a choice of camps, for there are always many different works in progress on a piece of railway construction. The headquarters camps, the ballast pits, the repair camps and the material yards are located on the steel; but the several grade camps which are frequently the headquarters of a sub-contractor lie out miles distant on the grade. Besides these there are, too, ahead of the steel, minor camps located at rock cuts, trestle-works, dams and excavations.

The repair camps, the ballast pits and the material yards usually pertain to the secondary stage of construction. They are busiest when the steel is being laid and the skeleton tracks are being lifted and ballasted. They are sometimes called finishing camps. The men employed at these are largely trainmen, and skilled mechanics of different trades. They are often union men, and are not ordinarily classed as navvies.

The grade camps are situated at ten-mile intervals and extend beyond the steel as far as the work is in operation—eighty, a hundred miles, or more. These camps are large, comprising a group of from six to ten good-sized log buildings. They may be operated directly by the head company, who employ a foreman and men at day labour, but more usually they are the local headquarters of a sub-contractor. The permanent officials at a grade camp are the sub-contractor (who may be an absentee), the local foreman and clerk, the cook, cookee and the barn boss. The sub-contractor engages capable help where possible to fill these positions. They are paid a straight monthly salary, which includes board as well.

But circumstances are very different with the man in a distant camp who works by the day. He soon finds himself in the matter of pay up against certain obstacles. In order that work conditions in such places may be studied from different angles, one example is given of each of three varying types of grade camps. These examples are all taken from works along the National Transcontinental, yet they are applicable not only to other camps both along railways, in the woods and at mines during that period of construction, but also to most camps similarly situated even to-day.

Let us look in turn at:

I A grade camp operated directly by local officials of a head-contractor, but under unfavourable circumstances and in an adverse location.

II A grade camp operated directly by similar officials of a head-contractor under favourable circumstances and in a good location.

III A usual grade camp operated by a sub-contractor.

In the case of 'I,' subjoined, exact names of places are given. This is not intended as any undue reflection on the operators of that contract, but the reader, with an exact mental survey in this case of what is really involved when a navvy undertakes to reach camp, is better fitted to judge fairly statements made of similar cases in further sections of the book.

Wages at a grade camp operating under unfavourable conditions

Three men, Canadians, a little above the average in physique, hired at Montreal to work with a railway contracting firm who were opening up a piece of work on the National Transcontinental Railway, one hundred and fifty-eight miles running east of where the town of Cochrane has since been located. McDougall's Chutes (now Matheson) was the end of the steel, being the farthest point north then reached by the Temiskaming Railway.

Along with the other members of the party, and conducted by a scout from a labour office after they had left North Bay, the men reached McDougall's Chutes the evening of the following day. After a night in the company bunkhouse there, the party was taken next morning by tug and scow down the Black River into the Abitibi River and as far as Iroquois Falls, a distance of about twenty-four miles. There the company had a cache camp.

The campman is fond of new scenes and frequent changes, and in a land where winter frosts are followed soon by heats of summer, a river trip throughout a June day is to be desired. The little tug ahead struggling with the tow-line pants vehemently; around sharp bends and straight from point to point it keeps its way, its dignity displayed occasionally by a shower of fiery sparks which sprinkle the men in the open scow behind. The sun is hot, and the sky shows clear between the fringe of spruce and hemlock which lines the river banks. Warmly clad, the men recline on bales of hay or squat on bags and boxes. With weather bright and crisp, the tang of health and life bounds on every hand. There are days and times when northland rivers beckon most strongly to those who eschew restraints of more ordered living, and the ensuing response in the hearts of sturdy men helps to maintain that steady supply of migratory workers for the camps of the frontier.

By two o'clock that afternoon the river cache was reached and a dinner was hastily prepared of canned beans, bread and tea. The tug went no farther, but the freight from the scows was transhipped across the portage to the pointers on the river below. Loaded with supplies and crowded with men, these boats, the same evening, reached the second cache at the Buck Deer Rapids distant some eight miles down the river. Here camp was made for the night.

By late noon of the next day the men arrived at the company's main camps situated where the right-of-way of the new transcontinental crossed the Abitibi River. This camp – Abitibi Crossing as it was called – was a bustling camp that summer, being the distributing point for the company. The grade was under way thirty miles east and about ten miles west of that point. Here the party was broken up, most of the foreigners in it – Bulgarians newly arrived – were retained at the Crossing, eight others (among whom were two of the Canadians mentioned) were destined for a grade camp out near Mestongo Creek, about nineteen miles distant, east of Abitibi Crossing. The grade being practically unditched at the time, and not even stumped, the trip was slow, for creeks and streams, then in flood, had to be crossed, and more than a day was consumed before the camp was reached.

The terms of engagement for the men at Montreal were: $2. a day as railway workers, with $4.60 deducted each week for board, and fare allowed if a man stopped six months. This was the verbal agreement with the employment agent, for, in this case, no paper had been signed.

What was the condition of these men, as far as the company was concerned, when they started work at the camp? All three were practically under the same obligation, but let us take the statement of one. He owed to the company:

(a) Railway fares	$15.60
(b) Meals served en route at company's camps (11 meals)	5.50
(c) Cost of conducting	2.00
(d) Blankets	6.25
(e) Doctor and mail	1.25
	$30.60

In this particular case the men were not charged for sleeping in the bunkhouse, as is sometimes done.

This amount $30.60, stood against the man as charges before he did a day's work. He started in to work on June 22nd. He worked three days, rested Sunday and then worked till Wednesday night, when wet weather stopped things for a couple of days, and so the month of June closed.

This is the account with the company at the close of the month:

June 22	To charges as shown	$30.60	
30	Board from 21st to 30th	5.50	
			$36.10
30	By work, 60 hours at 20c per hr.		12.00
July 1	To balance from June		$24.10
	Mail and medical fees (for July)		1.25
	Balance (due company)		$25.35

With this considerable camp deficit, a start was made in the new month.

July of that year had a great deal of rain. The wear and tear and mud began to tell on the men's outfits. In the case of this particular man, who was one of the most industrious and saving in the camp, it was necessary to get a pair of boots, $6.50, a pair of overalls, $2.25, leather mitts, 60c. The flies, too, were bad, and fly oil, 25c., tobacco,

$1.00, matches, 25c., paper and envelopes, 25c., and painkiller, 50c., stood against the account before the end of the month.

But some overtime had been obtained, and, in spite of wet weather, two hundred and six hours were put in during the month.

At the end of July the wage account with the company was as follows:

July 30	To balance from June	$25.35	
	Purchases (as mentioned above)	11.60	
	Board	20.00	
			$56.95
	By work, 206 hours, at 20 cents		41.20
Aug. 1	To balance	15.75	
	Mail and medical	1.25	
			$17.00

August was started with $17.00 still in arrears for charges. Before the end of August, however, the discouraging pay and the monotony, the mud and the isolation of the camp produced dissatisfaction and the man decided to quit.

Upon settlement at the office his account showed as follows:

Aug. 27	By 235 hours work $47.00		$47.00
Aug. 1	To balance owing Company		
	from July	$17.00	
Aug. 27	To board for August	16.00	
Aug. 27	Purchases from Company store –	3.95	
	Shirt $2.00, Socks (2 pr.) $1.20, Tobacco .75		36.95
			10.05
	Refund on blankets (50c deducted for washing)		5.75
	Balance due on wages		$15.80

On August 27th he was paid off with a time cheque for $15.80. He had left Montreal on June 15th, or, in short, after two and one-half months he had less than $16.00 and his board to show for his work and time.

But that was not all. He was close on twenty miles from Abitibi Crossing and there were two rivers to cross. When at Abitibi Crossing he had still before him forty-two miles of water and rapids to

McDougall's Chutes – the end of the steel. Only the company had boats on the river. A canoe would cost $5. a day.

He had another alternative; to take a trail which led from the Crossing and hit the Temiskaming Railway construction at a point a few miles below where the town of Cochrane is now located, then follow the Temiskaming Railway right-of-way for thirty-six miles to the steel at McDougall's Chutes. This also implied paying ferry charges at exorbitant rates to men attached to *residencies*, who were often using government-owned canoes. Being charged fifty to seventy-five cents for each meal if he eats at a cookery and forbidden the use of the company's bunkhouses – he is in every way made to feel the exactions of the company, exerted on the man who quits work. In the face of such alternatives he took the trail.

What portion of the $15.80 is in his pocket when he reaches the end of the steel? What percentage of that, again, will be left by the time he waits a day or two for a train and $6.00 is paid for a ticket back to North Bay, or if, by chance he has enough to reach some place where he can in time get work with real wages?

That summer an English-speaking foreigner had been six weeks out on the grade for the same firm. He arrived in McDougall's Chutes with sixty-five cents in his pocket. A few cents for six weeks' work! Financially outgeneraled, for the exactions made on him had all been perfectly legal! It's a case where the experience may be worth something, but, to those who have been through it all, the possible explanations will scarcely remove the burning sense of the injustice.

But just here the objection may be raised that all of this is an old story, that these work conditions were abnormal, and that this particular company was hard hit in many ways. It may be affirmed, too, that to mention this company is to select an extreme case, for its contract was one of the first in the Abitibi country and that conditions of work improved in the following years. If that were so these incidents would not be recalled – the sooner forgotten the better. Nevertheless they are referred to for two reasons: first, that they offer a plain representation of how things actually evolved in the matter of pay for men in grade camps during that period, and, second, as has already been indicated, such forms of settlement are still too common for the workers in isolated camps.

The figures here quoted were not the exception, due to untoward conditions on a particular contract. They were the rule at many grade camps of the period, similarly situated. For, wherever the

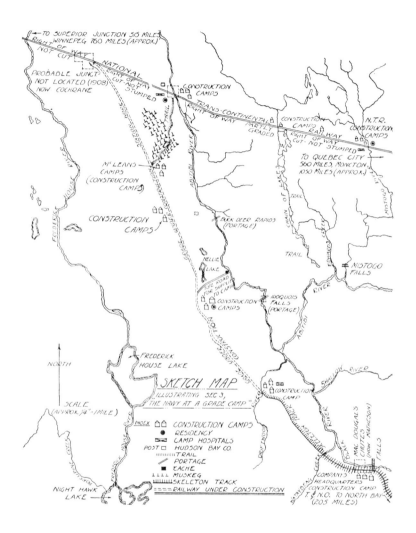

Map illustrating locations in chapter 3

conditions are such that, in order to reach camp, it is necessary for
men to follow the tote-road and rivers, with many delays and
stop-overs, precisely the same charges will be booked against them as
outlined above. It cannot be otherwise, the navvy shipped to a grade
camp is much in arrears before he ever gets started to earn.

But one need not draw conclusions too hastily. Let us look at the
working of the system some months later on another section of the
same road.

Wages at a grade camp operated under
favourable conditions
A group of men, nine in number, hired in Ottawa, at a private
employment office and under the usual terms. In this case pay was
to be $1.75, with a raise to $2.00 a day if their work was
satisfactory. There was also the promise of a refund of railway fare
to those who remained on the work some months.

These men, shipped in September, reached the frontier town in
northern Ontario the evening of the second day. They were met at
the station by a clerk of the head office, who conducted them, by
lantern light, down a trail to the headquarters camp, about two miles
distant. There they were fed and bunked. Next morning they were
told that the camp for which they were destined lay thirty-three
miles farther out the grade – a two day's trip at that particular
season, for the steel had been laid only a short distance from
headquarters. This was a surprise to the men who had been led by
the employment agent to infer differently, and who had heard
nothing, when engaging, of a thirty-mile walk, with time lost and
attendant expenses accruing.

They had been told, also, at the employment agency that they
would not have to 'muck,' as the foreign-born navvies did all that
work now. But of that promise, too, the foreman at the camp knew
nothing – his orders were to put them all in the clay cut, and there
was nothing else to do. Workers under such circumstances have no
alternative tasks.

Even in September, in the north country, warm strong clothes
and footwear are needed, but the prices which confronted these men
were astonishing. Although two of the men had had experience in a
lumber camp that same year they found the prices charged for the
van goods, at a grade camp, nearly double: low shoepacks $4.50,
worth $1.75 to $2.25 at the front; three-quarter length packs, worth

ordinarily $3.50 to $5.00, selling at $8.00; the prices of mackinaws, heavy socks, top shirts and woolen underwear were in similar proportions.

The men started to work the second week in September, but the month was so wet that there was a great deal of lost time and the men hardly held their own. Here are the charges entered against the men in this camp when they started work:

To advances —
Railway fare	$11.40
Meals en route (9 meals)	4.50
Blankets	5.00
Mail and medical	1.00
	$21.90

On October 1st the statement of one of the men with the company was as follows:

Sept. 30	To advances		$21.90	
	Board at camp	$11.40		
	1 pair shoepacks	4.50		
			15.90	
			$37.80	
	By work for 108 hours at			
	17½c per hour		18.90	
Oct. 1	Balance due company		$18.90	
	Mail and medical (for October)		1.00	
	Still due the company on			
	Oct. 1			$19.90

This man was offered $2.00 a day in October, and he started in again. But colder weather began to tighten things up. To work with any degree of comfort he had to buy warmer clothes and underwear. But, because of the prices charged for such supplies and the apparent hopelessness of ever getting square before months of work, the man asked for his time. Trouble then arose, for, according to the books, he was still in debt to the company. Finally a settlement was arranged. He was paid $35.00 a month straight and board, losing no wet days. This proved more satisfactory. He remained at the camp till February, and saved something, too, once the leakages were stopped.

Wages at a grade camp operated by a
sub-contractor
But were conditions of work and pay more favourable in a camp not
directly operated by the head-contractor? Outside a private
employment agency in North Bay during the period now being
discussed, chalked on a sloppy board, was the following:

MEN WANTED: FOR CAMPS
Day work	$ 2.00
Cooks	60.00
Carpenters	4.00
Blacksmiths	75.00

The above prices were very fair in that locality, considering the
supply of labour offering for work of that nature. In a few hours a
number of men, twenty-eight in all, were signed up by the agent.
They comprised the active, well set-up class of men who follow
frontier works, not quibblers over what is offered, ready for
anything, once their stake is spent – that nondescript lot common
to the camp trails in that period, with numbers in due proportion of
hasty speech and loud assertion, others with native wit and grouch,
and yet withal, when traveling in groups to camp, not uncongenial
with whom to tramp and bunk.

The men were promised work at different occupations and with a
monthly pay according to the class of labour performed – at least
that was inferred – but in the bland manner of the employment
agent, the matter of individual pay was stated in this fashion: 'Now,
all you men will get work, some as cooks, some as blacksmiths, some
as stable-bosses, but I'll just put you all down as labourers; then,
when you get to camp, each of you will be placed at your own line
of work.' This was agreed to. The twenty-eight men scouted, and in
this case outscouted, by an extra man from the agency, were landed
late the following night at a construction hamlet farther north.

The men spent the next two days tramping the broken grade to a
camp thirty-two miles to the east, for their agreements, when now
more closely scanned, disclosed the fact that they were hired by one
company but were intended for a sub-contractor.

Arrived at camp the foreman, who, in this case, was a Swede from
Minnesota and who had been tied up for days by want of muckers,

ordered the men next morning into the gumbo cut which for weeks had baffled the camp. Then the uproar began: 'I hired as a cook,' said one. 'I was promised work carpentering,' persisted a man with a Cape Breton accent. 'I'm no Dago – I'm a blacksmith,' declared a man in irate tones who hailed from in back of Pembroke. But the foreman, somewhat heated himself over the turn of events, assured them he was not looking for dudes, pencilmen, or experts, it was pick-and-shovel men he wanted.

'You men have all signed this here paper as labourers and you get to work and pay for the charges against you or I'll have you locked up,' continued the foreman, now furious.

But numbers were lacking to enforce his threats, and the new arrivals derisively defied him to set about carrying them out.

Later that day the men started their tramp back again to the construction town they had left two days before. Upon arrival there the whole of them were rounded up, and those who would not go to work at the company headquarters camp, and thus pay off the charges against them, were locked up in the primitive jail for a time. Finally all were released after promising to work for another contractor.

It is not intended in the above quoted incident to hold the men wholly blameless, but rather to show the friction which results at a grade camp because men when being hired are told only half-truths. They are deluded by plain misrepresentation which later affects wage conditions at the camps.

Nor are these incidents bald examples chosen at random. They are intended to show that the campman under such surroundings of work and pay is handicapped in three ways:

1 The isolation of the camps.
2 The excessive charges made for his supplies.
3 The misrepresentation which often underlies the wage agreements of workers in frontier places.

And, with the whole system unchanged, things are not prone to be otherwise. Who is to lose the time consumed in reaching a camp – often more than a week elapses on such trips? Who will provide the meals? Where will men sleep when en route to camps, and who will provide the blankets and pay necessary transportation across lakes and down swift rivers, with attendant delays, sometimes of days? Certain it is, the head company will not! All these charges must, in some way, come out of the men! At least that is the view commonly held by employers of such classes of labour.

The promise made, that if a man stops six months his fare will be refunded, looks fair, but, out of every hundred men who engage at manual work and sleep in the bunkhouse, you can count on the fingers of your left hand all that will be in a camp six months after they have entered it. The conditions previously mentioned – the monotony, the shifting, the camp-ennui – will drive them out. Indeed, too, cases are not unheard-of where things are made so uncomfortable that men are forced to leave a few weeks before the six months are up. Any such clause inserted in an agreement for work in camps is often but a veritable bait and both the company and the employment agents know this full well. To what proportion of the navvies in a grade camp is it ever refunded? How many workers, other than lesser officials, who start work in May at an isolated camp, will still be there at the close of September? That is the final test!

Rain and loss of time from inclement weather are a big factor in any campman's pay. Where men are hired by the day and lose wet weather, Sundays, and whole days while the machines are being repaired, they will struggle manfully if they are to keep even with the board. What with the different charges, five or six weeks may elapse before navvies so hired will have a dollar to their credit. It cannot be otherwise, figure as you will. A good healthy, strong man employed at a grade camp, in the September month of one of the years here under survey, was twenty-two days in camp and had only eight working days to his credit. In that particular month there had been eleven wet days and three Sundays during that period. That is not wages; it is practically a form of wage perversion – as well be paid in cowries.

In August, 1911, a trusted Russian was advanced money by a sub-contractor with which he went back to his native village and brought out sixteen of his stalwart countrymen. It cost $64.20 to land each of them in Montreal. There was then a further railway trip of five hundred and fifty miles, costing $24.00, and then a five-day tramp to the grade camp beyond the steel. When finally landed each man would be close to $100. in debt to the sub-contractor. It would not be difficult to show that these men, under the best of conditions, would work many months before they were quite square with the board. It was a good stroke for the latter to expend even $2000. to get seventeen good men who were articled and forced to stick until all advances were paid. But, under the system, as pay worked out practically for the navvy at a grade camp, it meant peonage and nothing else; conditions not befitting Canadians, nor even a Carib of the Windward Islands.

The workers at such camps may be recruited from two sources: the foreign-born who have yet to find out how the trap is sprung; and the English-speaking campman who, perhaps after a big spree, does not care where they ship him for a few months as long as they send him far enough from the drink, which, for the moment, he has learned to loathe.

It is no uncommon thing in railway camps to see some stalwart officer of the line exert pressure of his office on a bunch of foreign-born navvies, and force them to resume work at a camp where, after days and weeks, they have little coming in pay and wish to quit. But who, with experience of any length in far-out camps, will say he has once seen the law exerted similarly to give these same campmen the protection of simple justice? Truly, British law never seems so shabby as when raggedly enforced by some petty officer on railway construction.

In the face of things as they too often exist, in out-of-the-way camps, is it not absurd to read often that good wages are being offered but men refuse to work? Why? Because too many hard-headed campmen with strong hands have grubbed and laboured and worked under unjust conditions in distant camps and then found themselves outfigured at the office. Once bitten, twice shy!

HOUSING THE CAMPMAN: THE BUNKHOUSE FROM WITHIN

All camps imply bunkhouses. The housing of men on any frontier work is of prime importance. Buildings erected for this purpose constitute the most prominent feature of any camp. In fact a camp on an isolated work may frequently be designated as an aggregation of bunkhouses. Except during the meal hour, when the cookery claims undisputed precedence, the bunkhouse shares in the daily routine of the men, serving in the off hours not only as a dwelling but as the common meeting place of the camp.

There is great uniformity in the outward appearance of all frontier camps. A great similarity, too, distinguishes their appointments on whatever class of work, whether it be in the woods, on a mining prospect, or along railway construction. One pattern seems to have served the purpose for all future building. The same staid lines which first marked buildings in the timber limits adjacent to the St. Lawrence and along the tributaries of the Ottawa two generations since, are still retained. This uniformity in camps is apparent not only in northern Ontario and Quebec, but farther west in the wooded parts of Manitoba as well as in Alberta and northern Saskatchewan.

This rigid adherence to previous designs may be accounted for by the exigencies of all work in frontier places, particularly by the usual lack of facilities for profitable transporting to isolated camp sites the necessary building material, but combined with this there is also the conservative attitude toward changes of any kind that marks the functioning of life in camps.

Practically the same number of buildings are found in each camp, the office, cookery, bunkhouse, warehouse, stables and a blacksmith shop. The buildings may vary in size, but they are usually built of logs and are rectangular in shape. Along railway construction, a residency, with its neat group of buildings, is often located near the grade camp, and, if the situation is an important one, a building is erected somewhere adjoining to serve as a camp hospital.

With the exception of the office and the blacksmith shop, the buildings are quite large; the average size of a bunkhouse being thirty-four feet by fifty-two feet. They are built of logs, generally large spruce or dead-pine, with the walls of a height of nine or ten good-sized logs. Board floors are used if the location is near the steel, but the more distant camps have large poles, adzed down to make a rough floor. For the roof, small poles of uniform size are placed side by side, reaching from the ridge pole to the walls. The roof is then covered with strong tarpaper or rubberoid. The big cracks between the logs of the wall are chinked and mossed inside and plastered outside with a mixture of clay and a little lime; then, after a good bank of earth has been thrown up all around it, the bunkhouse is ready for the men to occupy.

Each bunkhouse has a 'chore boy,' often an elderly man who has a 'stand-in' with the company. His duty is to fill the water barrels, sweep out once a day and see that the fires are well looked after. The sweeping is usually attended to daily, but the floors are rough and a great deal of dirt accumulates. Bunkhouses are well supplied with water; three large barrels are filled every day, and six or eight washbasins, with plenty of cheap soap, are always at the disposal of the bunkhouse men. The men wash before going to meals; that is a form of camp etiquette duly observed. The quantity of wash water and soap provided and the big stoves with their warm fires are the two redeeming features of the average bunkhouse.

The bunks are of a common pattern, double-deckers; two sleep in each, making four in a section. The bunks extend along both sides of the building and across the back end. A large stove occupies the centre of the floor. Back in one corner will be the jack-pot, a spare bunk into which is tossed outworn apparel, boots, old socks, rubbers, caps, torn overalls, cast-off underwear, discarded clothing of all kinds, and not always clean. The jack-pot provides pickings, too, for the less fortunate who reach camp somewhat down on their uppers.

The bunks are bedded with hay and two or three pairs of heavy blankets are supplied to each bunk, which remain there until the camp breaks up. The blankets may be clean for a few weeks when first put in, but, with the coming and going, the shifting and jumping of these nomadic men, it would be a wonder if the bunkhouse blankets remained clean for any length of time. Vermin are rampant in camps long used, the blankets themselves smell heavy and musty, and, even though one changes underwear every week, it is impossible to keep clean, for lice and nits are in the bedding. There is danger, too, in using camp blankets, of contracting some abominable skin disease, carried by unclean men, for vice is not far distant from construction, and immorality lurks in frontier towns as well as in the congested centres.

The most striking thing about bunkhouses is the absence of light, due to two reasons probably — the difficulty of getting glass to some of the camps in part, but chiefly to precedent. The old-timers, who generally put up the company's camps, never knew such buildings to be well lighted, except perhaps the office. Besides, such men will tell you, windows make a bunkhouse cold. The result is seen in the dungeon-like buildings, camps sixty feet long and thirty feet wide having only two small windows in either gable. On wet days, or on a

Sunday, it is impossible to read or write in such domiciles except in a limited space under the lights.

Bunkhouses when erected, and for months following, are usually dry. Care is taken with the roofing of all camp buildings, with the exception, sometimes, of the warehouses for the coarser supplies. The whole of the roofs, as well as the gables, are covered carefully with thick tarpaper held in place by lath cleats or close-set rows of tinheads. This does well for a season, but it is sorely tested; the winds, the heavy rains of the wet spells, the snow, the freezing and thawing of the winter months soon tell on the papered roofs. It is the misfortune of the inmate, however, that once breaks are made in the paper they are not always attended to, and continued neglect adds to the discomforts of the occupant.

Another fact may be mentioned here in referring to the housing of the men. Camp buildings along railway construction are erected to do duty while a piece of work is being completed, but should something go wrong in the calculations, their provisions run short, a forest fire destroy part of the plant or alterations be made in the plans of the engineers, the occupancy of the bunkhouse is extended for months longer than was originally intended. Meanwhile, instead of fixing up the bunkhouse where the men sleep, the aim is to hustle the work, get through with it, and let the roof take care of itself. This shows up worst in the distant camps; the farther out, the poorer is the accommodation.

There are regulations, stringent enough on paper, requiring clean sanitary conditions in the housing of campmen, but such, too frequently, is the laxity with which these are enforced that bunkhouses tend to become unclean. In spite of the care exercised occasionally by a conscientious foreman, the whole surroundings of a camp tend to deteriorate.

The social life in a bunkhouse community is self-contained. The very work of any distant camp is performed in comparative obscurity. The men themselves dwelling in a camp often miles remote from the nearest hamlet are thrown largely on their own resources during their spare hours. This continues often through varying weeks and months at a time. Life for the individual under such circumstances is often solitary and humdrum, with little change of scene or incentive toward the finer things of life. Monotony predominates even when due allowance is made for the occasional recreation in camp, the passing jest of hardy men engaged in common tasks, or the pipe and story at the close of the day as men half-recumbent on hewed benches gather in groups to while away the evening hour with passing tales and gossip of the camp. A mental sluggishness can but accompany life continued under such environments. This is accentuated throughout the hours of the long days, which, whether due to the weather or for other causes, are spent in idleness about the camp.

Even with healthy men, this manner of life exacts tribute of the innate powers of mind and body. Workers under these environments are allowed to give but not to take. A restlessness pervades their days which ultimately infects not only their thinking, but their habits of life. As the months drag on there is a weariness of heart, a blank feeling that gets the better of the whole man. Take any set of men, however carefully selected, and let them be thrown as intimately together as are the men in a bunkhouse – hearing the same voices, seeing the same faces day after day, and they soon become weary of one another's society and impatient of one another's faults. And these be men who under ordinary circumstances would be able to dwell at peace with their fellows.

The natural reaction is shown in the current unstableness of labour so common in camps. There is the frequent desire to shift work, 'jumping' it is called, even though the move lead to little betterment for the individual. It is the fact of a change that is desired. Restless, 'taking his time' on the slightest pretext, the casual labourer in camps is in some respects the legitimate offspring of the bunkhouse.

The material comforts, tending towards wholesome methods of housing, have been but tardily bestowed on bunkhouse men. Taking one form of frontier work with another throughout the Dominion, it is apparent that little recognition has been given to the need, so frequently existing, for improvements in camp surroundings.

There follow here some descriptions of camps and bunkhouses which have done duty in housing workers in frontier places. All six pertain to the country through which in 1906-14 the Canadian Government was building in successive portions the National Transcontinental. These camps are not the worst that could be mentioned, neither are they the best, but they may be taken as a fair average of what one could have found in any twenty consecutive camps along that railway construction. The showing would not be bettered if the shacks of intervening station-men were also included.

It is well, too, to keep in mind that a cross-section taken of any score of bunkhouses today, whether along railway construction, in bush camps, or other frontier works would show a surprising analogy. With the exception of certain mines, and pulp towns which have been laid out to a plan, the housing of the men engaged on seasonal works in Canada still leaves much to be desired.

Leaky buildings in camps
In May, 1911, four men passing along the grade stopped for the night at a camp twenty-three miles from the steel. It proved to be one which had been singed by a bush fire the previous summer and which had since been but roughly repaired. The winter weather had not bettered the roof and it dripped from every quarter during the frequent spring rains.

Being not unused to camps, they cleared out two of the lower bunks in the large sleep camp and prepared to pass the night. Before morning their top blanket was soaked from dripping water which had first passed through the upper bunk. Why not change? Because much of the camp was leaking, one bunk was as wet as another; yet forty men in that camp, the greater number of whom were foreign-born, had been sleeping for three weeks during the break-up under just such conditions. Livable perhaps for the man newly arrived from the Balkans, but hardly a wholesome environment for the shaping of a future citizen of Canada.

Overcrowding in camps
The camp at No. 52 was the headquarters of a contractor with one hundred miles of the National Transcontinental. The buildings were closely grouped on the bank of a deep clay cut, the bunkhouse was not oblong (as is usually the case), but square. Two small windows lighted the building.

The bunks were built to accommodate forty-eight men, but, on train nights when a fresh lot arrived, it would often have a hundred men. This, with the men coming down the grade or waiting for a settlement at the office, caused the building to be always crowded, the overflow being forced to find the softest spot on the floor for a bed. Hardly could one sleep a night in those bunks and be clean in the morning. A man who used them admitted, 'I'm lousy; I'm good and lousy; but what's a fellow to do? Got to sleep! And I don't think they will let a "wiper" have a bed in the office during the day!' The whole surroundings were fitter far for the stabling of cattle than the abode of men; at a whiff therefrom a well-reared pig would grunt disapproval.

Two men who, about the first of May, were forced to spend three days in the bunkhouse there, preferred the hay tent. Bales were rearranged, a good-sized pocket was made and blankets secured which had been well shaken and aired in the afternoon sun; at least a safer bed was obtained.

A few weeks later, in June, the Legislature of Ontario on excursion bent, and in quest of first-hand knowledge of the northland, leaving their pullmans at the rail-head, were safely guided, on flatcars, down past that camp by agents who were showing them life on construction. But they are an easy lot to handle on such occasions; they can be shown by the contractor only what is desired, and the details of how men are housed may be of minor importance. Would that some titan power might have grabbed that iron horse in the clay cut there, throttled it, thrown it back on its haunches, and complelled the touring law-makers to pass a night in such surroundings! What would it have meant for the increased comfort of workers in camps on construction?

Neglected camps

'G. & K.'s' second camp was a small one. They had three such camps built on a sub-contract of less than fourteen miles. The camp had been a busy one for months, and was drawing to a close. It presented all the aspects of a camp which is 'hanging-on,' expecting every week to be the last.

To approach the camp in the dusk of a June day was to awaken at first-hand differing impressions of camps. The path led sideways down from a very steep grade, across a pole bridge and into the bush about two hundred yards. It passed close to the stable-tent, where the foot sank deep in spongy manure, down to the small-sized bunkhouse which squatted, low and dark-shaped in the shadows, like a stranded barge settling in the waters.

On the upper side of the bunkhouse the water lay, thick and foul-smelling, in a wide trench, while at the front the ground was damp and wet from the low-lying situation of the camp. The bunks were hung with canvas bags and blankets, for the fly season was at its worst. One lantern shone dimly in the back of the bunkhouse from a low box around which was gathered a group of heads engaged in a game of cards.

The night air had the damp chill which quickly settles down in the twilight stillness of a northern clearing, no matter how hot has been the day. Approaching the door, the air of the interior had that close, musty, vapid smell which prevails in all bunkhouses where blankets are dirty, the fresh air excluded because of lack of windows and openings, and where spittle and throat clearings and mud incase the floor: surely no entrance to the palace of Ahasuerus the King, neither befitting Baghdad in Haroun al Raschid's day.

It need not be expected that such camps will be free of vermin. 'Don't sleep here, partner, if you are clean,' was the manly rejoinder of an inmate as to chances for a flop. 'You had better try the cook, he is sleeping in a tent near the creek.' For the campman, too, is not without a rugged code of integrity.

Fighting flies in a sleep camp
This was a busy camp, a typical construction community on the bank of a big river. For three months it had served as the end of the steel. There were three large bunkhouses, one was occupied entirely by Italians. The other two were crowded with men of different nationalities: Russians (Lithuanians and Poles), French-speaking Canadians, and English-speaking navvies comprised the majority. There was among them a goodly sprinkling of machine men engaged with the steam shovels on the work.

There is no need to make reference here to any particular one of the bunkhouses at the camp. There was little difference in size, and conditions were much alike in all three. Experience, however, obtained sixteen times between the end of April and the middle of October of that year in the large bunkhouse, where most transients flopped, permits one to speak of the sleep conditions to be encountered there.

Take three nights in the first week of July. The building itself was large, as camps go, but miserably lighted with two low windows in the wall and a gable sash. It was located in a place which, even in midsummer, owing to the heavy rains, abounded with muddy pools and stagnant, undrained water. The board floor was lower for the front half of the building than the level of the ground outside. To pass from building to building was to make a detour, or splash directly through the puddles.

The bunks inside were draped with all kinds of fly protectors and screens, from coats and dirty shirts to the usual old blanket or oat sack, which can generally be secured at the stables. For it was in the midst of the fly season, and a week spent there should best serve to show the disadvantages under which the bunkhouse man gets rest during the eight or ten weeks of such a period.

The men, when working overtime, come in from work about 8:30. The foreigners go at once to their end of the bunkhouse, talking incessantly, while puffing away at their rough-made cigarettes; others, casting off their heavy military boots, sit stolidly thinking. The English and French-speaking workers – mostly cart drivers, machine men or carpenters, put on their 'stags' and seek comfort in their pipes; and all the time the camp is noisy with the tones of many talkers.

But, in July, the hour just before sleep, is the time the mosquitoes seem most vicious in a bunkhouse, and the content of a smoke is broken by the repeated drives at ubiquitous tormentors. Little real comfort is to be had. One by one the men creep into their bunks and draw their improvised curtains, for another long day lies before them and rest must be procured. Extra precautions are made to combat the mosquitoes. The chore boy closes the openings in the building and lights a bundle of old straw and rags to give the place a thorough smudging. Soon the whole interior is filled with heavy smoke and a rancid smell. This drives the mosquitoes down close to the floor and the men, tired by twelve hours with the pick and shovel, their senses dulled by the smudge and fetid air of the camp, have heavy slumber till three or four in the morning. But, even before the grey light of the long northern day is lighting up the camp clearing, the mosquitoes are again at work, for the cool of the morning has driven the pests in greater numbers into the buildings. To sleep is impossible; men walk abroad for a while in the morning mists as far as the trestle; others march up and down the floor, stamping and cursing, crazed with the pests and the lack of sleep.

How are such men fitted for work? It is only their good physical strength, the rejuvenating effect of work in the open air and sunlight, as well as plenty of good plain camp food, which counteracts the enervating influence of nights so spent.

Two things would have bettered such conditions: cleaner, brighter, more wholesome camps, and a plentiful supply of cheese-cloth, which makes a bunk fly-proof. Cheese-cloth is cheap, and the amount of extra work which men will do after a good night's rest would pay for such a small outlay in two weeks. Seventy cents per bunk would have given each inmate comfort for the season. It was amply supplied to the half-dozen men of the office building not fifty feet away, but for the navvy in the bunkhouse cheese-cloth was as scarce as silk veiling.

Camps hastily constructed

The camp at 'L' was not a large building, but it was crowded. There was but one door. During the night the cage-like bunk which occupied the centre of the floor behind the stove took fire; the flames quickly spread, licking up the inflammable hangings which hung about the bunks. As there was only one opening to the building, those at the rear had to pass the burning mass in the centre in order to reach the door. Six Austrians, in an attempt to gather their meagre belongings, delayed too long; they were forced to creep on their hands and knees to pass the fiery mass. Five of them escaped, two with horrible burns, the sixth met death, his whitened remains showing next morning where he had vainly tried, as a last resort, to reach the opening of the little camp window.

Camps poorly located

Camp 'G' was the construction camp of a sub-contractor who was running behind. His camp tents lay on the hillside, sloping down to a swift-running river, which, at the trestle-work below the camp, broke into rapids.

In spite of regulations governing the building of camps the cookery was lowest down near the water, the bunk tent was above that, while higher up lay the stable. The whole drainage of the camp was from the stables down past the sleep places and the cookery to the river. Inside the mess tent the men could dabble their shoe-packed feet in the mud while seated around the pole tables.

Who was to blame? The sub-contractor in this case was pushed so hard by the head-contractor that he floundered around in his efforts to save and scrimp. It was cheaper for him so to place his tents; it saved a man or two. But what of the campmen who undermine their health and wreck their capacity in life by just such surroundings?

Seven men went out of that camp with symptoms of fever in less than four weeks, one of whom was eight months before he was again able to earn enough to keep himself.

It is not to be wondered that darts, with barbed points, enter the souls of men who work in such places. They view with deep hatred a system which holds life so cheaply. Men who, through months, have suffered from the selfishness too long countenanced in the camps of Canada, can speak with truth. Not superficial reports, accepted as final in higher quarters, but facts from the bottom can best show the state of things encountered by men in bunkhouses.

These six camps were not all found on any one piece of work, nevertheless they fairly represent the type of bunkhouses which commonly housed the workers, particularly in camps ahead of the steel. Speaking of such sleep places as he knew them previous to 1915 the writer will here make two asseverations:

1 That they invariably presented living conditions which were a disgrace to any so-called inspection whether federal or provincial.
2 That hardly could a man live continuously in the average bunkhouse then commonly found on frontier works, throughout the weeks of six consecutive months, and not suffer in health.

For two generations and more, even as late as the present decade, the people of Canada have apparently condoned the lax conditions of housing in camps as being incidental to the very nature of the tasks. Meanwhile, the romance, latent in many forms of frontier work, is generously extolled in song and story. Thus the campman himself, whether as a lumberjack or a navvy, lauded as semi-heroic in the robustness of his personal qualities, has long been deemed to disdain .the need, even, of the common physical comforts. This attitude toward the life and work of men in camps continued throughout the third period of railway expansion. These years, busy in material development, seemed but to accentuate some of the worst features pertaining to the herding of men in bunkhouses. All too commonly the men with strong arms and heavy boots who builded on the grade, crept of a night into bunks, the sleeping surroundings of which would put to shame a well kept kennel.

'But,' says a camp foreman, 'What about it? You can't expect perfection on construction; it's as good as these men ever had; they're not fit to put in a clean place; it's impossible to put up decent buildings so far from the source of supplies, especially as many of them will be used only a little more than a year at best!'

'Yes,' and one opines in thought, 'Did not marshals of the Emperor there on the Prussian plains, in those dreary weeks preceding Eylau, for warmth seek heat in dunghills?'

You cannot better these conditions, it is affirmed. Such is the opinion of practically all employers of camp labour, particularly on railway construction, and from one point of view this does seem conclusive.

Yet an answer to this objection lies often within a stone's throw of the very camp where such an assertion is heard. It is a common fact that both isolated residencies and other headquarters for the engineers may be fairly comfortably equipped. A trend toward some solution surely lies in this.

Lining the right-of-way, at intervals of ten miles, are the residencies. At each will be a resident engineer who has charge of ten miles of the grade. The engineer sees that the trestle-work and grading done on his section are up to the requirements. Over every four or five residencies is a divisional engineer, and these in turn are subject to the district or chief engineer.

The engineer at a residency is generally a well-qualified man, usually – though not always – a graduate of some university. Under him will be an instrument man, a leveller, a rod-man, and so on, down to the chain-man and the two axemen.

The usual residency has from eight to eleven men, including a cook. Their supplies are put in independent of the contractor. Because it is a government branch and the probable demand on a residency being pretty well known, the supplies are ample and well assorted; the best of canned fruits, jams, pickles, oysters, prunes, apricots, peaches, dessicated potatoes, smoked meats and pork is supplied.

In 1912 the average residency, including the pay of the cook, cost about $300.00 a month to grub. However, as little criticism can be made of railway contractors on the score of the meals they supply the men, it is only fair to admit that the staffs of the residencies, too, should be given the best. Any favourable comparison, however, ends when the provision made for the housing of the man at the residency and the navvy at the bunkhouse is considered.

It is a grateful sight, after packing for hours along the wet trail of a newly-stumped right-of-way, to come on a residency – its five or six buildings standing shapely and uniform, in a clearing, on a hill, a river bank, or in some chosen spot near a lake. There is a spic-and-span air about it all, the buildings themselves are well put together, often hewn inside and out, the walls chinked regularly and neatly plastered. The whole surroundings have an air of consideration and thoughtfulness for the comfort of the dozen or more who dwell there.

The cookery will have good drains to carry off the water and refuse. The meats will be protected from flies by neat frame buildings covered with a fine wire netting. Ice will be stored in the winter, and the residency has earned well the name for good food, hospitality and bonhomie from those whom it shelters: passing engineers, officials of the line, contractors, churchmen, the mailmen, any one with a carte blanche, are made welcome. The chain of residencies, at ten-mile intervals, is a splendid system of hostelries stretching for hundreds of miles.

The men of the residency have single bunks with plenty of good, clean, heavy blankets. The cleanly surroundings have their effect on the inmates, who invariably reflect these conditions by rigging up box spittoons, thus helping to keep the floor clean. Five to eight men at the residency will have a small bunkhouse to themselves – whereas, on the other hand, a building of similar size in the construction camp, just across the river, will do duty in housing thirty or forty inmates.

The chain-men, axemen and workers, who do practically the same manual work as the navvies, have a good roomy building. There will be plenty of windows, higher doors, good level floors and walls whitewashed or covered with white lining-paper. These will be brightened, often, with pastings from some magazine or weekly paper.

It is no uncommon thing for a man who has been working at a construction camp, living in all the squalidness of the bunkhouse, to get an appointment as an axeman up at the residency. Why is it that

the surroundings of this man, when employed at the adjacent camp
are hardly considered, but when he passes to practically the same
kind of work as a helper at the residency he at once drops into a
clean, well-lighted bunkhouse, a warm comfortable berth, with
papers to read in spare hours, and partakes of a dozen conveniences
denied the man who is forced to live the bunkhouse life? In the case
of the National Transcontinental the same money is sustaining both,
yet this man is unheeded until he passes into another form of
employment. Solicitude is then, apparently, shown at once for his
proper housing, and other conditions of work.

'But, surely, you don't class residencies with the bunkhouse, do
you?' 'Yes, and no!' No, in that no one would expect a residency
staff to live under any deprivation of whatever necessary comforts
they now have. Considering the monotony and isolation of the life,
they should be well-provided, and when it is considered that their
work at a point lasts from three to five years, their buildings require
to be well put together. But, on the other hand, suppose a
bunkhouse only does work for fifteen months, it houses in that
period many hundreds of workers. Why should these bunkhouse
men be huddled like pigs? Should common decency, even, be denied
the navvies on whose backs falls largely the building of the road?
The thing is too lop-sided. Do not deprive the residencies of one
essential, but give the bunkhouse more!

Even the bunkhouse, such as described above, can be quite
comfortable, and many of them are so, at least when the work starts.
They suffer from the fact that too much latitude is allowed in the
matter of observing hygienic conditions. Camp foremen and the
different walking-bosses are not held rigidly to the regulations
enacted both by the provinces and the Dominion for the welfare of
men who work in camps. There are restrictions definite enough in
these matters, but too often existing conditions are at variance with
the printed regulations.

The happy solution for all camps would be smaller bunkhouses.
Buildings accommodating eight and ten men would best meet the
needs. It is quite noticeable in camps of whatever kind that men
with a stripe desire, where possible, to get into a small building by
themselves. On the Pacific Coast where the Loggers' Union has
succeeded in wresting recognition of this preference, the camps are
usually composed of many small-sized bunkhouses, accommodating
six and eight men. Nor is it conducive to Adamhood that sixty,

eighty and, at times, one hundred men be huddled pellmell for months at a stretch bunking in crowded quarters.

The writer, as has already been stated, has no desire simply to prove querulous. He should be first to admit that in recent years there has been a pronounced tendency toward the betterment of camps in Canada. Particularly is this so in the past five years: many company towns builded in out-of-the-way places are models as such. Even in the camps themselves the old order is changing; the iron bed and mattress for individual use is displacing the old double-deck bunk with its blankets and hay. The provincial governments have also enacted more stringent regulations pertaining to isolated works, and camp inspectors are giving more heed to proper enforcement. But while this change for the better is welcomed, the reader is again reminded that the great majority of bunkhouses across Canada have undergone but little change. This applies particularly to the smaller companies' camps on temporary works, initial developments in mining, and jobbers in the woods. While figures are not to be had easily, it is probably a conservative estimate to place the number of old-type bunkhouses in the provinces of Ontario and Quebec alone for the season of 1925-26 at 2000-2500. Such places vary but little from buildings in camps during the previous quarter century.

With the hope expressed that the men in bunkhouses will ultimately have more livable conditions, let us add here a few suggestions for betterment in the housing of Canadian campmen even under the existing system. These are not new – the writer is well aware that he is saying nothing new – but let us have a consistent observance even of these standards of sanitation, particularly in the back places:

1 That more windows and windows lower down be provided, and roofs kept intact. That an opening be provided in the rear of every big bunkhouse.

2 That bunkhouses be aired and ventilated for a certain period each day, preferably for an hour after men leave for work in the morning. Blankets should be systematically aired – not left to the personal whim of the campman himself. Floors of large bunkhouses need washing at least twice a week.

3 That a chore-boy be provided for every thirty men at a camp. In the face of so many duties heaped on one man acting as such, the bunkhouse itself is neglected.

4 That during fly-season the sites of busy camps be raked every ten days, also the ground about be sprinkled with a cheap and suitable disinfectant.

5 That printed regulations governing sanitary conditions in camps, whether issued by the Dominion or the particular Province affected, be posted always in some prominent place, for all to know, preferably in the bunkhouse.

6 That, to a limited extent, the foreman be held personally responsible for the sanitary conditions of his camp.

7 That all inspectors of camps sleep only in the large common bunkhouses alongside the men — let them not be ashamed of their work.

Chapter 4

Some ethnic groupings among campmen

BEFORE discussing further the activities and daily work of men on frontier works it may be profitable to obtain a clearer conception of the racial elements which go to make up the body of workers in camps. In this section the campman will be discussed from a more intimate angle, his personal traits, some of his ethnic qualifications, and his usual form of employment, as observed during the building of the National Transcontinental.

There are two distinct groups of workers at once apparent in camps on a piece of railway work, the 'whites' and the 'foreigners.' This semi-racial demarcation is not a pleasant distinction; it may not even be just, but it is always in evidence on any hundred-mile piece of new construction.

THE 'WHITES'

Among the whites are included always the Canadian-born, both French-speaking and English-speaking, as well as the new arrivals from the British Isles, and Americans from different states of the Union, engaged on the work. The term foreigner is not applied always simply as a sobriquet for non-English-speaking workers; included with the whites are usually the Scandinavians also, and sometimes the Finns, and in fact any other foreign-born nationals who by their intelligence, their skill as workers, or sheer native ability, have earned a recognition on their individual merits.

To the white-man falls most of the positions which connote a 'stripe' of some kind, officials in one capacity or another — walking-bosses, accountants, inspectors, the various camp foremen, cache-keepers, as well as clerks who perform the more routine work of checkers and timekeepers. This class also includes the cooks and helpers in the cookery, the tote-teamsters on the hauls, the drivers of scrapers and dump-wagons in the mud cuts and on the fills. The white-man, too, does much of the rock work, where more than ordinary skill and practice in the use of powder are essential for effective blasting.

The most remunerative part of railway construction, in so far as it gives opportunity for bigger pay to the worker, is the secondary phase, and white labour congregates in the busy camps which mark this stage of the work. They man the pioneer which lays the steel, operate the big steam shovels, supply the crews for the several ballast trains engaged in hauling gravel for the first lift under the skeleton track and make the runs as train crews on the 'local' which plies its semi-regular trips over the portion of the contract already completed. The men of this class, too, are mostly employed at the repair camps and machine shops on construction where there are frequent calls for locomotive mechanics, boiler-men, pump-men, engine hostlers and machinists of parts.

The different bridge crews and a preponderant part of the gangs who build the wooden trestles on the line are whites. There are few foreigners on such works: not that the man from Central and Southern Europe is unacquainted with the art of bridging great rivers by huge spans of steel, for he is prone to criticize the seeming haste with which, in Canada, the long trusses are soon girded into great arches and tracked with level crossings, but too frequently at a sacrifice of the solidity and finish of workmanship which characterize those in his own land. Many newcomers to the Dominion from Central Europe would prove useful on structural work, but have not the requisite knowledge of English so essential in the conduct of these hazardous tasks. The lack of it is a barrier to employment with a bridge-crew even as a rivet-heater. As for trestle-building, that means further the skilful use of the peavy and axe for which the foreigner is not usually fitted.

First let us consider briefly the English-speaking Canadians — the native-born, they may be dubbed. They represent that virile type of man common to the frontier works of woods and mines. It is safe to say that the majority of them are not without experience in a bush camp before they drift to construction. In fact the railway camp is often recruited from the woods at the break-up in April.

The English-speaking navvy is seldom illiterate, but has nevertheless eschewed the school-house and its restraints at the earliest opportunity. Few have taken work beyond the third grade in a public school; fractions to them are a mystery, but can be solved in a practical way, quickly enough, and accurately, too, when hours of work and total pay is the point at issue. Their reading seldom gets beyond the newspaper or the stories of the cheaper magazines; of such some read assiduously; recreation of this form being snatched even at opportunity between spells of work during the day's activities. Nor do these men usually become wholly untethered. Mail day is always anticipated, its welcome letters bearing the postmark of the home town or a village community, somewhere in the more settled parts of the country.

But knowledge to the highbrow! Textbooks to such men are taboo: strong, self-reliant, reckless at times, the English-speaking Canadians hold tight most of the machine jobs on construction. Particularly is this so of work with the locomotives; the hiss of steam, the throb in answer to the pull of the throttle, and the heavy pounding on the poorly-ballasted track all find a response in the hearts of men who delight in action. Nor need one, in such work, wait years for promotion; often mere youths, still in their early twenties, gaze proudly out from the cabs of the ponderous locomotives used on the ballast hauls.

But the Canadian-born as a worker in camps may be unstable. For a time, following his arrival on a work, and while his stake is low, he is, if anything, too subservient while thus confronted with adversity, but his self-assertion mounts rapidly with the size of his stake and his independence quite in proportion. Gains at cards or subsequent losses will accentuate his restlessness. Then anything may happen; under such circumstances it requires only a word in reprimand from one in charge to serve as a spark in the tinder and to produce a sudden shift.

The Canadian worker, too, particularly in large camps, has a tendency to submerge his individualism. He is prone to follow a leader. If a camp is dominated by different men with pet ideas, cliques arise with attendant cleavages and sometimes friction among the men. On the other hand, a sudden unity of purpose may arise among this class, which, under the influence of some extremist, results too frequently in a swerve toward the left. Then radical talk is cozened and acts countenanced which disrupt for a time the work of the camp. The English-speaking Canadian-born do not necessarily constitute always the best labour for frontier camps.

There is, in turn, a noticeable delimitation between the Canadian navvies on railway construction who speak English and those native-born who are of French descent. Even in their occupations the offspring of the two primal Canadian races seem to gravitate to different kinds of work on the line. The French-speaking navvy is usually more accustomed to frontier conditions and is invariably an axeman. While he engages sometimes in the routine work at machine camps and busy pits as a car-knocker, a brakeman, a helper or machinist, he predominates more usually in the trestle gangs or at the camps. Frequently, too, numbers of French-speaking navvies are found at a grade camp where a compatriot is operating on a piece of work or where the foreman in charge is of their own tongue and race.

The French-speaking Canadians in camps have marked personal characteristics. Possessed of sound constitutions, they are stronger and bigger commonly than the average English-speaking campman, particularly those from the British Isles; in this respect they compare favourably with the Scandinavian races. Hard workers, they are also good feeders. No other class among the navvies seems possessed with the lightheartedness and cheerfulness of these men. Even in serious moments exuberance is not far distant; some trivial pretext soon forms the motive for a digression – there is a push one of another, a shout, a little run – the spirit of youth seems not to desert them. True, these qualities may also show in the more ephemeral tendencies of quitting work on some slight pretext or jumping camp. But usually the French-speaking Canadians are steady, and while they dislike restriction and must have their own way occasionally, they are consistent, at least during the period of the seasonal work on which they may be engaged. Contentment with things as they are is with them an asset which makes them desired as workers by various contractors.

The French-speaking Canadian who navvies on the line is not usually literate. In this respect he lags behind the Italian, the English-speaking worker alongside him, and particularly the Scandinavian and Finn who engage in the same class of work. It may even be questioned if the mental attainments of members of the Slav races who work on construction are not superior to those Canadians of French extraction found in the bunkhouses and camps.

For as was commonly observed in the Canadian camps, during the period under consideration, there was in evidence a wide gap in educational attainments between the mass of French-speaking workers of the isolated places and their compatriots who had received the advantages of a special training. The former continued but hewers of wood and drawers of water, and were desired as labourers because of these inherent qualities, while the latter, often selected from the same homes and parishes, became, owing to a centralized system of education, the well trained products of special schools and local colleges. Few of these, however, gravitated to the bunkhouses. Eager, acute, affable, and equally at home whether conversing in French or English, they were to be observed in distant camps in some official capacity. As a reuslt there was lacking between these two extremes a proportionate number, comprising a body of well-informed workers, commonly apparent among other nationals.

Then, too, there is a further, if perhaps more extraneous, reason for illiteracy on the part of French-speaking campmen. Such men, recruited so frequently from frontier settlements, and with the lure of the chase and the woods tingling in their blood down through whole generations, are prone to display a distaste for schooling of whatever kind.

In the larger camps, where men of different nationalities coalesce as navvies, the French-speaking Canadians at times appear to disadvantage. Speaking their own language where possible, they are naturally thrown largely in association among themselves. The foreign-born campman meanwhile does not always distinguish clearly what is the place and relation of the French tongue in parts of Canada. Certainly he has no desire to learn it; English as the common medium of intercourse is sufficient task for him. Indeed he esteems French of no more account than his own tongue and those who speak it but as rival nationals seeking like himself in Canada the opportunity of a fresh start. One result is that the French-speaking navvies are often in disfavour with the foreign-born in the larger camps. While pliant as individuals, the Canadians of French extraction are assertive in numbers; proud of their lineage, yet perhaps conscious of a discrepancy somewhere, they vociferate most often about the place of the white-men on the work and often to the disparagement of those who are foreigners. But any masquerade of race superiority to be effective even in camps must correspondingly have attributes which command respect, or meet with open scorn from the many capable nationals of other speech who may be loath to acknowledge any such distinction.

There are phases of new construction in which the French-speaking Canadian excels. Much of the earlier work beyond the steel is performed by him. He prefers to be in the vanguard. The space and freedom of the trails and water routes appeal to him, whether carrying the mail, running lines with the engineers, building corduroy roads in the low places, toteing supplies up the grade, or assisting with ready axe to erect the big log company camps. He is seen to advantage at the portage where for the time the canoe and pointer must displace the heavy haul on the cache-road. With loaded back he rotates in quarter-mile trips from the 'dump' to the lake, his well-greased shoepacks slopping along the muddy trail or through the muskeg, bearing his balanced loads of flour, sugar, meals, beans, tinned goods or other urgent supplies. True, flies abound and mosquitoes torment and grouch increases with every untoward delay: his sacré-ing is furious, and it were not well just then if some unobtrusive snag or root in path should cause a further spill. But once the load is tallied, strong arms push the pointer out through the reeds and into deeper water, the headland is rounded and the lake breeze blows fair. A rough sail of tarpaulin is soon improvised, all hands relax, pipes are filled, the pleasant nod and joke displace the erstwhile petulance of the portage trips, and a song, *Malbrouk* perhaps or *A la Clair Fontaine* – chansons heard two centuries since on the rivers – bursts from the bronzed throats of care-free men. Who of the camps has not known these men in all their moods and not learned to love them?

For these men of Breton stock are still the pathfinders on our frontier works. They delight in leading over unproved ways. Blessed with physical alertness and perseverance, they eagerly confront in their tasks any sudden obstacles of woods or rapid. Their native qualities of sturdy endurance ensure success. Scions of those who shouldered closely with Mackenzie in his exploits, these men still possess the indomitable spirit of Brûlé, of Radisson, and the Vérendryes, or of those holier men whose lives and efforts made known the contours of the Lakes. In the construction of the Canadian transcontinentals they have occupied their own fields of activity, and these are not the least important.

Most camps on railway construction have also a considerable number of newcomers from the British Isles – Scotch and English. There is a noticeable tendency at times among the other Canadian railway workers to resent a new arrival from over home as an intruder, but, even as workers in obscure construction camps, neither these English nor Scotch workers are the kind to say 'by your leave!' Their industry, their experience, often, and their natural aptitude for machinery, as well as their fondness for tools, usually assure them a permanent place. They throng the temporary machine shops and do much of the repair work. It is a fact that sometimes they find themselves competing with men among the native-born, who, by hasty assertions of superiority, would seek to hide a conscious deficiency in skill.

Then, too, among the workers in the camps is a considerable sprinkling of American-born. Ever since the seventies when Canadians in large numbers wrought as navvies on the building of steam roads in the fast-settling states beyond the Mississippi, there has been a give-and-take between the two countries in the actual work of railway building. Both countries have profited from this relation. Not alone has the exchange been in the matter of railway builders – the Hills and the Van Hornes – but it is particularly in evidence among the gang-foremen and local bosses on construction. These men have an experience gained anywhere – on new roads in Montana or branch lines on the prairies, in the heavy construction of the mountain sections or in the iron regions about Lake Superior. Their activities are not delimited by national boundaries.

The gang foremen on railway construction are navvies who have been promoted. They have risen from the ranks. Big, strong, hard, clear-headed, quick-thinking men, sometimes expressive in word, they take hold of a group of workers and get something done. Effective at their tasks, they are the real pivots in the practical work of construction, and they usually know their worth; they esteem themselves to be the salt of the line, if not, indeed, of the whole earth.

Such is the real camp foreman. He is easily judged by one common test: What proportion of his gang desires to follow him to another work? For the capable foreman interests himself in the men of his crew. He realizes, too, that his own advancement depends upon their ability to work.

But there is, on frontier works, another kind. It is the 'push' or 'driver.' God, surely, has seldom made a more offensive creature than the foreman-bully. Such a man has an innate pride in his capacity to coerce. It is his boast that his father before him has handled men. He is not susceptible and may prefer to be feared on the gang. Courting disfavour locally, he covets commendation only from the company, nor does it misbeseem that such a man in turn is usually humble enough with higher officials. The native-born and rugged men with American experiences, both north and south, usually constitute this class. But such foremen are not restricted to any one nationality. Perhaps the sternest taskmasters in camps to-day are the foreign-born – men who, after the experience of a few years, have been promoted. Their own lives, fostered often in adversity, have produced exceptional traits, but they not infrequently expect in others the same mastering qualities that have shaped their own wills and purposes.

Prominent, too, among workers on railway construction is another distinct group, the itinerant navvy, commonly known in the camps as the 'bo' or 'floater.' Seasonal work begets this man. Usually under thirty-five years of age, he hibernates, perhaps in a machine shop or at other temporary work somewhere in the larger centres of the East or Middle West. He knows much, and not always in one channel; this may be the motive of his shifting. With the approach of spring he drifts to the North and to the prairie country, where railway activity usually marks the long-day summer and busy fall months.

The real bo has no one dependent on him, or at least has forgotten for the time being any one who might have such a claim. He has not strong family associations – that where lie his children, there he hopes to lay his bones. In that he is happy; he finds it a hard enough task, with his frequent moves, to keep himself intact. He disdains steady work. In the first years of his vagabonding among camps, before the seamy side has quite been evidenced, he boasts of his attitude towards life; he is a bo and proud to sign himself as such. He knows equally well the railway environments of Chicago, the yards at Kansas City or the wheat haul from Fort William. Much-traveled and free in expression, he carries weight with the younger campmen about him. But only for a time, for, though often capable, he is very unstable. Like the Arab, he folds his tent in the night and suddenly disappears from the line. Shifting is his weakness, and by that he is appraised among the steadier navvies on the works.

Of such a type is also the tourist navvy, who always winters South. When first in fall the heavy frosts show signs that winter now is close at hand he heads for the coast as the land of promise. Later he may drift southward as far as the park benches of Los Angeles. He will attain his purpose if it means 'riding the bumpers'; but, with a stake in hand, he does not disdain to buy a ticket part way and ride in state. The money necessary for winter clothing will serve to land him where he does not need an overcoat. The English-speaking navvies, Canadian and American-born contribute almost entirely to this class.

But it should not be overlooked that even the migrant seems to meet a social need in the camps. More or less talented he provides often the spice that enlivens life on an isolated work. His very versatility is his passport. His wit at times and his repartee, when his own experience and worldliness are not unduly paraded, enhances him with his fellows. Vivacity upon occasion makes of him the jester of old, transplanted from the baron's hall to the walled spaces of the bunkhouse. He serves to offset the vacuousness so prone to beset all discussions in such surroundings. For the drifter among camps is not solely a vagrant. While at times he may display the characteristics of the tramp, that by-product of the battlefields in the early sixties, he can claim readier kinship with the man, not without gifts – careless and indifferent, but nevertheless acceptable as a visitor – whose songs and mirth helped beguile the days of homestead life in bygone settlements.

There are no finer types among the navvies on railway construction than the Norwegians, Swedes, Danes, Icelanders, and, to a lesser extent, the Finns. They have much in common, and seem to take naturally to frontier work. At one time, perhaps a thousand years ago, these peoples spoke one language – the old Norse, though for many reasons on construction they are all commonly designated 'Swedes.' They have played a big part in the later period of railway construction in Canada. The Scandinavians usually work together in groups as distinct nationals, using their own language, but they readily assume their place with the best workers on the line. Their splendid physique, their willingness, and their prodigious capacity for work are big assets in performing the heavier manual tasks of the camp. Their services are eagerly sought for rock work and excavations. Many of the Swedes, also, become camp foremen and company officials on the grade.

Much of the Scandinavian lands is mountainous, and the climate at times is severe. There is, too, a sterile soil to combat. Sea-faring shares largely with the cultivating of small farms in giving occupation to the people of the home countries. Nothing in the conditions of life there suggests effeminacy. On the contrary, the call for strong personal traits produces in these sturdy men staunch characteristics of frugality, initiative, and self-reliance. Men of such stock are not usually found looking for the soft places in camps.

The Swedes, even those found as workers in camps, are a literate class. Coming from a land with a wealth of literature there are frequently cultured men among them, employed along the grade. They are lovers of music and influenced by the songs of love and sacrifice, and mirth or pathos peculiar to the Scandinavian countries. These men suffer nothing in comparison with the English-speaking navvies, whether Canadian or American-born, engaged beside them on similar works, nor indeed with the higher officials often with college attainments.

For in Scandinavian countries few youths can elude the minimum requirements of the schools. The population of these lands, too, is not composed so largely of workers recruited from large industrial centres, neither have they, with the possible exception of their chief port cities, the extended slum areas of large urban places. When emigration does take place it is the natural overflow of the large families, too numerous for the opportunities at home, to the wider fields in other lands. Such men, even as campmen, are of a high average. They have been healthily reared, and are comparable rather with the young men who compose each year the migrations westward to the Canadian prairies from the well-kept homes of old Ontario, and the maritime provinces.

An ancient and a proud people, the Scandinavians bring to the camps the spirit of the Viking race. Even in the days of Pytheas the longboats of their forebears threatened the ports of trade in western Europe. Unchallenged in the history of peoples, even by the Phoenicians, they first abandoned the shoreline and took navigation away from the coasts and into the ocean spaces. In open craft, with rattling oarlocks and square-rigged sails, ancestors of these men quartered the seas from the Baltic even to Baffin's Land. This was their Dominion. Not for five hundred years later did ships of other nations make their way into the same regions. What have these races not taught the world in seamanship for a thousand years? Let us think of these things as we watch their descendants of the centuries gathered in groups on some isolated work, loitering, skulking, if one would call it – men of massive frame, slouching about some obscure Canadian camp – these be no scions of an upstart race.

There is a clannishness about the Scandinavians, and a keen sense of personal independence which does not desert them when, as navvies, they labour on railway construction. They have long lived under the best forms of representative government. They do not readily assent to Czarism, whether it be in a Baltic province or under a jobber in camp, or some railway contractor on a Canadian transcontinental.

As a campman the Scandinavian works hard. He always uses his head in his tasks. His weakness is that in the seclusion of some hotel room he games and drinks in the off-spell of a fortnight between works. He may not always be popular, for he shows at times a tendency to buck the job and quit. He may have to be humored with promises of increased pay or lower prices on the stores supplied him. If a grouch is being nursed on the line one can look for its first appearances among the Scandinavians.

Not uncommonly the Finlander employed on frontier works in Canada has been associated in name with the various Scandinavian peoples. While there are many physical and social traits that lend themselves to such a comparison, there are nevertheless very pronounced racial divergencies.

Offspring, also, of an old ethnic stock in Europe, the Finlander has been called upon throughout the centuries to defend his place and existence as a people. Not only was the might and power of the Russians to be withstood, but continued pressure, too, on the part of Sweden at times, so powerful in arms on the continent. That this small land in the face of continued aggression preserved itself as a distinct race is a tribute to its people.

An impress of this may be gleaned in the camps. The Finlander wherever found is assertive of his nationalism. It becomes with him a personal factor that makes him at times almost bitter. No Finlander is flattered to be called a Swede even in a bunkhouse. His racial pride is supersensitive, not unakin in its intensity to the yearnings of the Macedonian in his long struggle for recognition.

The Finlander is an individualist. He is fond of music and very keen for education. These new arrivals, though possessing a very fair education in their own land, are easily the most eager to acquire a working knowledge of English even under the handicaps of the camp conditions. Age does not debar, adults of forty-five may be found with the men of earlier youth. The strides made by the Finnish people, however, in social legislation is reflected occasionally among these workers in the expression of radical ideas. They appear loath to abide the slower constitutional methods.

As campmen the Finlanders have proven their worth. Strong and willing, they have claimed a foremost place, particularly in rock-work and with the axe. Their services are sought for particular jobs. The men themselves, as encountered on frontier works, are taciturn, silent but reliant. As a race they possess the clannishness of the Scandinavians, but even the closest friendship of a work group en route to camp, disrupted by the presence of high wines in tins, may lead to stolidness, quarrels and brutal personal onslaughts.

Reared under climatic conditions not unlike those which prevail over the greater stretch of the Dominion, the Finlander has shown native initiative, and ranks among the most virile of all bunkhouse workers. Not even the French-speaking Canadian can show more adaptiveness in encountering the physical drawbacks of life in the northern lands, than do the Finnish people who come to Canada.

Before discussing the so-called foreigners found on frontier works, mention may here be made of the Indian. Strange as it may appear, men of this primal race seem exotic to camps. The bunkhouse itself in the Canadian hinterland signifies an intrusion upon his former domain. Camp activities of whatever kind mean ultimately a narrowing of privileges and customs that for so long have marked his mode of life.

The Indian himself draws apart from the continued labour in camps. The ordered complexity with which considerable numbers of men are handled effectively, the big machines that in their ponderous efforts awaken to new life the solitudes that he so long has called his own, may awe, or even attract for a time, but his stay in a bunkhouse is usually temporary. The Indian more than any other campman is rooted in his own ways, and the methods of the past.

It is not every foreman who can handle the Indian to best advantage. Moody in disposition, he has to be studied. While wiry, tenacious and strong, the Indian not infrequently displays indolence. He leaves much to be desired, too, in matters of personal cleanliness. The Indian by nature is not a campman, neither is it easy to weld him permanently in the routine ways and life of the bunkhouse.

True, there are exceptions: young men, from a nearby reservation perhaps, or who have had some contact with civilization in another form, excel occasionally in particular phases of camp work. Men like these may persevere in works during a full season, but it is unusual. There may be an incentive in such cases through a desire for new clothes or some ambition to gratify in the purchase of jewelry for personal adornment. It is quite possible, too, that in the case of an Indian, new-found revenue from work at a camp will be supplemented by the sale of moccasins or other leather goods from the work of his women-folk in a not distant cabin or lodge.

The camp cookery is always a great attraction for these men of the woods and the wastes. The copious meals there provided mean, for a time, a welcome change in food and diet, and they proceed to satisfy their wants with childlike avidity.

But wherever encountered, a shadow follows the Indian of the St. Lawrence and the Lakes. Be it in any camp, he occupies but a lowly place, and this in the face of the fact that he should be found among the foremost. For was he not favoured among the native races of the lands? Here are men whose fathers first on this continent were carefully fostered in the arts and sciences. Men of parts and wholly devoted, from that court dominated by the Grand Monarch, then the centre of real achievement in Europe, moved through the years in and about the Indian villages, sharing their accomplishments unstintedly and weaving culture, by daily contacts, into the lives of the people. But with what meagre results! Opportunity now close at hand in the forest clearings was contemptuously brushed aside, and Wisdom spurned in their picketed encampments.

For the Indian is not even an imitator. With little desire to improve, he has stood still for three centuries. His native craft in evidence about the camps remains today similar to those that glided streams in eager quest along with La Salle and Marquette, or formed in entourage at Frontenac's behest. How different from that other race, also a dependent people, whose color makes of them an Ishmael even in a bunkhouse but who with opportunity at length to hand, have fared so promisingly in spite of an ignoble beginning.

THE 'FOREIGNERS'

It has already been pointed out that the name foreigner, applied to navvies, is an epithet not necessarily implying a slur at nationality. It is a generic term, used by the supercilious among the English-speaking workers and commonly applied to those campmen, of whatever extraction, who stolidly engage in the mucking and heavier tasks.

Among such groups, men of the Slav races greatly predominate. As workers on construction they display definite characteristics; slow and immobile, lacking initiative; rather careless of personal appearance; with but limited mechanical ability; not quarrelsome except when liquor is about; easily brow-beaten, for the foot of despotism has cowed their spirit; just plodders in the day's work – withal, that pliant type that provides the human material for a camp boss to drive.

When seen to advantage the Slav as a campman is of medium stature, thick-set, with moustache usually, not graceful in motion, and with something of a sullen expression on his broad face. There are other things that impress one when first meeting him in the mud cut on the grade; cowhide boots smeared with gumbo reaching to the knees, a peaked cap that bespeaks the barrack life not far removed, uncouth trousers and coat with old-land fastenings, unshaven face – with the dull resentment of the hard-heel showing from eyes, joyless-looking and suspicious. But, on further acquaintance, there is latent there the quiet strength, the unpretending courage, the perseverance and the staunchness which we like to think of as the very essence of our own Canadian character. By virtue of these good qualities, and given fair conditions, the Slav can and does succeed even as a railway navvy.

Such men herd together in shacks hastily improvised near their work. They live much among themselves, and while there are clear-marked distinctions not only of nationality, but of ideals among these Slavs, such are not always apparent. Too often fellow-workers in camps neither know nor care enough to note any differences. In a hasty moment or as a term of reproach they are locally dubbed Russians, Bohunks, Galicians, Douks maybe, and occasionally Hunkies.

Why have these foreigners been so anxious to emigrate? We all know how much misery and hardship men will undergo in their own land before they can determine to desert it. How often have the most tempting proposals to embark been rejected by people who appeared to be almost starving. Few persons will readily leave their families, their home scenes and their communities, especially where the village life is so entwined in daily contacts, to take up anew the struggle for life in the untried ways of a new land without some strong underlying cause for uneasiness.

In emigrating, these strong-limbed men experience a great change. They leap from environments where the dumbness of tradition too long has tended to make them inarticulate, to a land with opportunity for individualism. Coming into contact with them only as navvies and in the other forms of heavier unskilled work, have we too quickly condemned them? What have we learned of their home country, their literature, their music and their aspirations? We should consider, when prone to criticize, that the fathers of these men stemmed finally the Turkish advance in Europe when continued successes for two hundred years seemed to have doomed the lands drained by the Danube. Behind this barrier, made by the Slavs, western Europe in security progressed in commerce and art.

We know too little of these peoples! Is it wholly to our advantage that these sturdy men, gifted often in age-long trades of smithing, weaving, pottery, or what not, forego their native arts to become ditchers and muckers on the seasonal works in the camps of Canada? We are prone to regard as commonplace their efforts as workers in far-out places, yet somewhere behind each day's work there lie solid qualities of human strength and purpose — attributes that among the varied craftsmen of the cities would be esteemed a virtue.

Of the eastern Slavs, large numbers surged on the work of Canadian railway construction for several years. The Ukrainians were particularly in evidence. There were few new arrivals of any race who took so readily to the hard manual work of the grade. The railway work with them, however, was only a way-station. Sooner or later they intended to have farms of their own in the new land. At first opportunity they gathered their earnings and located on a prairie section in the west. Kind-hearted, generous and devout, and with the traditions of a great literature behind them, the Ukrainians represented the best type of Slav groupings among the navvies on the National Transcontinental Railway.

Members of the western Slavs, now comprising largely the countries of re-established Poland and Czecho-Slovakia, entered Canada during the third period of railway construction under diverse names. They were commonly listed as Slovaks, Bohemians, Poles, Austrians, Lithuanians and, in some cases, Ruthenians. But, while constantly divided in Europe for political reasons, they were very unwillingly a subject people. Their patriotism was always intense. Even as navvies in distant camps they talked much of readjustments in Europe which some day would mean the granting again of their national aspirations. Many thousands of these people came and went on the line during the ten-year period of construction. Less purposeful in their plans and life, they shifted frequently from work to work.

Occasionally in evidence among the various Slav groups, but noticeably different, were the pure Austrians, or Hungarians, as they preferred to be called, upon an acquaintance. Invariably refined and lacking not in personal dignity, they displayed even in the isolated camps of the hinterland those inherited qualities that had contributed to the prestige of the Magyar. Conspicuous in bearing, supercilious even, among the other workers, they were sometimes known as the 'aristocrats.' Men palpably transplanted – a remnant of that remarkable people, restricted in area along the Danube, who, for long, provided the leaders that fashioned in power the loose-hung hegemony of one hundred million souls which made of Austria the dominant power in Europe for half a century and more.

The southern Slavs, including Serbs, Croatians, and other mountain races, now known as the Jugo-Slavs, were also employed in considerable numbers as labourers in the camps on railway construction along the National Transcontinental. These are a darker people than those already noted among the other Slav divisions. Discords are in evidence among them springing from rivalries of race and accidents of geography. While they are industrious plodding workers and aggressive, they suffer from a lack of English, a working knowledge of which they are not always willing to acquire. There are men of middle age among them, more accustomed to the use of arms than of tools for useful pursuits. These men are seldom wholly detached from the lands beyond the Adriatic. In thought they continue to dwell there, and thither they hope to return.

Bulgarians also, and a few Macedonians, so closely allied in their personal traits to the southern Slavs that they may be included as members of this grouping, were frequently in evidence on construction. They, too, can make good as navvies but they are hard to hold. No amount of drudgery causes them to take an eye off things as they are back in the Balkans. In unaccounted ways the latest information pertaining to events in Europe seems to reach these men in distant work groups. During the months of threatened hostilities in the Balkans, in 1910-11, the new arrival at a grade camp – whether the mailman on his rounds, the transient with newspapers, any one with information – was besieged by these eager-eyed men for news from the front. For like all other Jugo-Slavs, they nurse resentments, the accumulation often of lost generations. Even in the hinterland they would attempt to settle rooted differences; violence on a railway work, in the James Bay country, has shown how the bitter antipathies of these pristine peoples may be transferred to the grade camps of a new land. Following the outbreak of the Turkish war in 1912, the Bulgarians gradually melted from the line.

The Balkan Slavs, too, carry their sentiment to the camps. All their emotions find expression in their primitive tunes and dances. They would influence us by their urns. Songs, abounding in love and war, enkindle their hearts with the memory of the age-long struggle against the Turk. In the late twilight of a Sunday evening, when the dark is settling about the camps, the pent-up surgings of these home-lorn men will break forth into song – the old familiar airs of their own mountain villages – caught up in turn by their fellows in the distant shacks and carried in echoing diaphasons along the grade. And in such modes of self-expression, simple in desires, lies the germ of the drama.

Men of the Levantine peoples – Turks, Syrians, and Armenians – are found only occasionally and in small numbers throughout the camps of Canada. The Turks, when employed at all, are usually located at grade camps and on clay-cut excavations. The Turks are big men, peaceful and industrious. They seldom remain long, however, on a work. Canada is not, at best, a place to their liking, the whole environment here being unnatural in many ways. That he is here at all proves that he has been transplanted, and at a tremendous personal disadvantage. Few of the Syrians and Armenians found on construction are employed in manual work. Following the customs of their fathers, they engage as shopkeepers and small dealers. Much rivalry exists between these peddlers and the Jew vendors of the little railway towns.

The Jews, while not numerous, are always in evidence during any period of railway activity when large numbers of men are employed in camps. Few Jews engage in manual work. There are exceptions, however, and persistent able workers they are even in the most strenuous tasks. But they usually prefer to do their own planning. As tailors, peddlers, jewelers, and small traders of various kinds they follow the steel, locating temporarily in the small towns which spring up in its wake. It is only occasionally, or by special permit from the head-contractor, that peddlers are allowed in the camps ahead of the steel, so these small dealers, ensconced in their tar-papered shops at the small construction hamlet, wait to do business with the man going in or coming off the line. Quite frequently, too, the Jew is ubiquitous at a frontier town as the proprietor of an employment office for shipping men to camps and works.

The German as a distinct national was somewhat obscured in the Canadian camps previous to 1914. This was particularly the case along railway construction. Many new arrivals from the Fatherland were associated with Poles and Austrians of Central Europe, while others aligned closely with the Scandinavians of the west. There was no pronounced influx of Germans to frontier works such as marked the presence in numbers of 'Swedes,' 'Bulgarians' and 'Russians.'

Invariably competent, willing, and possessing reliance, the German-born worker was an asset to a foreman. He applied himself earnestly, his industry marked by quiet reserve. Such men in camps were steadying factors among the migratory labourers.

The bunkhouse to the German-reared was not entirely new. In the life of each the barrack still loomed in the background. It was plainly the desire of these newcomers to forget those years of enforced military service. But while they had no love for the army as such, they remembered it still with awed respect. One type, however, of an opposite temperament was occasionally in evidence among these German arrivals in camps: the conscript or petty officer released from service, who still carried in his heart bitter enmity toward all things military. Sensitive, as they usually were, the mention of arms and officers was to these men repugnant. It conveyed the memory of stringent punishments for minor infractions of discipline involving isolation, black bread, and the squeak of rats in dungeon-like cells. Germany to such as these was but a bitter remembrance.

Occasionally, on the other hand, one encountered in the camps at this period the German reservist. Life in the barracks, or training on board ship with him, too, had left its impress. But it was of another kind. He carried an air of assumption, nor did he hesitate to boast of the future. In the bunkhouse groups, even though greatly out-numbered, and by nationals not always friendly in their listening, he would amplify at opportunity an Old World matters and coming readjustments.

The Italians in turn comprise an important constituent among the workers in camps and on railway construction throughout Canada. Each nationality on a frontier work seems to fit into some particular form of activity: the Slavs usually become labourers' helpers, the English-speaking delight in machinery, the Finn excels in blasting, while the newcomer from Italy displays an adaptedness for work with cement – whether on excavations for concrete, erecting massive piers, or building abutments. The Italians, too, engage quite frequently at ballast pits or are found in large bodies with lift-gangs on railway maintenance, particularly when they may labour under their own countrymen acting as bosses.

The Italian navvies must go about their work in their own style. While not fast, they are, nevertheless, very steady and consistent, and accomplish much in the day's labour. While, usually, men of small frame, it is surprising what physical adaptiveness they display. They do not hesitate to undertake the heaviest manual work, and, although at times their physical tasks seem beyond them, yet grit and purpose seem never to desert these agile men.

There is something in the companionship of the big gang that appeals to an Italian. He works best alongside his compatriots where he can still dwell within sound of his mother tongue. Invariably the campman from Italy is peaceful, very methodical, well-behaved and drinks little. While often illiterate, he does not disdain to study, and will display much eagerness, even in mid-life, to acquire in the off hours at camp a working knowledge of English.

Nor are the Italians of the camps always homogeneous. A sharp cleavage shows too among this class of workers; there is the 'Naples' type, or southern Italian, and the northern Italian.

From Naples ships the man, short, swarthy, alert, and keen, his sensitive and suspicious nature in evidence even among his fellow muckers at a bridge camp. The human traits are always near the surface among this class of Italian workers; noise and talk, general contentment varied with an occasional song and with laughter, usually marks their working hours; this, however, may be varied as suddenly with words of irritation followed as quickly, at times, with acts of revenge.

The northern Italian is different. Bigger physically, he is distinctive in appearance; also fairer in complexion, he is usually quieter-toned and invariably he is literate; he brings with him the instincts of his race, artistic, genial, and versatile, but passionate too. These men are accustomed to tools and engage often as carpenters or handy men; but in whatever line, their ability with a trade of their choosing assures them steady employment while at a camp.

One needs only a superficial acquaintance with men on frontier works to note at times the love of the aesthetic that lingers with many Italian labourers. Even while mucking, or employed at other heavy tasks that seemingly would demean culture, there are not wanting to the observer evidences of genuine refinement among these men. It is the Italian worker rather than the Greek to-day who is prone to blend the grace of Athens with the sterner mind of Sparta.

Orientals, at least outside the Pacific province of the Dominion, are not numerous in the Canadian camps. Occasionally they may be found in gangs on railway work on the prairies but seldom are they employed in the eastern provinces. The fear of unfair competition due to their lower standards of living has united labour throughout the Dominion in a phalanx against the employment of Asiatics to any extent. In the charter granted the Grand Trunk Pacific, provision was made by the Dominion Parliament to prevent the employment of Orientals during the construction of the road. Some years later, in view of the disinclination of the Canadian-born to navvy under the conditions which then pertained in camps, guarded suggestions were made that Chinese coolies be admitted temporarily to the Dominion to complete the delayed work on the mountain section of the new road. The idea, however, met with little favour. While some Chinese were employed, it was not to an extent that gave any appreciable competition.

There is, also, a similar attitude toward the Sikhs, whose sudden influx, 1906-8, threatened to dislocate labour in the mills and camps of the Coast. Big, well-set-up, likeable, possessing the air of confidence born of centuries of free men, their worth as fellow citizens of the Empire can be appreciated by the people of the

Dominion, but Canadians will resolve, at the same time, that no portion of their land shall be made an outlet for the masses of India.

Back of all lies the racial instinct, a desire on the part of the Dominion that no large settlement of peoples from the Orient be permitted in any of the provinces. 'A White Man's Country' has found an echo as a slogan in the hearts of most Canadians. 'They shall not pass' seems in Canada an inexorable law against the yellow races. This fact alone precludes the possibility of their working in any numbers in camps or as navvies on any new railway construction.

Chapter 5

When the campman becomes a contractor

The navvy at station-work

SUB-LETTING is the bane at times of camp employment. It rears its head in many shapes. In chapter 2, mention was made of station-work. It will be appropriate here to enter more fully into the details of such methods as were observed along railway construction, for jobbing under one form or another is still commonly in vogue in the different frontier works.

A sub-contractor seldom undertakes more than ten miles of work on a new grade. Such a stretch offers about the maximum amount to be handled safely, considering the outfit and equipment usually at his disposal. He has, too, to keep always in mind that untoward events may tie up his work for days at a time. Nor can he afford to imperil his relationship with the head-contractor by being behind with his particular contract when the steel creeps toward his work. Delay then means further expense, if not indeed ultimate confiscation, according to the terms he has made with the head-contractor. These things serve as a damper in checking any undue ambition on the part of a sub-contractor to undertake too much work.

In any ten-mile section the bigger clay-cuts and much of the rock work, requiring as they do, horses and machinery, are usually completed by the sub-contractor himself. He will build his camps centrally near to the biggest cut on his piece of work, and the heavier operations will thus be undertaken by his local foreman with gangs of men employed at day work. But wherever possible the sub-contractor hastens to let out in station-work all the lighter pieces of grade.

A 'station' is one hundred feet of the right-of-way in its native state. The term, too, usually implies that clearing and stumping have already been performed. On such a strip of right-of-way the road-bed is to be raised to grade level. This height varies in places from less than two feet, to five and six feet in others, but the average height of a road bed to be built by station-men is usually under forty inches. This class of work is accomplished by small groups of men working with shovels, grub-hoes and barrows, wheeling from the pit up long planks, hewed in tree lengths.

In England, during the middle of the last century, navvies working in bands like these were known as 'butty-gangs.' They were composed of men possessing size and great strength, labourers from Lincolnshire and Lanarkshire, who worked long hours. Some of these men even in the fifties made good pay at work undertaken in this way, but as was then proven, it was disastrous for workers lacking exceptional physical endurance.

The size of a station-group varies much according to the number of stations attempted; from two men working as partners, who take perhaps five stations, to as many as eight, ten, and fourteen men in a group, who may undertake twenty stations. In case of rock work fewer stations are allowed to individual groups.

Station-men receive a minimum amount per cubic yard for the material they heap-up to form the road bed. The prices to be paid will depend, too, on their bargaining power with the sub-contractor.

Having in mind current rates paid for such work during the railway activity of 1911-12-13, the allowance per yard for muskeg or light soil was around twenty-seven cents; five cents more was usually paid for clay, while loose rock brought a still larger sum. Provision was also made that in case hard-pan was encountered or should some showing of rock when uncovered prove a detrital, a proportionate increase per yard would be made over and above the prices paid for ordinary excavation. This was known as the promise for 'classification.'

Since station-work is commonly practised where muskeg abounds, an understanding of some of the characteristics of the latter gives a clearer conception of the nature of the task assumed by station-men.

Throughout whole stretches in parts of Canada is the muskeg. Ever present on the landscape it is dreary in its desolation even to the healthy-minded. It is, to the eye, a fairly level stretch of wet moss and grasses grown rank, dotted at intervals with low shrubs in thick clusters, while here and there, in the open, stand straggling clumps of stunted tamaracs, their knotted limbs frowsed in furze. Sometimes a low-lying lake or thick, brackish pond occupies a depression in the centre of the area. Though wet, the muskeg is not a marsh, neither is it a bog or a swamp. But it is full of meaning to the man who is forced to cross it without good footwear.

In those flat wastes only such herbs survive as are adapted for living in cold, damp bottoms. The Labrador plant is invariably present in abundance throughout the muskeg. This small shrub weaves its roots about and through the moss, forming hummocks firm enough in wet places before the grade is ditched to give dry

footing to the man en route to camp. While the dense spongy covering of the muskeg does not retard the downward movement of the
frosts in fall, it hinders its realease in summer, and frozen ground
will be found below the thick padded mosses even in the weeks of
June.

There is no rock in the muskeg. Its soil is a dark, spongy loam
extending from three to five feet below the surface, then white clay
or hardpan is usually encountered. Scarce in a four-mile strip will
sufficient land high and dry be found to give a suitable site for a
shack. Where possible the navvy eschews the muskeg during the early
summer months as a breeder of flies. Its redeeming feature, however,
is that once it is drained, the soil of the muskeg makes excellent
shoveling, and is particularly adaptable for station-work.

Muskegs abound throughout the watershed of the mighty Moose
and whole portions of the National Transcontinental traversed this
tract. Across such areas the new line coursed in long sweeping
tangents, its road bed in the initial stages shaped by the arms of
sturdy men who wrought in isolated groups at station-work.

Let it be noted here that all station-work on railway construction
is not confined to muskeg alone, yet the constant presence of these
wastes, in commanding places, both in the North-western States as
well as throughout northern Canada, has been a direct incentive
toward the promotion of petty forms of sub-letting.

Since station-work as a practice presents the crux of all sub-
letting, let us consider some of the phases of work conditions that
develop under its actual operation. Take the case of a group of
navvies, eight in number, who ship to do station-work at a camp,
forty miles in advance of the steel. Several days, not less than eight,
will be consumed before they finally reach the headquarters camp of
the sub-contractor for whom they hired. Their stations being
allotted, they will require an outfit – tools, barrows, dynamite for
frozen muskeg and for blasting obstinate stumps, grub-hoes, not to
speak of a generous supply of chuck, all of which is procured from
the stores of the local sub-contractor, whose supplies have been
brought in during the sleigh haul.

The list following gives an idea of the sundry articles required to
start a fair-sized station-group under ordinary circumstances:

4 wooden barrows

8 axe-heads and handles

4 rolls of tar paper

6 lbs. tar paper nails

10 lbs. 2½ in. nails

10 lbs. 6 in. nails

8 shovels

1 pair hinges

2 boxes dynamite

1 stove (4-lid camp stove)

4 bags flour

50 lbs. bacon

30 lbs. coffee

25 lbs. sugar

25 lbs. bread (for immediate needs)

2 cases condensed milk

50 lbs. butter

1 case tomatoes

50 lbs. beans

8 tin cups

8 tin plates

10 knives and forks

3 boxes matches

10 bars cheap soap

3 bread pans

24 candles

1 coffee pot

1 granite pot

1 box prunes

1 box raisins

24 plugs tobacco

1 half-barrel pork

1 half-barrel sauer-kraut

Outfitted in this way, these men assume a relation to the sub-contractor very similar to that which he, in turn, occupies to the head-office. They, too, start handicapped by a considerable debt, due to advances, but their credit will remain good with the sub-contractor as long as they continue to pile up the grade. Their work not only pays for replenishing their own supplies, but also serves to warrant advances and credits to the sub-contractor at the main head-quarters of the head-contractor.

The station-group will spend the first few days on their work in erecting a shack. This does not take long, for plenty of trees of the right dimensions, suitable for building the walls, line the right of way on either side. Care is taken to locate their building at a point convenient to water. Then the barrows are assembled, and half a dozen long shapely spruce are hewed for portable runways which rest on wooden horses.

And how do things work out? Figured on paper the station-man should fare well. Each man will excavate in a day and wheel up the long plank onto the grade, from one hundred to one hundred and fifty barrow loads, depending upon the height of the fill. With an

average of ten barrows to the cubic yard he thus removes ten to
fifteen yards daily.

At the prices paid for station-work when the National Transcontinental was under construction, this would mean a pay per day
of from $2.50 to $3.75, and at times under favourable conditions,
an average of even $4.50 and $5.00 was not uncommon. When the
fact is recalled, too, that good workmen, even in the towns and
cities, during that same period were seldom receiving more than
$2.00 per day, it is apparent that station-work looked attractive to
certain classes of virile workers. Meanwhile the daily cost for chuck
per man on a station-group ranged, at the time, from thirty cents in
the case of the Poles, Russians and other Slav workers, who lived
more cheaply, to fifty and sixty cents apiece for the Swedes who are
not only great feeders, but vary their food and always buy the best
to be had.

There are many things, however, which militate against the big
pay. There is the outlay for suitable clothes and, especially,
footwear. When the men go on the work they must first surface and
ditch along their stations; this involves working in water often for
days, at the start of their jobs as station-men. Waterproof shoe packs
or long boots must be secured. Only the strongest and warmest
clothing will suffice, and such goods cost very high away out on the
line. The men coming new on the work are generally down on their
uppers and thus in addition to the initial debt for grub and outfits,
they incur further current obligations for boots, for heavy topcoats,
for socks, shirts, underwear and the many sundry necessities so
essential for men while at work of this kind.

It is by the cost of all such supplies that station-men are cramped
in any attempt to make good. They start heavily in debt, and often
the machinations of skilful figuring are employed to keep them
there. Their credit endures just so long as the amount of grade
upreared ensures ample recompense for the sub-contractor himself at
the office of the head-contractor, who in turn is reimbursed from
the Railway Commission.

The station-man is practically beholden to the local sub-
contractor in the matter of prices for his supplies. Nor does
uniformity in charges exist, among the nearby sub-contractors, for
prices will vary considerably on adjoining contracts. Camp stoves of
like material will vary four dollars within ten miles, long clear pork

fluctuates with the different supply depots, while canned goods in boxes – tomatoes, condensed milk, corn, and other goods vary most of all. It is a case where the seller is in no way restricted. Whatever may be the initial costs, these are accentuated by local conditions of transport, and in some cases owing to the personal whim of the owner, all of which detracts from the earning power of men at station-work.

Station-men often have difficulty in getting the bills showing the charges made for their purchases. On one pretext or another the clerks will withhold them when issuing the routine supplies from the stores of the sub-contractors. Yet these bills in themselves are the only signed papers the foreign-born navvies have as a check on the office for supplies procured.

Then, too, the sub-contractor has other sources of income from his station-men. Occasionally he hires out a part of his outfit to these groups of men. A horse, maybe, and a few rough-made carts are loaned a station-group to help complete a piece of heavy work. So often however it happens that long spells of wet weather with ensuing trouble from gumbo, and other interruptions of different kinds prevent the use of a horse for days at a time, and meanwhile the charges incurred for pressed hay and oats are necessarily very high.

There is also another form of revenue which the alert sub-contractor may command. It arises from rents for housing quarters used by station-men in places where it is not practicable to build a shack. Occasionally a disused company building is given and without any charge, but if a tent be loaned, the men occupying it will be charged from fifty cents to one dollar each per month for the use of it. New tents are hardly to be expected under such circumstances, and there are cases when the first monthly rent so collected will repay all that the tent is actually worth.

There is much uncertainty about station-work. While the men of a group have a signed agreement, stating exactly the prices being paid for different classes of excavation, they never know definitely just how they stand in the matter of pay until the day they are 'measured-up.' The only thing positive is that the sub-contractor will see to it that they are doing enough work to clear their van account.

Much of this indefiniteness is due to the promise usually made the men for classification and increased yardage. This, like the sword of Damocles, always hangs suspended, a direct incentive for increased effort. It does not, however, always bring a corresponding remuneration. The matter of measurement and classification rests entirely with the engineers. This leaves too much opportunity for collusion at the expense of the illiterate foreign-born station-men, when very cordial relations exist between the office and the residency.

It is common for men, who have had experience at station-work, to leave intact in the midst of their particular piece of excavation an 'island' or sample section. These are upright columns of earth about eighteen inches square at the base. When any doubt exists as to classification these pillars remain as tangible proof verifying not only the depth of the excavation but giving a cross section that shows the nature of the soil already removed.

There is a legal aspect about station-work which many groups of men learn to their own cost. When men undertake work in stations they are no longer navvies but become contractors themselves; true, they are many circles out, but the change is real nevertheless. They are no longer labourers, nor can they seek redress from the contractor if the condition of their employment denies them even meagre wages for the time so spent.

The men doing station-work assume the bulk of the risks themselves. The weather will intervene. Even under the best of circumstances such workers lose much during wet periods. Though station-men work through all but the steadiest rains, yet, even then, as many as five to eight days are lost each month. Meanwhile expenses accrue for grub and other needed supplies. Sickness, also, is not unusual: the close, fetid quarters of the shacks, the heavy feeding on pork and strong foods, while offset by the open air and immense physical exertions, wear down the strongest constitution. Potatoes soon run short on the line, even the canned tomatoes may play out, and there is little green food to counteract the heavy unvaried meals of salted and smoked meats, bread and syrup and beans – the result is a camp ennui – a mild form of scurvy often, or a staleness which few escape during months at station-work. The intolerable pests of black flies and mosquitoes, too, poison the system and make the work for five weeks in June and July extremely arduous. This all seriously impairs the earning power of the men engaged in station-work.

That some men occasionally do well at station-work is not surprising. But it results from an expenditure of energy and time which would easily bring a good wage at the front in more civilized surroundings, let alone out on the fringe of things. They work very long hours, often from four or five in the morning until darkness settles down on the long northern day. One barrow keeps its turn with another, and the work proceeds with unchanging monotony. The men who engage in it are men in their prime, and if they do, occasionally, make a stake it is often at a serious sacrifice of their health and their efficiency as workers. Only men strong and physically fit can undertake it at the best of times.

Sub-letting in stations is an unhealthy form of employment for any man's work. By means of it labour is unduly cozened with promises. As has already been indicated much depends upon individual effort; when thus engaged the navvy is his own boss, works when he likes, rests an hour at noon, or shovels unrelentingly till nine at night. This in itself appeals to a self-reliant type of worker and brings a corresponding compensation. For a fortnight at a stretch one may even make good pay under the conditions. But this is the rosy side, it is the bait that lures; taking the whole summer through, the big pay to the greater number at least is as elusive as the pot of gold at the foot of the rainbow. Neither the head-contractor nor his subs are going to be so easy. If station-work were always likely to prove such an assured thing there would be nobody ready to undertake the daywork at the camps.

With what the reader has now gleaned of the general methods which underlie this particular system of sub-letting on railway construction, let us look further at a few concrete cases of station-work along the National Transcontinental, which show fairly its results under actual operation. Examples are here given to indicate:

1 Station-work at its best
2 Station-work as a partnership
3 The human factor in station-men
4 Station-men in default
5 Station-work under normal conditions
6 Station-work at its worst

STATION-WORK AT ITS BEST

Eleven men, Austrians, constituted a working group which took five stations in the end of April, 1911. There was quite a heavy cut on the work for station-men to tackle, but the sub-contractor supplied them with four dump cars and rented them a horse, and the gang went at it.

They worked steadily through the midst of the fly-season and finished by July 26th. They were then measured up, accounts were straightened, rents for car and the horse were paid, and after a settlement these eleven men had each made an average of $4.15 a day, as well as his board.

That is the pleasing side of a wage bargain between the sub-contractor and a group of navvies. Would that it had more often terminated that way!

STATION-WORK AS A PARTNERSHIP

'Can I get a bite here, boys?' said a quiet-toned man, middle-aged, stepping into the cookery at a grade camp about ten o'clock one morning. 'I've worked five months up the grade and I haven't got a cent – but, money or no money, I've got to get out when I'm able, or I'll be a dead dog.'

Even a camp cook may be non-plussed as to who is beating his way, but this man was given a hand-out, few questions were asked, and the incident was forgotten.

A couple of days later, thirty miles farther up the line, a man with ragged overalls, a long dirty shirt down to his knees and face smeared with lard and coal-oil, on account of the flies, was chopping away at a root in the muskeg.

'Hello, old man – you must like working alone,' said one in passing.

'Can't say that I do, but the way things are going I'm in a pretty pickle.'

'Why, what's up?'

'Well, it's just like this, my partner left me four days ago. We came in last March, here it is the end of July. We took seventeen stations and had ten finished when Bob jumped it the other day; if I quit we get nothing after all these weeks, for our contract calls for us to complete the whole seventeen stations.'

'Bob got dry, I guess, and quit,' suggested the passer, raising the tump-line and resting his pack for a moment on an upturned barrow.

'No, not a bit of it! Bob's a good worker, wouldn't want a better partner. We worked a year together on the branch, near Superior, but he took cramps, and no wonder,' said the station-man, filling his pipe, 'No oatmeal, no matches, no sugar — station-men here for eight miles living on pork, bread and tomatoes; a fellow's stomach won't stand it. Not even a raspberry to be had, and the flies they are just simply unbearable!'

'Will Bob get any pay for what he has done?'

'No, not a cent, unless I can hold down and finish, then he and I can come to some arrangement.'

'Well, what if you both quit with only the ten stations finished?'

'We would get a little, later on, when the accounts are adjusted — some of the leavings would drift our way; meanwhile we could live on wind till such time came around,' said the station-man in disgust. 'Yes, and I'll tell you what's more, I honestly think those clerks at the office there would like nothing better than a freeze-out for the whole of us, once we get the grade well under way for them. They'll not put themselves out to get supplies for us at any rate.' Whether right or wrong in his summing-up of things, such was the impression the system of station-work not infrequently made on the navvy.

THE HUMAN FACTOR IN STATION-MEN

1 Less than twenty-three miles from the end of the steel, a Finlander, for some years resident in Canada, took a piece of station-work. Abounding in the physical vigour requisite for such enterprizes, he possessed also that balance of mental equipment which means, in any worker, not only ability but the greater gift of initiative.

His particular piece of work, carefully planned by him, and performed with persistent diligence, was finally completed in twenty-six days. His venture proved successful, and netted him, after measuring-up, a stake of four hundred and ten dollars.

His departure soon after, for the nearest frontier town, some hundred and sixty miles from the rail head, where was to be found a considerable colony of his own countrymen, was not unnoted and with a degree of envy by fellow station-men of nearby groups who were not so fortunate in their own tasks. Not five days later word trickled back to the men on the station-groups that their erstwhile fellow worker, penniless and sorely beaten as the result of debauch, was confronted with a term in the district jail as a vagrant – just one case among the hundreds, showing that a campman, like ourselves, is not to be unduly tempted when new-found gains are jingling in the pocket.

2 At the risk of tiring the reader let another typical incident be mentioned which shows, from another aspect, this same tendency to squander a stake.

Scotty was not new to Canada. For eight years he had followed the camps both East and West. Experience gained on the prairies and in the mountains, as well as along construction where, north of Lake Superior, new roads skirt the shores of lakes or hew at times their sinuous way through jagged courses of pre-cambrian rocks, and acquainted Scotty with the meaning of a big stake. Station-work for him, many months at a stretch, had meant ample returns. His weakness was how to keep what he had made – and he was frank in his estimate of this frailty.

All workers in camps have ideals, and dream dreams. Scotty's objective was a snug farm for himself in a river valley at the coast. The climate there with its rain and mists would remind him always in later days of the land he still called home.

After repeated defeats in his different efforts to hold his well-earned stakes, he took, along with two companions, in 1913, one more piece of station-work. This promised well and would require nine to eleven months for completion. To circumvent his weakness he arranged with a bank manager, in a town at the head of the Lakes, that whatever money was received from his contract should be placed to his credit at the local branch, and on no condition was it to be released even to himself, unless sober.

For months the little party grubbed incessantly, and with some measure of success. Within a full year, the work was finished. With a substantial credit awaiting him and happy in that reliance which comes from the possession of ready money, hard won from toil, Scotty started westward.

But there intervened the subtle wooing of a frontier town. When the head of the Lakes was reached Scotty was anything but in the mood for farming. His demands for the money lying to his credit were at first consistently refused. His insistence finally became abuse and he was told to take his money and be gone. Ten days later he was stranded with $1650.00 spent, and himself in possession of a disposition somewhat akin to that of a caged bear. The farm in Okanagan was still a mirage.

Then was heard the war drum, and Scotty to the sound of the tocsin moved with men eastward to where, above Quebec City was the gathering in ranks for the armed conflict beyond the sea.

THE STATION-MAN IN DEFAULT

Nor is the station-man always devoid of deception. Of his perfidy at times toward the sub-contractor the writer is not unaware. Scales in the balance may tilt to either side. The contractors however have this advantage that they can usually forefend their interests locally. They have the rail position at least until displaced.

One concern of the sub-contractor and his clerk is to keep a station-gang, once it is supplied, at work. A tendency may be displayed among some workers to den-up in the inclement weather. Well provided with food from the nearest depot, the shiftless among them display an inclination to sit by the fire for days if unmolested, particularly when Boreas without, in no uncertain way, is challenging all and sundry who intrude on his domain. Whiling their hours with smoke, and chat or games of chance, men under such circumstances apparently ignore any obligations to the company that has provided for them.

Forceful methods are sometimes taken to drive the indolent among such groups to their tasks. But unwilling work at best is the result, and men so circumstanced will barely excavate enough to pay for their provisions. Gradually the gang melts away; first one face, then another, is missing from a group whose members bear so much in common resemblance. Stealthily they join some gang of fellow nationals, perhaps on an adjoining work. Fed by one sub-contractor they prove of advantage to another. Incidents of like nature encourage a wide-spread distrust by many contractors toward whole groups of station-men.

STATION-WORK UNDER NORMAL CONDITIONS

Take the case of a group, five Canadians, who engaged in station-work. They were not new on construction, had followed the line for years; splendid, able and active, their attitude toward the whole matter of station-work serves properly to appraise the working of the system in general.

If one of their number, and once the work were well started, we should probably commune with ourselves somewhat as follows:

'There are five of us in our party. We have eleven stations, but it is heavy fill. We have been here now six months and a half and hope to finish by the end of September, six weeks hence. We can take out ten yards in ten hours, and we are getting twenty-five cents a yard. With the prices of grub here, it costs $1.00 a day for board of each. So we make fifteen cents a yard clear – a dollar and a half a day and our board; but any man at the front, suffering no inconveniences, can make that. To make allowances for lost time we have to work fourteen hours a day whenever possible – then go back to the shack, cook for next day, or seek shelter from the mosquitoes behind the canvas bags. We are in our prime, but another five years at this and we will be broken-down men. The sub-contractors know well that if they did this work by day-labour it would cost them thirty-five to forty cents a yard.'

STATION-WORK AT ITS WORST

At 'K' Camp, forty miles from the steel, eleven Russians took a piece of station-work on March 11th; their contract calling for twenty-three cents muskeg and thirty-two for the clay, with classification. They worked without let-up, week in and week out, and finished July 20th. After a few days they were 'measured-up' by the residency men and went to settle at the office of the sub-contractor. There was less than thirty-three cents a day coming to them. What could they do? Nothing! They had hoped for a favourable classification, at least thirty-seven cents per yard instead of thirty-two on the clay, but were disappointed. Like 'buying a pig in a poke,' they didn't know till the last day how they stood. It is in the interest of sub-contractors to keep them so. How long would a man work arduously in fly-season if he knew that he was making $32\frac{3}{8}$ cents a day? But, then, other such similar groups have ended seriously in debt – cases in point where the pencil got ahead of the shovel!

'Hell sure will go a-popping some day,' said old Harry, the chore boy, who had followed camps for forty years, as he stood at the water barrel rolling the ragged sleeve of his smock and slowly studying the disappointed faces of that group outside the office window. 'Time and again, every few days, this same thing goes on,' he said in rising tones, 'doesn't matter if they are Russians, Canadians, white or black, yes, even if yellow-bellies – the poor devils worked hard, didn't they – and get little, if anything!'

That bunch left the camp in sullen Russian style. There were four large rivers they would have to pass before the steel was reached. At one of these a man with a 'pull' at the residency, using a canoe belonging to the engineers, would take them across for fifty cents a head; at the next river a student fire-ranger, advised of their coming, would similarly oblige them, and at the other two rivers, men, locally posted, would ply the ferry-trade for all it was worth. With their awkward packs and hand bundles of bread and fat pork they would reach the steel in two days. A further charge of $5.50 each would land them, after a hundred-mile run on a contractor's train, at the nearest construction hamlet. There they could rest a time and ruminate on the strange new kind of servitude countenanced in the camps of Canada: Labour in such forms is sunk to low estate! Even the Roman slave, tethered to the land, received his daily portion of bread and salt and oil if not an allotment of sour wine. Is it as of old the battle to the strong? But then it has been better put, and long since:

Stick, stick, beat dog;
Dog, dog, bite pig!

The employer under such a system has little to lose. He makes a clear profit on every yard of earth removed, as well as on the goods supplied. The more station-men the better in many cases. Meanwhile, if the men make well at times it is through the fine meshes of a sieve. The very uncertainty of such remuneration bears out the saying credited of old to the Norseman, Havamal, 'Don't praise the day until the night, a sword until it is tried, or ice that has yet to be crossed.'

For it follows, as the day follows night, that given opportunity, aspiring man will ever advantage himself of labour that is dependent. It was so when throughout those continued centuries of feudal exactions the Church alone was the protector of the worker; it was evident in the many legal contortions and adjustments that sought to hamper the hireling in the years following the Black Death, as it was, later, when the members of the Swabian League, in fealty sworn, would hold in subjection the peasants of the Upper Danube.

What may we conclude from these recitals? Perfection cannot be looked for under the conditions, and many men have more capacity for kicking than for making the best of things. Discrimination must be used, but the fact remains that the system of station-work is ruinous to more than half of those who engage in it, particularly when the amount of energy and time and work expended is considered. Surely but another branch of the upas tree showing in the wage bargain.

Station-work as exemplified on the National Transcontinental, and still pursued on branch building in Canada is a denatured product of labour. It is a struggle at best against environing circumstances. There is a natural recoil from the compulsion of such conditions. The whole tendency is to make of these workers a prey to sullen resentment, bitterness and crime. But it is treated lightly as one of the inevitable defects of the transition stage in a country's development — that with the navvy and the campman it was always so — and precedents are hard things to master.

Chapter 6

Shacks and shack-men on railway construction

STATION-WORK necessarily involves shacks. Each group of station men will have a shack-centre. These may be located at distances of one mile, two, four or eight miles from the office of the sub-contractor, according to the location of their work. Few station men, however, are farther than six miles from some source of supplies, whether at the sub-contractor's office or at a temporary depot situated conveniently to the station men.

A few of the shacks used by station men are very neat, particularly those built by the Norwegians and Swedes. These people when engaged in station work generally take big portions of the grade in a lump, they prepare to stay for months or a year, at a time, and are more careful about the buildings they put up. In general, however, most shacks are hastily constructed, crude and with no pretense at even the most meagre precautions for sanitation. Occasionally two shacks are built side by side, one is used for cooking and one for sleeping, this arrangement having an immense advantage in the fly season. But, after all allowance is made, the number of clean, tidy little shacks, when account is taken of the different nationalities on any sixty-mile stretch of new construction, will not number fifteen per cent of the whole.

The Scandinavians once they had experienced the actual conditions under which station men wrought on the National Transcontinental gradually left that phase of construction. Latterly they were found at the larger excavations and at rock-work. Their places were taken by the Slavs who were being brought to Canada in large numbers for such purposes. Much of the station-work on the Transcontinental was performed by these peoples.

This type of navvy, the Russian or Bohunk, crowd the shacks ahead of the steel. Their ignorance of the country, their stolidness, their willingness even, combined with the group quality of blindly following a leader, all contribute to the fact that their earnings from the performance of those heavy manual tasks are scant. Yet, imbued with the hope of gain under new conditions and endowed with that tireless energy and stubborn purpose which takes no heed of time, each day to these men is a work day, and, in spite of flies and heats and rains, they fill it to the brim.

The shacks of Slav station men, hastily constructed of small-sized trees, stand at the edge of the right-of-way. They are uniform in shape, and in the case of the larger groups will average eighteen feet long and twelve feet wide, with the front wall eight feet high; the roof made of long poles side by side, slants toward the back, resting midway on a substantial ridge-pole. Tar paper covers the roof. There is one small door, and, usually, a single pane of glass carried carefully from the nearest depot gives limited light to the interior. In such shacks nine to sixteen foreign-born navvies will dwell, somewhat on the principle of the modified padroga of their own Slav villages.

Bunks occupy the interior of the shack; double-decked, they line the whole length of the structure and extend across one end, if the gang is large. A small, rough table is propped against the wall under the window, the remaining space being occupied in cold weather by a stove. Food supplies, clothing and personal belongings fill every available nook. The only way in which the usual shack can comfortably accommodate all the inmates at the same time is to have half the men recline for periods on the bunks.

Outside, in the small clearing, is the large clay oven, semi-oval in shape and about half the size of a hogshead. These ovens are usually arched over with a pole frame and tar paper to protect them from the rain. Bread is baked three times a week. The oven is first fired red-hot, the coals are then hastily scraped out and a large portion of dough is placed on the heated clay bottom. There it slowly cooks. The loaves thus baked are very large, tapering in shape, sometimes two feet long, and often eight inches thick. The bread itself is well-crusted and most toothsome. It is a luxury to men who in their own lands fare on black bread, or other mixtures of barley, rye and coarser meals.

The shack group purchases its provisions at the depot of the sub-contractor. The packing of supplies for four or five miles over a heavy, undrained right-of-way is not an enviable job, so the task is rotated among the men. Once a week, usually on a Sunday, two men make a trip for the needed supplies of the group.

The Slav workers who dwell in shacks do not live as well as the Swedes. The latter deprive themselves of nothing and the amount of work performed by them shows up in proportion. The Slavs stick closely to the fat pork, beans and bread. Their meals are coarse and strong and have much sameness, varied upon occasions with sauerkraut, syrup and canned tomatoes. Stchee, a boiled pot of meal and beans with little squares of pork, eaten along with plenty of bread and weak tea, is the common diet. In many cases each member of the shack group, provided with a long spoon, or wooden ladle, helps himself to the stchee from a common basin in the centre of the poled table.

What is the daily routine in a shack? Let us take the case of a small camp of five to seven men. Their building, framed of small spruce or poplar, is chinked inside with slabs, or moss, the seams on the outside being plentifully encased with mud. The roof is made of poles covered with thick paper or sods. The floor usually is of hardened clay. A door like that of a chicken-coop opens into the shack and light struggles to enter by one small pane. For sleep there is to the inmates the hours of rest between the lights of the long northern day. Advantage is taken of the extended twilight to work late, and invariably an early start is made as well at the morning tasks. In the grey dawn the cook arouses first, takes a stretch, reaches for a cigarette and puffs vigorously while his senses collect. Soon all are astir, the air is heavy and the chill of the muskeg makes the blankets damp and musty. The clothes and boots of the men, left wet and smeared in mud the evening before, will be stiff and hard, for seldom is frost long absent from the muskeg wastes.

In all small shack groups the men take the cooking week about. This means that one of the party puts in a heavy week every month or so; not only does he do much of his usual day's work out on the grade, but he also looks after the cooking. On rising the others begin their work while he prepares the morning meal. Breakfast is served about seven, then work, with half an hour for dinner. Supper comes about five, then work again, the men seldom returning to their shack till dark; then a smoke and into the bunks once more for the short night's respite.

The off-period for rest, or the opportunity for recreation of any kind, is not easily had by any shack group. Good tobacco is always plentiful, and for further relaxation, in the larger gangs, there is the concertina with its strident notes, played of an evening at the week-end; but work, lots of it, through the long hours is the order for the day in a shack group of whatever size.

It is of interest just here to mention another phase of life in camps that bears a close similarity to that of shacks along railway construc-tion. It pertains to the practice which some nationals display as labourers to co-operate for their mutual advantage in the matter of housing and food. This is characteristic of the Bulgarians and Macedonians, but it is also particularly noticeable among the Italian workers.

The Italians, while often quite prominent along any piece of construction, do not commonly engage in station-work. They prefer to work together in larger numbers, and nearer the steel. There they are assured of regular supplies and at more reasonable prices. Working usually in large numbers they can act collectively; seldom are they coerced as are the more illiterate Slavs. Having a longer acquaintance with the methods of this Western world they have learned their bartering powers in certain kinds of work when acting together, and they use them. Thrift unallied to sagacity is of no practical use.

There are, however, phases of their work as navvies which correspond to the life of the shack groups. Take the case of, say, one hundred Italians engaged in building abutments at a river camp twenty miles ahead of the steel. In such places some will dwell in tents provided by the local contractor; others, rather than pay tent rent, will improvise shelters of some sort. And fantastic they are – oat bags stretched from pole to pole with a covering of tarpaulin or tar paper, or an evergreen lean-to arching the mouth of some pit on the hillside.

The Italian navvies, although disposed toward community life, do not usually dine in whole groups. They are individualists in their meals. Two, usually, cook their food together. After the day's work is done a busy hour follows in any Italian camp. Many small fires, nursed by handfuls of twigs and chips, are lighted in the open. Not only is the evening meal partaken but a start is made in the preparation of dishes intended for the next day. There is washing, too, for, personally, the Italian is the cleanest of all navvies. Seldom will an Italian, no matter what the circumstances, start the week's work at a railway camp without a clean change in shirts and undergarments. An Italian camp is always noisy. The clamour, the occasional song, the excited talk, the fitful fires and the darkening background of the woods on a night in July speak not of construction life in Canada, but of the dwellers on the slopes of Vesuvius, or of villagers in the poorer districts of Catania.

At works along the National Transcontinental the Italians were seldom paid more than $1.75 for a day of ten hours, yet they actually made fair wages. How did it work out?

Italians grub in pairs. Two of them would lay in a month's supplies as follows:

1 large wooden box macaroni	$3.50
1 bag potatoes	2.00
Bread, 1 loaf each per day	4.50
1 pail lard, 10 lbs.	2.50
Smoked bacon — side, 22 lbs.	4.00
Tea, incidentals, etc.	2.00
	$18.50

Thus two Italian workers, cooking for themselves, would live quite well, and for less than $10.00 each per month.

When we bear in mind that the same class of workers on the Transcontinental got plenty of overtime and Sunday work, their monthly pay-check during the summer often exceeded $56.00. thus, allowing for grub, the Italian navvy counted it a poor month that he did not clear from $40.00 to $45.00. Many of these same men were remitting money to families in Italy. Its purchasing power in southern Italy at that time, when the price of many necessaries and general living conditions were compared, was as five to one. The Italian navvy was no fool! He was living, in his own way, on the same plane as the higher-paid machine men and officials on the line. The Italian as an individual profited most from his work as a navvy.

There is the danger, however, that the Italian in his efforts to economize may unduly lower the standard of life for the other more healthily-reared navvies. Large numbers of Italian nationals, during the long periods between seasonal works, tie-up in some adjacent town in what are really communal stopping places, run by one of their own countrymen. These buildings are large tar-papered structures which for fifteen to twenty cents give the inmate floor space on which to spread his blankets, with the further privilege of cooking meals on one of the half-dozen stoves. As many as forty men are not infrequently roofed over night in such places. Slightly improved houses will be found in the larger towns where the foreign-born navvies spend the winter months.

Such buildings were in use in New Liskeard in 1904, McDougall's Chutes in 1907, Cochrane in 1908-11, Nipigon in 1912-13. It may be questioned if they are entirely absent to-day from such centres as

North Bay, Sudbury, Sault Ste Marie or Port Arthur. These rooming tenements are, in their own way, the corollary in the railway town of the shacks out on construction.

Not all the foreign-born navvies dwell in ill-constructed shacks. Even among the Slavs there are exceptions. Practical men are found in all such work-groups who, by their native ability and skill can, with a few tools, construct from the meagre materials at hand — pole-trees, moss and clay — very creditable shacks as temporary domiciles. But even when this recognition has been allowed, the fact remains that the great majority of the shacks occupied by foreign-born workers could be classed only as squalid and unsanitary, a menace to the morals and health of the inmates.

With this in mind we may examine fairly closely a typical shack such as was used in 1912 to house a group of workers on railway construction who had come but a few months previously from Central Europe. It is typical of the shacks which for successive years lined active construction in that thousand-mile stretch of trans-continental extending across the many-rivered lands of the James Bay country.

Out where the river W. rolls noisily across the grade and where the S., by another channel, some four miles distant, hastens north-ward to join the mud-washed Moose, was a shack for station men which housed nine foreign-born navvies. The pole-built shack was little more than seven feet high in front, with a back wall less than six feet in height. A narrow door four feet high hung from the one remaining hinge, while a small window-pane admitted light to the crowded interior, revealing the roughly-made table and row of sleeping-bunks down the side.

A stone's throw from the grade, the shack was easily reached by long poles, strung in three, to bridge the ditch and low, wet ground that edged the clearing wherein it stood. The ground about was littered with empty tomato cans, condensed-milk tins, old bits of smoked meats and refuse of all kinds, and, now that summer heats had come, the stench was almost unbearable.

Let us enter this shack to get an idea of the abode of the men who had left it for work two hours previously. There, on the pole table beneath the window, were six large loaves of burnt bread; a chunk of pork simmered in a pot over a slow fire; in the corner was tossed half a bag of flour and about twenty pounds of sugar, with

some barley, and spare pieces of salted meat. Empty snuff-boxes
were in plenty, littered about on the earthen floor, for 'Copenhagen'
seems an essential to station-men of all degrees.

Down the grade in a small clay cut the group of men were at
work who made of this their living quarters. They were filling dump
cars and then, six men to a car, four harnessed in front and two
pushing from behind, they would take the cars to the dump while
the others would remain to loosen clay for the next load. From the
experiences of other groups it would be pretty safe to infer that
those same men finally finished that cut and left, after months of
work, with little more to show for their labour than the grub they
had received. But, as has happened before in these chapters, this is a
digression verging on bitterness, which may not be justified in the
mind of the reader.

Yet for fifty-two miles on that piece of work shacks in succession
had been passed of just such description. Was it that a difference of
dialect and language produced grades among the navvies, resulting in
an estrangement which had condemned these workers to such
abodes? Coverts of gosherds some centuries removed! The rush-
strewn hovels of Lancastrian days were no fitter breeding places of
Asiatic plagues. To dwell therein was to stem the swirl whose under-
tow drags always down to fever and disease.

One wonders what malady affects these older peoples that they
must submit to such blood-letting. Are these foreign workers, in
their shack groups along railway construction, any better off than
their forebears, two generations removed, who wrought as serfs for
other masters? Liberty is theirs in a new land, and the handling of
coins, hard won in servitude, but what about the sacrifice?

After all, the recompense of life varies but little for the toiler.
Throughout succeeding centuries the hewer of wood partakes of the
crumbs, and camps in their baldness but reveal again the taskmaster
of another age. The artisan of a city state by the Aegean, the peasant
of the Palatinate, when yet the eighteenth century was young in
years, or the operative in England when the machine and factory had
displaced the labour of the home and shop may find a parallel to-day
in the bunkhouse man on different forms of frontier work in
Canada.

Each year there enter, through the ports of the Dominion,
foreign-born workers who in many cases go direct to camps. They

are soon engulfed in some phase of frontier life; working, grubbing, finding their bearings in a young country, these men live among us but share too little in any real benefits of the new land to which they have come – a refractory substance in the matter of assimilation.

To trudge with pack ahead of the steel along the Transcontinental where in broken stations shack-groups of foreign-born men were heaping up the grade in the land where broods the Begatchewan, was to pass through sixty miles where passive, listless nonchalance prevailed: some of these men cheery and talkative with a good-natured smile on their sweaty faces, others morose, suspicious and uncommunicative. There one dwelt apart from the happier life of the older Canadian communities – a wanderer at the portals of the strange land of Muscovy.

What are the social out-croppings? Time spent around any of the frontier towns reveals this in all its crudeness. The situation is simple. Men, both English-speaking and foreign-born, are deprived during months at a stretch of the companionship of women, of home ties, and all that elevates life in a man; they are starved by isolation and monotony. When they again reach the outskirts of civilization the frontier town with its 'aurer' lights, its music and noisy hilarity entices them from their deepest resolves. Vice too frequently pervades such places and, in divers haunts, drugged potions aid in 'rolling' the victim.

The all-night orgies, the drunken sprees lasting for days in some top room of a hotel or lodging house; the busy rigs with their pimpish outriders who ply their ghoulish trade, the snake-room with half a dozen forms crouched upon the cot or dirty floor, spuming and snoring off the poisons of a protracted drunk; and then the group silent, sore, sick, and seamed with debauch, rounded by a 'pilot,' who gather in the zero weather late of a December night to catch the train en route for months more of life at camp, such is the vicious circle in which these men are held helpless – the obverse of life conditions in camps and shacks through previous months of work. It is a characteristic of Canadian life which produces a shudder: the curse of hardness overspreads it, and the price of hardness is hideousness.

Chapter 7

The medical system on frontier works

Sanitary surroundings in isolated camps

NO DISCUSSION of the bunkhouse is complete without some understanding of the medical system provided for men in grade camps and
on isolated works. Vital as the lumber camps and other frontier
activities have been in the industrial life of Canada, the sanitary
conditions of such places, even as late as the beginning of this
century, were but primitive.

The bunkhouse man for an extended period was even denied the
common decencies of life. From the days of the shanties, when cook
and men slept and ate in the same building, on through a transition
period of twenty-five years marking the turn of the century, men of
the camps were herded in low-walled buildings, ill-lighted, and with
but scant inspection of any kind. Quite commonly sixty to eighty
men occupied the close quarters of the bunkhouses. With the sodden
clothes of the inmates, steaming of a night over a hot fire, and the
ventilation but meagre, the air of a sleep camp was invariably
tainted, if not noisome.

Even the washing of clothes, continued for long a matter of
personal whim with the men themselves. There were no baths of any
kind, and natural facilities, if at hand, vanished once the ice had
covered over the river or lake.

The legend, too, passed current with many hardy foremen that
such privileges were needless, in fact they made a good bushman
effeminate. Whatever the reasons, and doubtless they were many, so
far as one may gleam from health reports, or the statements of older
men, living conditions in frontier camps were bad –lamentably so,
until well toward the close of the century. For fifty years the bunkhouse man was ignored in matters of housing and sanitation, as
though his tasks, isolated in location, pertained to a remote or
mediaeval period. Like the Cyclops of Homer, the shanty-men were
treated as giants and fanciful perhaps, but far out and alien.

And the occupant of the bunkhouse might have continued under
such environments were it not for the periodic outbreaks of small-
pox and other infectious diseases that year after year ravaged the
camps. It became apparent that the continued neglect of the
bunkhouse threatened to take toll of older communities: the dis-
persion of men each spring at the break-up became frequently a
menace to lumbering towns and hamlets.

Then came signs of needed stirrings. Late in the nineties there was
some indication of a medical service. Between the years 1901-10, the

Province of Ontario, by succeeding enactments, gradually established a system of medical supervision for camps. These regulations, even though belated, were a step forward, in the interests of the bunk-house man. They served in turn as the prototype for similar rulings pertaining to frontier works in other provinces.

The initial legislation of this kind was necessarily somewhat limited. Certain regulations, however, were set forth for the betterment of life in camps. Stated briefly, three things were enacted: Vaccination was required of the men; the visit of doctors to local camps was provided, and the inspection of all bunkhouses became compulsory.

But, while provisions of this kind were clearly set forth in statute, there was lack of efficiency in carrying them out. The machinery provided was inadequate for such an extended area, and many of the enactments were systematically evaded. Thus, while formal compliance would be made with the regulation requiring medical visits to camps, the doctor, himself, might fail to reach many of the camps included in his contract.

Under the circumstances, the observance of regulations governing sanitary conditions in camps was often very lax. Not uncommonly, and as late as 1908-9, camp buildings, quarantined for small-pox in March, have been used to house 80-85 men in the cutting season of the following fall, the necessary cleaning and disinfection meanwhile having been very perfunctory. With some personal knowledge of medical supervision in such camps, particularly in the Province of Ontario, during the first fifteen years of the century, one will affirm that sanitary conditions in the bunkhouses, even then, were such that the work of the provincial authorities can only be described as having been superficial, if not positively neglectful of the real welfare of the workers in camps. So far as the bunkhouse men were concerned, the existing departments of health continued an anomaly.

There are indications, however, that needed changes in camp conditions of work are at hand. Doubtless some of these are an aftermath of the World War. Many modes of life, long established, were dislocated by that cataclysm and, among others, indirectly perhaps, the status and housing of the campman.

The present-day worker in camps varies from the old time lumberjack or shantyman, in that his mode of life does not tether him so completely to one company. Readier means of communication, too, have made him more versatile. This, in turn, has a serious drawback, in that it may tend to make him migratory.

It was doubtless some phase of this inherent desire for change that caused the men of the camps, in 1914 and the years following, to enlist in such numbers. Be that as it may, the bunkhouse men in thousands responded to the call to arms. Military service in its routine, and the barrack life with its strict observances – and none more so than those pertaining to sanitation – gave to the man, whose life had been spent on frontier works, a clearer conception of existing conditions. His return to camps meant the doom of the crowded bunkhouse. There was open revolt against the dark, dirty, and unsanitary camps.

Nor was this episode, tremendous in itself, unique in the annals of the camps. Some thirty years before, men selected from various frontier works in Canada, had served under Wolseley in those lengthening months of tortuous advance on Khartoum. The deeds of campmen in Europe, during the Great War, whether denuding old forest of timber or laying skeleton track on the Western front, had been antedated, a generation before, by the feats of their sires, who, as voyageurs had doggedly surmounted the cataracts of the Nile or poled, with supplies, the swift waters at Atbara.

But the return of the men from the Soudan, with experience gained in older lands, the Mediterranean, France, and in London, wrought little change in the life of the distant camps. Their number, a few hundred, at most, was insignificant, when the men had scattered once more to different works. Being barely a unit, they were submerged in the bunkhouse by the mass about. To make comparisons meant the inevitable twitting that life in the East had unfitted them for the shanty. These men, encountered occasionally in later years, big-boned, silent, and slow to age, were first to claim a healthier mode of life for men in the Canadian camps.

Quite another factor, also, has contributed in a material way toward needed improvements of the old-time camps. Even during the World War, and particularly in those years immediately following the Armistice, Canada experienced a sudden expansion in frontier works of various kinds. Mining had already shown definite signs of development before 1914. This was followed through many years by the erection, at a huge outlay, of great plants for the manufacture of pulp and paper, as well as the accompanying harnessing of water powers for hydro-electric purposes. The strides made in such activities, particularly in the hinterland, have meant an expenditure of one and one-quarter billions of American, British, and Canadian money on frontier works (see Appendices C and D).

These later companies, most of them operating on a big scale, have introduced many innovations in the matter of housing workers. With plants in places transforming what erstwhile was but an isolated wilderness, they have builded neat company towns, and caused the erection of camp buildings, better lighted, more sanitary, and sometimes steamheated.

Accompanying these changes there has, also, been more concern evinced by the provincial governments and their departments of health as to the conditions existing in bunkhouses. The strange lethargy toward life and work in isolated camps that marked the legislatures of eastern Canada for whole generations seems to be passing.

True the loggers of the Pacific coast, some fifteen years since, had been aggressive enough to obtain for themselves fitting recognition in matters of camp employments and housing, but in older Canada, the bunkhouse man has had a long fight for even the barest recognition of clean, healthful, and sanitary camps.

Since 1920-22, however, stringent regulations have been enacted in the Province of Ontario, and also in Quebec, relating to the housing of campmen, in the unorganized districts of these respective provinces. The leading features of the new statutes pertain particularly to the erection in future of camp buildings of standard designs, varying in size and requirements according as it is the intention to house twenty, fifty or one hundred workers. Overcrowding, at least such as existed in the old-type bunkhouse, is lessened, and single bunks are provided. Increased lighting, and ventilation add greatly, also, to the physical comforts of the inmates.

There has been, too, a rattling of the dry bones in the valley, and a change for the better has been effected, at least in the Province of Ontario, in the matter of medical supervision in camps. The goal now is preventive service to men, rather than the former method of collecting monthly dues from campmen over a whole area, and making but a minimum outlay in return. Sanitary inspection is now governed from one central source, and has become more effective. It is no longer possible to follow camps for successive seasons without ever meeting a health officer. The district officials concerned with local enforcement are alert, and much to the personal advantage of men who find domicile in the bunkhouse. The costs of the present medical system are shared jointly by the provincial government, the company directly concerned, and by the campman himself.

These measures are to be encouraged. They give promise of an awakened desire on the part of the official Boards of Health to render some bit of real service to the campman. Let it be hoped they are indications of a permanent policy that will some day ensure for the worker of the bunkhouse some of the advantages, medical and otherwise, enjoyed, whether by the machinist in the factory or the student at his college.

In view of what has already been stated, it is apparent that the medical system at present in operation throughout the great majority of camps in Canada is but a development of very recent years. Midway between the old camp days, that extended into the nineties, when but meagre provision of any kind was made for the men of the bunkhouse, and the later enactments of the various provincial legislatures particularly since 1921, which give promise of more fitting consideration of living conditions in camps, was a transition period of two full decades or longer. These years marked the beginnings of a systematic effort to regulate sanitary conditions on frontier works.

The detailed study which follows is of the medical system as seen in operation during the period following the turn of the century. The facts relate again to the camps on railway construction, but the details presented, apply also to the practices generally followed at that time on other frontier works, whether lumbering or mining, and particularly in Northern Ontario and Quebec, which area included then, as it does still, a large proportion of camp activities in Canada.

During the construction of the National Transcontinental Railway, the Dominon Government required of any head-contractor, that he provide a medical doctor and all necessary hospital facilities for every five hundred men employed by him on the work. This meant, usually, the presence of a head doctor, or medical contractor, and of from two to six medical assistants on each railway contract of one-hundred miles. It involved also a medical headquarters, called the main hospital, and several subsidiary hospitals at thirty-mile intervals out on the line where operations are in progress. The main hospital on a railway contract is seldom shifted, but the secondary hospitals, in following each year the centre of activities on the grade, are moved, as required, to different points.

The head-contractor allotted the medical contract on his work, just as he did the other contracts – clearing the right-of-way, cutting ties or grading. There were many doctors, too, who were glad to get a medical contract on construction, and the head-contractor in consequence exacted pretty much his own terms. In fact, the doctor was selected for the line just as was the general manager or some of his abler clerks.

Having obtained a medical contract the doctor proceeds as follows: If the railway contract is a large one, extending three hundred miles or more, he makes preparation for six years' work at least. His main hospital will be erected near the base of supplies. Quite often the offices of the head-contractor have already been located at this point. If this centre happens to be the town where the medical officer has his practice, that is a further advantage to him; by renting a house of ten rooms, putting in some necessary equipment, engaging a nurse and an assistant, he soon has his main hospital well started. This will be enlarged later, as the railway work extends, and as men are employed in increasing numbers. Some creditable and complete little hospitals are maintained by medical contractors as their main hospitals.

The subsidiary hospitals are often situated at or near one of the grade camps. They are usually log buildings, sometimes an unused company building is utilized, but where possible they are built new of lumber, and well tar-papered. Quite frequently tents with a peak roof, sixteen feet by twenty-four feet and having side walls about four and one-half feet high, are utilized to serve as subsidiary hospitals. These when double-roofed or covered even with a tarpaulin to secure an air-cushion in the roof as a protection from the heat usually prove quite satisfactory.

These secondary hospitals contained from five to seven camp-beds, supplied with mattresses and blankets. Cotton sheets were provided at some, but such provision was exceptional at least in subsidiary hospitals. In the rear of such hospitals was a small room partitioned off for cooking purposes. In one corner, too, was located a room for the orderly. It contained a few supplies and a couple of camp-beds, one of which accommodated the itinerant doctor when off his route.

How was the camp doctor paid? Each campman on the whole work of a head-contractor, whether within reach of the doctor or not, was charged $1.00 to $1.25 per month for medical fees. This item in cases included, also, a charge for mail, but as the mail service in distant camps was only perfunctory, and very irregular, the men generally attributed the whole deduction made from their monthly pay, to the requirements of the medical system.

The doctor himself deals only with the office at head quarters; the books there show not only the total number of men employed for the month in the camps run directly by the head contractor, but the names also of those at work in the camps of all sub-contractors. He is entitled to dues from every man who has been on the line during the month.

From the very nature of things in camps, men are coming, and men are constantly going, and this semi-nomadic shifting only increases the more when pay is good. There are times when one man, in less than six weeks has hired for work on as many as three different contracts. This means that the medical fees in that time will be deducted, successively on each contract.

If a campman remained at a camp for only five days the medical fee for the full month was deducted from his pay. Some men have been known, even, under the medical system then in vogue, to pay the doctor's fee three times in thirty days.

To keep a working force of twenty-eight hundred men steady for a month on a railway contract as many as fifty-one hundred names have been entered on the books at the head office. And from each of these the medical fee is deducted. This shifting of men, due to various causes, is an advantage to the medical contractor. It makes the listing of names for the medical system more intricate but tends, in the end, toward increased returns.

But all the fees paid by workers for the medical service, did not go directly to the doctor. The office of the head-contractor got a percentage. The amount of this deduction varied according to the agreement entered into with the head-contractor. The amount to be paid under such circumstances, however, may safely be put at seven to twelve per cent of the total.

Each medical contractor in camps previous to 1914, employed two to six students as assistants on his work. One usually remained with him at the base hospital, and one was stationed at each of the subsidiary hospitals. Occasionally these medical assistants were graduates who had yet to take their Council examinations, but oftener they were undergraduates barely in their final years who engaged temporarily in this field of work, offering as it frequently did many latent opportunities for advancement. Student assistants were commonly paid by the month and at a rate corresponding to that received by a walking-boss or good camp foreman on the same piece of work. Along the National Transcontinental this ranged from ninety to one hundred and fifty dollars per month, with board included.

Each student doctor on the National Transcontinental had usually a subsidiary hospital as his headquarters. From this he made regular trips fifteen or twenty miles on either side, among the men of the shacks and other work groups. During the first three months of spring and early summer, when the right-of-way is in bad shape, these side trips going and coming will often consume a week in each direction, depending both on the condition of the grade, and the number of men employed.

For these young assistant doctors had often a difficult place to fill. Usually they were inexperienced in camp life, but carelessness was the exception among them. Earnest and keen, they did the best under the circumstances, tramping the grade, calling on isolated work groups, dispensing pills of one kind and another, and in case of accident giving first aid. The student doctor was not overpaid for his services. More of the monthly dues collected could profitably have gone directly to him.

And how often acts of personal sacrifice and even heroism have marked the devotion of these obscure medical assistants in the performance of duty in far-out camps. Acts unrecorded abound, where a navvy, his limb mangled in an untoward blast, or some campman long wasted in fever have gradually been nursed back to health and strength, in some crude improvised subsidiary hospital, through the personal care and untiring attention of these young doctors. Such deeds brighten the whole period of railway building on the frontiers of Canada. They are the one redeeming feature of the medical system in camps. Such particular cases are told and retold in the bunkhouses, and the knowledge of them, echoed in different places, has earned for the student doctors a place safely ensconced in the hearts of all workers in camps.

But assistant doctors, like the men of the bunkhouses, are hard to hold; jumping is chronic even with them. About four months on a distant piece of construction and the student, too, is ready to 'go out.' When the medical force is short an assistant or two, it is the subsidiary hospitals that are left unmanned. The nearer points receive the first consideration. Thus, for months at a stretch, work groups at distant points will be deprived of the near-by presence of any doctor, although even under such circumstances deductions from their pay are still made regularly each month for the usual medical fee.

If the medical service on frontier works had any reason at all for its existence, it was surely to guard carefully the health of the camp-man. Yet, in their attitude toward the unsanitary conditions at many camps both in the woods and on railway construction, the doctors and their assistants were either glaringly careless or purposely negligent. No one expects of a camp the well-kept conditions of a modern suburban district, nor even that of a company town nurtured by some near-by industrial plant; the exact interpretation of sanitary laws pertaining to camps may even be given much laxity where common sense demands it; but, due allowance having been made, what excuse can be offered for the men who held medical contracts, or for the wholesale disregard of sanitary standards at so many camps, which, at that period, were presumed to be under government supervision?

The health of the navvies, at least along the National Trans-continental Railway, was made the direct concern of the Dominion Department of Public Health. Was a real interest ever evinced to maintain fitting camp conditions? If so the occupants of the bunk-houses knew little of any such activities. The filth of some grade camps on Canadian railways would barely be surpassed by that reported on Siberian construction during the same period.

Already in chapter 3, section 3, when speaking of the housing of workers in Canadian camps, particular mention was made of the living conditions too commonly encountered in bunkhouses on frontier works. It becomes necessary in the next few succeeding pages to indicate the sanitary conditions of camps from another angle – that which would show the direct responsibility of any doctor holding a medical contract, for the cleanliness and health-giving surroundings of all camps comprised in his territory. A further enumeration of incidents displaying insanitary conditions in camps does not make pleasant reading; it unprops, too, the romance commonly associated with life in such places. To develop a flair for noting only the drab is uncouth, nor would it betoken a healthy mind; but while that is to be avoided, it is necessary to point out that men holding a medical contract of whatever kind, owe in turn very real obligations to the bunkhouse men. All too frequently duties in this respect have been overlooked.

There follow here, more detailed remarks about camps, common enough in the Canadian hinterland as late as 1915.

CONDITIONS WHERE THE CAMP SITE WAS POORLY SELECTED
Ninety men were at this camp. Situated in a low muskegy place, a small stream passed through its midst. The cookery refuse during the winter months had been taken by handsleigh back 100 yards where it was dumped on the snow. In the spring a large pit was dug forty feet away from the cookery and a drain led directly from the sink into the pit. In the loose soil, however, the drain soon plugged and no pretense was made during the next month to open it. Old tins and solid matter were hurled instead out of the back window, while other refuse from the cookery was carried by pails and dumped in the pit, now half fallen in. For weeks the contents of the pit, a rotting mass, lay there uncovered, a breeding place for flies: the whole, repellent as fever in the Athens of Aeschylus, or filth to Dante in the narrow streets of Florence.

The men at this camp suffered violently from dysentery long before the fly season had come. The student doctors in passing left medicine at the office. The trouble of the men was pronounced as the usual camp sickness. Navvies who had wrought there two months had never seen the medical man inside the large bunkhouse.

SANITARY CONDITIONS AT A CAMP FAR OUT
Take the position of things at Camp 'O.' This camp for the best part of one year was not nearer than sixty miles to the steel, and things progressed there as they always do in isolated camps. Before the summer

had passed fever was rampant in the dirty camp. A dozen cases of typhoid developed there, and ultimately the camp was closed.

Yet no deaths were reported from that camp. The men had gotten out and scattered to other points. Some went west, on the harvest excursions. Others, their bodies weakened by disease sown in the stricken camp, could only reach the end of the steel where, after lingering a few days, three of them succumbed. Yet one will search long to find any account of these deaths. They are attributed to other causes, and, above all, not credited to the camp where the malady was engendered.

SANITARY CONDITIONS AT A CAMP
WHICH WAS LATER INVESTIGATED

That same year, at 'L,' a point 300 miles to the east, a camp of less than thirty men was also allowed to go unchallenged until in the fulness of things, disease spread, and seventeen of the inmates threatened with fever were removed to an improvised hospital on the point, stretching out into a big northern lake.

Well founded report has it that this incident stirred even the health authorities at Ottawa. A representative was sent north to investigate. But there are wiles best known to the line; the company's officials will beckon and the staff at the residency can prove congenial. So artfully was the agent from Ottawa managed, that more than a week elapsed before he reached the camp. Meanwhile the stricken camp had undergone a remarkable change in its sanitary aspects, and there was little to report.

Few men die of fever in the camp hospitals, and the medical health officer may return a comparatively clean report to the authorities. But what of the scores and hundreds each year who, feeling out of sorts, quit work and go to the front, but later are forced to take to the hospital at Fort William, Sault Ste Marie, Sudbury or Ottawa? The camps are responsible even if illness develops months after. Too long, little more thought was given the workers in some forms of camp life than if they were swine or sheep; but even sheep may balk on the way to the shambles.

Do official medical reports of the period 1900-14 usually show a small-pox epidemic to have started at a residency? It was always in the low, unlighted, foul-smelling buildings into which men of the camps were crowded like beasts, where disease germs revelled

voiding in venom the lives of the inmates. Yet year after year in that
period scores of just such bunkhouses were passed and repassed
unnoticed, or unattended to, by students and assistant doctors who
represented the medical system in the camps and along railway
construction.

It has been claimed on the part of the medical contractors, along
the National Transcontinental at least, that they in their work were
not responsible for the sanitary conditions of the camps, that that
was a provincial matter and was the concern of the local inspector. It
is hard to see just where the line was drawn. It may be admitted,
however, that there was some overlapping. But if the medical contractors had no responsibility for the unsanitary camps, what about
the general class of buildings, designated hospitals, which were maintained on the different contracts in order to comply with the legal
requirements of the medical system.

The following cases are in point: they are typical of camp hospitals and will bear comparison with similar buildings on any 1,200
miles of construction during that whole period.

TWO CENTRALLY LOCATED HOSPITALS

1 The hospital at 'A' was composed of two small-sized log buildings. It stood high on a splendid site overlooking the whole camp. It
was an ideal location. Both buildings were kept scrupulously clean.
The few beds for the patients were enclosed with roomy mosquito
bars. The man nurse in charge had his heart in his work. His cooking
was a credit, and his uniformly good cheer was infectious. The whole
environment bespoke an interested attempt to give the patients
light, rest and contentment. Would that there had been more hospitals
like it!

2 The head hospital in this case was close to a frontier town. The
doctor had not selected the site. The building had been put up by
the head-contractor before the doctor arrived, otherwise a different
location might have been chosen. For the first seven months this
hospital was in operation, it had no water supply. The only water
handy was from a hole, half the size of a barrel, sunk in the middle
of a depression. Later, water was brought in barrels by a hand-car
from a fresh running stream in a muskeg a mile away. As the orderly
there said: 'This is not the first camp hospital I've been in, but it is
the first one I've seen without water.'

A NEGLECTED SUBSIDIARY HOSPITAL

Let us look for a moment at a more detailed description of a tent hospital and what it discloses in actual conditions:

The hospital at 'M' was thirty-five miles from the end of the steel; it was an old peak-roofed tent 16 ft. x 24 ft. x 5 ft. with a pole floor and a low pole wall. It had done service the year before as a hospital at another point, and when it was moved to the second camp to do duty the following year, it was in a ragged and leaky condition – a big tarpaulin such as contractors use to cover cement, or to protect stores, was thrown over the tent as an additional protection. The tent was pitched back in from the right-of-way close to the shore of a shallow, muddy lake, in a dense thicket of scrubby jack pine. The small-wood stumps stood close about the frame of the tent.

In the late afternoon of a day in August, a passer-by in search of water, left the glare and oppressive heat of the right-of-way to follow a trail through the thicket which, after 300 yards, led to the hospital tent in its small clearing. Used blankets were thrown across the stumps to catch the sunshine which in places broke through the thicket. The smoke from a smudge at the front drifted through the tent, while the heated air of the interior combined the odor of simmering pots with that of disinfectants.

Into that tent, one stepped reverently. Even in a wilderness a hospital, of whatever kind, is sacred. It speaks of man's concern for man. In a corner to the right were provisions, a side of smoked bacon, half a ham, one case of condensed milk, half a bag of sugar, some canned corn and tomatoes, a little rice and some flour – pitched topsy-turvy on the floor. In the other corner was a small camp-stove with two greasy pots and unwashed dishes littered about. Behind the stove was a lard pail filled with discarded scraps of food.

This hospital at the time had three patients, one of whom, a stalwart-framed Swede, wasted in sickness, was slowly passing out. An orderly was in charge, but a student doctor visited the tent when on his regular rounds. The orderly supplemented his pay by assisting the cook at the residency just across the lake, and his work there consumed the most of his time.

These incidents while but scanty in detail are intended to show the nakedness of the medical system that was afforded men in camps even until very recent years. The bunkhouse man from whom dues are collected expects greater concern even in far-out places for his physical well-being.

Back of each work in frontier places there upon the hillside was the place of crosses. That could be expected, life is not leased to any man and all camp tasks bring particular hazards; but of a dozen graves, mostly unnamed, situated in a birch grove, whose flattened mounds now scarce mark the place where once a busy camp was noisy with the sounds of construction, how many were laid there through accidents and other unavoidable causes, or were the greater number carried thence for sepulchre, having paid prematurely, the penalty of living conditions in unsanitary camps?

And it is meet just here, before closing this particular chapter to mention one other practice, formerly common enough in camps, which has also an indirect relation to the medical contractor. Let it be recalled that during the third period of railway construction in Canada, there was frequently a discrepancy in recording systematically the facts pertaining to deaths of labourers in isolated camps.

'Oh, some Russian is buried there!' was the passing remark that commonly designated an unkempt plot in the vicinity of an erstwhile camp. The epithet in these cases usually meant a foreign-born worker of Slav or Balkan extraction.

All too frequently, in such happenings, there was but little accounting of the personal belongings of the deceased. The fashioning of a rude box, and the digging of a grave apparently consumed whatever balance was due him. Later, if perchance, at the request of the family in Europe, inquiry was made through their Consulate in Canada, and thence through a local magistrate, for due accounting of the deceased's affairs, but scant trace remained. The little group of countrymen, who best would have known him have departed in the intervening months with the shifting of works. The name, even, on the wooden slab is barely decipherable – washed by the rains. All camps have short memories – a foreign-born man of the bunkhouse vanished from kith and kin, as though the waters of a northern lake, in an uneasy mood, had suddenly opened and taken him forever in its keeping.

Seldom had the campman who spoke his unbiased mind, words of praise for the medical system provided in frontier camps previous to 1920. This fact in itself was sufficient to condemn it. Nor was it reasonable, that the doctor any more than the district police, should, for so long, have been looped up with the employing company. The health of the bunkhouse man, quite as much as the due observance of the law, was the concern of the whole country. The medical officer was entitled to a substantial remuneration but not one made directly by monthly assessments on the workers in camps.

The following are some of the objections formerly made by men in bunkhouses against the medical system then provided:

1 That little was given the campman in return for the fee deducted each month from his pay.
2 That the service was irregular and uncertain.
3 That quite frequently the so-called hospitals were a pretence.
4 Lastly and chiefly, that the medical system suffered from its very relation. It was hamstrung right from the start: the medical men, the ones who could best have spoken were beholden by the system to the very parties responsible for the existing conditions.

And these in substance constitute the reasons why Canadian bunkhouses, even in a twenty-year period when camps were under a pseudo-medical supervision, remained so long neglected. The claim of the campman to common decency was retarded because the existing regulations pertaining to sanitation in camps on frontier works were from the very relation of things, often inoperative.

Chapter 8

Some alternative employments for workers in camps

THE IMMIGRANT from central Europe newly arrived in Canada has but a limited choice of works. Handicapped by language, at times, by prejudices, and usually without funds, he is fitted only for the heavier manual tasks. The bush camps, the mines, and the railway extra-gangs during the milder months, as well as camps on new construction, offer the most probable forms of employment, until he has become better accustomed to the country. But even in these occupations there are many forms of work, which from the very nature of the tasks are closed to the newcomer.

It is intended in this chapter to indicate briefly some of these barriers. The next few pages, too, will serve to give the reader a general understanding of alternative work in other camps, some of which, in themselves, may be deemed corollary to the tasks of the navvy. To this end a glimpse will first be given of routine work in a bush camp, followed by an outline of prospecting in the Cobalt country – work in this particular field was an actual alternative to the navvy on the National Transcontinental Railway. Extra-gangs are then mentioned as being a form of labour readily accessible to the foreign-born immigrant.

IN BUSH CAMPS

Migratory labour of the camps is not aimless in its flow. There is on frontier works a fixed rotation, it proceeds from the lumber camps outward to the railway work and thence to the mines and mills of the industrial centres. And seldom is this order reversed; the prospector is not going to revert to navvying until compelled by circumstances, while the navvy looks back on the routine hours of the bush camp as a memory of days to be forgotten: thenceforth his gaze is outward. When the English-speaking navvy does occasionally return, it is because of a stripe of some kind, or when a slackening of industry throughout the country causes him to fall back on the winter camps which do not fluctuate so readily as other frontier works.

On the other hand, the foreign-born worker signing up with an employment agent is quite willing to engage in bush work, for all kinds of frontier tasks are alike new to him. Then what prevents a newcomer becoming a first-class bushman during his first year in the country? Let us consider briefly some aspects of work in the woods which are a deterrent to the new arrival.

Somehow we have been prone in Canada to consider lumbering, as an industry, to be coeval with agriculture or even with the fur trade. But, previous to the last century little had been done throughout British America toward building a permanent export trade in forest products.

The settlers themselves gladly burned their timber – the quicker to hasten clearing. As late as 1806, General Brock made mention that much of the lumber used in Upper Canada came from Vermont.

Even the magnificent forests of the maritimes, situated often at tide-water, could not compete with those of northern Europe as a source of supply for bush products of various kinds. But before 1808 the long struggle with Napoleon had disrupted trade conditions among the warring peoples. The royal meeting on the raft at Tilsit particularly affected the commerce of the Baltic. England in her need turned toward her possessions in America for the timber supplies so invaluable to the Navy.

The provinces by the sea were the first to respond to this new demand. Before Waterloo was fought, New Brunswick had already built up a considerable export trade in pine and squared pieces. It was not, however, until 1840 that similar exports from Ontario and Quebec had assumed definite shape. But rapid expansion ensued, and by 1858 the shipment of lumber and stick timber from the St. Lawrence region and the Ottawa Valley through the Port of Quebec had grown to vast proportions.

Lumbering, thus, had taken its place as one of the basic industries of the country, and back in the mid-century all this meant shanty life. Bushwork then and for another forty years was largely performed by men working in gangs who were domiciled in small square-built log structures housing about forty men.

Before discussing the opportunities for work which confront a newcomer in the woods in the present day, it may be well also, at this point, to form in retrospect some conception of previous conditions of housing in the winter camps of Canada. For transition has marked even the buildings of an isolated camp; the shanty was the precursor of the large bunkhouse still so commonly used on frontier works across the Dominion.

The old-time shanty was of one rigid type. Constructed of medium-sized logs dove-tailed at the corners, it formed a quadrangular enclosure probably thirty or forty feet square. From end to end resting on the walls stretched two large girders, and upon these the roof rested. This was usually composed of the halves of trees, hollowed out. These scoops, as they were called, were placed concave and convex, thus to overlap, and usually they made a snug and dry covering.

The floor of the shanty consisted of small logs hewn flat. The walls were chinked well and mossed, making the building warm and weather-tight. In one end-wall a door was cut. Outside this stood a water barrel and an improvised trough near at hand served the men for washing.

Each of the long girders used for sustaining the roof was supported by two upright posts resting on the floor. This constituted a four-post area which occupied the centre of the shanty. In this space was located the distinguishing feature of all shanties — the large open fireplace or camboose, used not only for heating the building but also for cooking. Encased by logs, hewed square, it was substantially built up with layers of stone, sand and earth. From two of the corner posts were fitted wooden poles to swing at right angles. These served as cranes from which pots and boilers could be adjusted to any position over the big fire.

There was no chimney to a shanty. Directly over the huge fireplace was a large opening in the roof, surmounted by a square framed projection above the roof ridge, which served as an outlet. Smoke, however, was the pest of the shanty. Practice and much skill, even under the best of circumstances, was required to build an open camboose that did not vomit, particularly when there was foggy weather, or the wind blew from an off angle.

The shanty was self-contained. The foreman, cook and men housed under one roof. Double-decked bunks extended on three sides. The men slept with heads to the wall. On the fourth side were stored supplies of various kinds in bags and barrels with also a large case — or van — pad-locked, containing wearing apparel. Seated around the roaring fire, cheerful in the full enjoyment of rest after a day in the open, there was the contentment of a quiet smoke, the tale or song of an evening varied with the fantastic shadows and flickering blaze of the shanty fire.

Discipline, too, on the part of the one in charge was firmly exercised. This demanded peculiar tact and judgment, as well as physical prowess, at times. Shanty days, however, knew little interruption, and quarrels were the exception, for liquor was prohibited alike by walking-boss and foreman. It was when the 'drive' began in the spring that a change occurred. The life along the streams and in the vicinity of small settlements with their numerous taverns of riverside shebeens, did more to unsettle the shantyman than the regular routine of life in the bush.

A generation and probably more has passed since the last of the old-style shanties. But there are still old-timers encountered in the big bunkhouses even to-day, whose thoughts will revert to the life once lived about the open camboose. The memory, particularly of the bread and beans cooked under such conditions, still haunts, nor does the excellence of such diminish in the telling. It is the yearning as of old for the flesh-pots of Egypt.

The cook is ever an important figure at any camp, but in the crowded shanty he was supreme. There he was more or less of a despot among his pots and pans. And here, for a moment, we shall look a little more closely at the camboose in operation.

The variety of food that is now found in a camp cookery was unknown even in the best shanty. Until well into the sixties, bread, pork, molasses and peas designated the common fare of the shantyman. Tea as yet was a luxury at a dollar a pound, to be purchased from the van at the option of the worker himself.

But each ten-year period brought changes even in shanty fare. After 1870 beans were more commonly used, and barrelled pork, so long a staple food, shared place with beef, not infrequently brought to camp on the hoof. Tea, too, and sugar were commonly provided by the larger companies. The mixed diet was found to be cheaper; at any rate it was infinitely healthier and much more work could be done.

The bread baked on the camboose, however, remained the delicacy of the shanty. The cook, having prepared his dough of an evening, placed it in a large iron pot. This was swung on the end of the crane and buried for the night in a bed of hot ashes and sand at one side of the fireplace. The strength and fine qualities of the flour were not lost by this method, being condensed in the bread. The result was, when uncovered for breakfast, a great loaf, strong and firm, yet light and wholesome.

Methods of camp cooks varied, of course, but the common preparation of beans in the open camboose was as follows: The cook having sifted and washed ten quarts of beans — sufficient for two meals for forty men — boils them for a time over the fire. Then, large slices of fat pork and layers of beans are placed alternately in one of the large pots, the lid being hermetically sealed by a rim of dough. The whole is then buried alongside the bread pot at the side of the great fire. The steam does not escape: the fat pork, dissolved by the heat, compounds with the beans, and in the morning a succulent and nutritious mess is uncovered.

No dining table was used under these conditions. The shantymen, at a nod from the cook that the meal was ready, with plate in hand, helped themselves individually from the big pot of beans. Then, with a generous piece of bread, cut from the huge loaf resting on a shelf in the corner, they seated themselves on the logs about the fireplace or squatted at opportunity, their bread and beans washed down by copious draughts from mugs of tea. Strong food, of course, but not for men whose strenuous work in the keen bracing air enabled them to digest heavy meals.

It was the common boast that any first-class shanty could be constructed, using the axe alone as a tool; nor need a nail or any iron whatever enter into its structure. Doubtless this was true, but any questioning to-day among men who timbered in the earlier times reveals the fact that shanties were often hastily constructed and quite uncomfortable. Such buildings were usually low and frequently cramped for space. To stand on the shanty floor and, without changing his position, kick the scoops of the roof, was a test of physical power and suppleness for an inmate that merited great respect among fellow shantymen. This varied with the feat of him who, still fresh after the long hours of chopping, could on entering, deftly hurl his axe to ping with quivering stroke into a girder post.

Sanitary conditions, however, in and about the shanties were of the crudest. Things went along well enough in this respect during the months of severe weather, with low temperatures prevailing, but once the lengthening days of early spring showed frosts alternating with the warm sun of mid-day, small streams trickling from rising ground about, polluted often with ordure, endangered the health of the shantyman. The return of these men to their neighbourhoods, and the homes in the settlements, was not without its menace of smallpox, which ever lurked about the crowded camps.

Work in the shanties is usually associated with timbering operations formerly conducted along the Ottawa or its tributaries. The forty men of a shanty such as has just been described would account for about seven thousand sticks in a season. These were felled solely by chopping, for the shantyman was always an axeman. Few companies in the sixties and seventies operated more than five shanties. But in the nineties new methods came, the saw was used wholly in cutting, gangs were almost doubled, and the winter's cut averaged fifty to sixty thousand pieces, depending of course upon the size of the timber, the slope of the land, and other factors.

By slow degrees some improvements came in the shanties themselves. Early in the eighties bunks were restricted to one side of the building, while a long table occupied the opposite wall. A room off one side accommodated the foreman, while the clerk displayed his goods on shelves down the remaining side. Big box stoves, too, for heating were introduced, and found more satisfactory. With a separate building for cooking, the camboose gradually disappeared; whatever its merits, it was handicapped by its many defects.

But lumbering still remains the most conservative of all great industries in Canada. An exception is here made, of course, of the big-timber operations of the Pacific coast, where logging by machinery and the high-lead assumes, in places, gigantic proportions. The old East, however, due perhaps to climatic conditions, or to inherited prejudices, is slow to change its bush methods.

There are, in some parts of Canada, and not restricted to any one province, whole villages the families of which, French and English-speaking, have grown up in a like circle of activities – the winter camps, the spring drives, and, then, the sawmills for the summer months. There is a continuity of generations in the tasks; the grandfather timbered on the Ottawa, in Maine, or in the woods of Michigan; the father cut the splendid pine in camps about the Georgian Bay; and the sons to-day are found in the camps and mills of the North Shore. There is in some families, and often in the villages of a whole countryside, a tradition of bush work. Boys from such homes have handled the axe from very youth; they grow up in an atmosphere brimming with tales and yarns of the lumber camps. Any alert lad, fourteen to sixteen years of age, raised in such an environment, is of more practical use in a bush camp than some big able-bodied foreigner, willing though he may be, who has all the elemental force of one who dwells near the soil but who is strange to life in the woods and all its ways.

On first impressions it may be inferred that the work and activities of a bush camp in Eastern Canada consist largely of heavy unskilled tasks. That is but partly true. Physical outlay is there, and in plenty, but there is also what is much more desired, the skill and practice of years. Bush methods are not learned in a month, nor in a season. The successful completion of a winter's cut tests the worth of both the foreman and his men. Under an able foreman the routine of a busy camp is as nicely apportioned as that of any large factory. To land the required count of logs on the dump at the lake before the break-up in spring is the goal of the winter camp. The different work groups of the camp co-operate in a score of ways. They follow each other in orderly rotation at their tasks. The failure of one gang dislocates the others; any shifting and rearrangement of groups necessarily means loss. The man new to camp ways is a handicap to more than the men of his own immediate group.

But even a closer relationship exists among the workers in a bush camp as individuals. The very nature of the day's occupations calls for a responsiveness, one man with another; whether at felling timber or with hooks at the end of a skidway, bushmen must work in unison. The faculty of reading the other man's thought, the knowledge of just what to do and the right moment at which to do it will save much unnecessary labour. Injury, too, and serious accidents may follow the movements of the inept. Any capable bushman needs, in the first degree, the adaptability to fit into the ways of his working partner. Ignorance just then produces friction. Better even a third-rate man used to camps than a newcomer who, while endowed with bodily strength, does not always know how to use it to advantage.

Here in passing one reflects that lumbering is still, perhaps, the most romantic of all frontier works in Canada. From the week in early fall when first the camp operations begin, on through the cutting season with autumn woods, gorgeous in changing tints, into the snows of early winter, followed at the new year with the sleigh-haul that ends with the break-up only when the logs of the great skidways have been landed at the dump – these differing activities of the woods embody for strong-limbed men a distinctive fascination that does not vanish with succeeding generations.

And briefly will be noted but one phase of effort – the loading by torch in the early morning of the January haul. The bush camp then is actively in operation while yet the clear-cut stars show overhead and all about is wrapped in the shadows of the woods. The teams in line full hours before the day has shown, follow in relays the beaten tracks of the smooth-iced roads. Already voices of those at work are heard in the distance, but indistinct. Then comes a turn in the bush road and in the smoky glare of torches are seen heavy horses breasted in foam, and men, gnome-like figures in the uncertain light, some for warmth still muffled in their outer mackinaw, and others with breasts already bared to the zero blasts, moving methodically at their tasks with hook and line; shouts and curses mingle with the clinking of chains or the heavier crunch of big-end logs topped into place on the load. Surely these be the offspring of the light-haired race ever the frontiersmen of earth.

For woodcraft blends with, rather than destroys, what is picturesque in nature. There in the torches' light, amid the early stillness of the snow-filled woods, with trees in avenue, branching as jets from a fountain, giving impulses of symbolism and imagery, is action clear and sharp, strong and energetic, with human thews at bowstring tension. Is not this indeed workmanship – fit even and passionate with life about a form of art and that in abundance? For, if schools refine, it is true, also, that the sterner experiences in camps may give dignity in motion.

There are human factors, too, which are not to be overlooked that preclude ready employment for a new arrival in a bush camp. The foreman in a lumber camp is the king peg. He has full sway in his isolated bush kingdom. While generally a proved man and capable at his particular work, he is often, at the same time, very conservative and headstrong. He likes things done in his way only, and that way may not always be easily grasped. A breach of some detail early displeases and leads to prompt dismissal. This bears hard on the foreign-born, particularly if a prejudice already exists against them, for if there is a wrong way in which to hold an axe or to cut a trail the newcomer is sure to follow it. The bush foreman and the foreign-born do not usually take to one another at first; their friendship is gradually acquired.

The bush camp, too, has a social side to its community life. Even the 'dinnering-out' and other features of the day's work are not devoid of humorous incidents. But relaxation comes chiefly of a night in the bunkhouse chat, or the improvised games and songs of the week-end. Into the former the younger men enter with enthusiasm, while the older heads acquiesce by nods of approval, over well-filled pipes.

In surroundings such as these, tales abound of that mystical superman, Paul Bunyan, the forest Zeus, arbiter in all things, great and small, that comprise the days and work of the campman. What with the numerous episodes fittingly recounted of his titan accomplishments, surpassing as they do all others in the experience of man – his mighty feats, however, embellished always with a humanness befitting life and the lowly ways of camps, he has long remained the patron revered of all good bushmen.

True, the impress, uncouth at times perhaps, may reveal itself in camp hyperbole and vehement expression. But there is also in effect the throb and zest of quickened life. The earnest youth, by circumstance confined, hearkens in turn of a night from his log-hewed bench to the retold tales of this mighty man with his double-bitted axe, or of the ox, inseparable in all his log-making, whose strength, proverbial for half a century since, could, at need, remove the hill or straighten forest streams to drive the stranded logs.

For while this hero of the bunkhouse is simply the projection to the highest power of the campman's own human capacity, there is, too, latent in all his dealings, a goodly measure of the ludicrous. In the delineation of his idol the bushman in fancy is kin to Lucian of an early century, or even to Rabelais and Swift. But the prosaic giant of the Canadian camps is not inspired by animus, nor does he become a Gargantua, much less a ruler in Brobdingnag before whom the inhabitants of the earth are as grasshoppers. The Paul Bunyan of the hinterland, tremendous in resourcefulness and capable as he be, is nevertheless mirth provoking, the soul of jollity and humanly considerate of all his fellows.

Nor need such impulses be deemed of low estate. They simply react to their environment as did Themistes to the Aegean patriarchs. And Education before now has concerned itself with myths inherently of much less worth. The well-mouthed lines that shroud in mystery the brand Excalibur, or the tale of Cadmus, who tracks through Thrace with his spotted cow, progenitor as it be of mighty towns, are not removed in fact from the doughty deeds of this storied bushman and his blue ox. Even the Canadian pineries, in their inviting solitudes, may prove fertile for thought as were the groves of the Cephissus. For hardly is the idealism of the class-room dissevered from the dreams of the less favoured. Illiterate men who crowd the shanty and the bunkhouse are heartened not by annals of Arthur's court, with chivalry in profusion, or of recorded warriors in epic strife at Troy, but from the versatile doings of one with many human excellences, who shapes his deeds to the commoner rounds of the woods and camps.

True, the foreign-born congregated in a bunkhouse may have a place in forms of recreation, but seldom does he fully participate. There is the barrier of race and language. This, combined with his conspicuousness, if present only in small groups, sometimes leads to practical jokes at his expense.

In the lumbering industry there is a natural limit to the number of men, and the amount of equipment, that can be profitably used to cut the logs from a given stand of timber. On the North Shore the bush camp which gives the most effective results is the six-gang camp. Each gang has its quota of fellers, teamsters, rollers and trail-cutters. These, with the men more or less permanent in the camp, constitute a working force of ninety to one hundred and ten men. Among the fellers are men picked for their skill with the axe and saw. The work is dangerous and care must be exercised in placing the timber. The skidding group, too, needs men accustomed to the hook; this the foreigner has seldom used. And even trail-cutting requires practice, it can be made light or heavy, depending on how the axeman uses his head. As for the horses, no good foreman is overly anxious to have a newcomer handle the lines. So that the regular work of the bush camps does not readily offer an avenue of profitable employment to the man of foreign extraction just arrived in Canada.

But there is in all winter camps the road gang. This will vary in size from eight to fifteen men, according to the needs of the camp. The men of this group are employed in grubbing, ditching, leveling the main roads, and doing other routine work. In it are placed the younger men and those not particularly fitted for special tasks. The road gang is the general utility group, the catch-basin for all kinds of unplaced labour in the camp. The men of such groups, swampers they are called, with their grub-hoes, double-faced axes, and saws, are employed most frequently as muckers. This work is not unlike the primary stage of railway construction. The foreign-born can do this satisfactorily, and it is in such groups that they are first placed in bush camps.

The foreign-born have, moreover, good assets in their contentedness and usual perseverance. These qualities are in demand in any group of frontier workers. In the face of the constant jumping among white labour in the winter camps, which only increases the more during the good times, the fact that they are at least more dependable gives the foreign-born a further passport to the goodwill of the bush foreman, exasperated so often by the uncertainty and fickleness of the casual camp man. In view of this the foreign-born have gradually increased their foothold and have ultimately secured a fixed place in the work of the winter camps.

As a result, while few foreigners of Slav extraction were seen in the winter camps of Canada previous to 1902, and even for the next eight years were a curiosity in the bunkhouse, yet, before 1911, some of the most capable among the foreign-born were driving teams on the sleigh-haul, while others had entered the arcana of all good bushmen by proving their ability as fellers and logmakers. Many large companies now devote one whole bunkhouse in a camp to the use of the foreign-born bushmen. They have earned their place in the camps in the face of opposition. Latterly, too, the pulp camps, with their smaller timber requiring men of less experience, and having fewer of the customs to combat, which are so deeply rooted in the camps of the pineries, have attracted increasing numbers of the foreign-born.

It may be noted that while the bush camps do not pay as high wages apparently as are offered in the railway camps, yet in the end the real pay is fully as much. Compared with the railway camp, there are fewer deductions of one kind and another against the bush man. There is also much less expense incurred in reaching camp.

All in all, had the new arrivals in the Dominion, during the final decade of railway expansion, been more readily adaptable for the bush camps, the pay there offered would have given them an effective alternative in their choice of camp work.

AT THE MINES

During those years when a highway of steel was slowly being forced through the watershed of the Moose remarkable discoveries in the

Cobalt country had given rise to much mining activity. What effect did the new work at the mines have on the navvy in the railway camp, farther north?

There was one direct result; the silver camps lured the white labour off the line. Gradually the English-speaking and French-speaking navvies forsook the railway camps for the mines. Particularly was this true of the men who were being paid by the day and who suffered much from lost time. Even many of the men on the better-paid clerical staffs were hard to hold. They stuck to the works, some of them, from a sense of loyalty to their chief; others from the fact that they were receiving a pay comparable with what Cobalt could offer them, and much safer, in that they were sure of it six months in succession.

What was the attraction of the Cobalt camp? Why did conditions of work and pay there draw men from the railway construction farther north so that the camps of the line, deserted by native-born workers, were recouped year after year with new arrivals from Europe who knew little or nothing of Canada? Why was there a leakage of this class, at first opportunity, back down from the railway work, until irate foremen on the grade, as they saw their gangs depleted every few days, cursed the name of Cobalt?

Previous to 1911 little real mining was done at Cobalt. The earlier years were occupied in the staking of claims and the performance thereon of the required work in the initial stages of development. This called for men with a practical knowledge of the woods and lakes and trails. It meant also the frequent use of the canoe and many other experiences of the frontier which the foreign-born had yet to acquire. For it was the white labour which first took to the woods. Prospecting was the allurement, and the search for 'minerals in place' supplanted the more matter-of-fact work of the railway camps.

Nor are the qualities required of a prospector and a navvy dissimilar. Self-reliance and strong physical hardihood are prime essentials in either. Many of the early prospectors at Cobalt had been on occasions lumber-jacks or trappers for a season, and the great majority had come from the frontier settlements of Ontario, Quebec, and the Maritime provinces. Keen, alert, tenacious, daring, even if at times lacking in caution, many of them possessed the qualities so much in demand just then in the new mining fields.

These accessions to the ranks of the prospectors continued for some years to absorb the white labour from the National Transcontinental Railway.

For there be characteristics common to all those who require space. The navvy and the prospector in Canada are interrelated. The romance of Silver Islet one-quarter century before attracted men in great numbers as prospectors to the North Shore; most of these men were merged later with the navvies who were then building the Canadian Pacific around the rocky shores of Lake Superior. Not uncommonly, too, the navvy and the prospector have exchanged works in the boundary country and the Crow's Nest Pass. But, whether drawn from the mines at Rossland or from the camps on the National Transcontinental Railway, the instinct of the men who flocked to the Cobalt fields was the same; it was that which back in the later fifties had drawn men to the streams and gravel beds of Cassiar and the Cariboo.

The work of the prospector has ever appealed to the virile of the Canadian camps. There comes a satisfaction in wresting from nature first hand. That man who sleeps upon the ground, sees the stars by night in their places, and is lulled by the winds of the forest. Such as he, will readily wager his days and weeks in a contest with the elements. For daring is an inheritance of the intrepid, nor is it restricted to any age. The ancestors of such men fought the Saracens at the gates of Tyre. Their forebears cheered with Drake from the poop of the Golden Hind in the chase of galleons off the Chilian coast. In their veins courses the restless blood of the Canadian voyageurs and of the hardy frontiersmen who later in paddled craft threaded swift streams with the pathfinders of the North and West – Hearne and Mackenzie, Lewis and Fraser, and the undaunted Thompson belated in his attempts.

The grubstake, in the Temiskaming country, involves a third party – one who agrees to outfit a group, usually two men, on a hurried investigation of a likely field with the object of staking new claims. For this the men are assured of their maintenance and necessary outlay with pay. Other inducements, a percentage on the number of claims staked or a small interest in the properties, are sometimes added as an incentive to the men. In such deals the third party usually assumes further, all expenses of recording and development. Compared with pay in the railway camps, the remuneration seems large and the work, while strenuous, has not the monotony of life on construction.

There is another difference. The navvy on the grade has no share in what he produces. His interest is bounded solely by his pay. But a prospector is, to a limited extent, a partner. That means a further remuneration. It is psychic; always just at hand, lurking around the corner, is the smile of the fortunate find; urgent, haunting, it was as potent in the clay belt during these years as at any time since, through the centuries, the men of the blood races have poured out at the North Gates.

But the prospector has no light job. His work is measured not by the day or by the month but by the completion of a task. There is not the steady grind, yet the day is never done. Every hour may occasion fresh demands for the exercise of strength, vigilance and native experience. The canoe is the common form of transportation. There are whole days of paddling against the current of a northern river, varied with poling rapids, or fighting at times in a sudden squall the whitened waters of a wind-swept lake. Portages, too, must be made; many of them are more than a quarter of a mile in length and the trail is not always cut. Packing and re-packing increase the hardships of the trip. This is work to which the foreign-born is not accustomed. Nor is he friendly towards the canoe.

To camp for the night is quick work for practised hands. The small tent is disentangled from the pack. Soon it is suspended from a horizontal limb and tethered. Balsam boughs or dry reeds with the blankets at hand readily provide a bunk which needs no coddling to invite sound sleep.

The prospector carries but limited provisions. Only bare essentials are taken. It could not be otherwise in the face of much packing and frequent shifts. Impediments of all kinds are eschewed. Bacon, flour, beans, rice and tea constitute the minimum. If fuller supplies are taken it follows the blancing of many personal whims. The prospector has not the choice for a meal which confronts the navvy in the camp cookery. It does not take many weeks in the woods for the best prospector to feel the monotony of his limited fare; beans and bacon and bannocks, meal after meal, soon become commonplace. Disaster, too, is surely imminent if the tobacco runs short. It is then the game of staking becomes very drab indeed, and the work of the prospector bristles with difficult human problems.

But how does the actual pay work out? The prospector receives approximately the wage of a good camp foreman (in 1910 rather less than $100 a month was recieved). Added to this will be pickings for the successful when the bonus is paid and when, if desired, he disposes of his small interest in the claim. On the other hand, it should not be overlooked that the work of a prospector is not continuous. Three trips in five months would be a good average. Living expenses, too, are high in any new mining town. While the prospector handles more money he also spends, between trips, much more freely than he would if in a railway camp. He dwells in the midst of opportunities to squander his earnings which the navvy on the grade escapes.

Occasionally a real measure of success does attend the prospector. But ready money thus procured means, often, as quick an outlay – a visit back home, a trip to a distant city, Montreal, Toronto or New York perhaps, new sights and high living for ten days; his waking dreams, never far distant amid the discomforts of the trail, seem to be realized. But the prospector seldom makes more than a good living. Compared with the station-man on the line his chances for gain seem bigger, but when his work for ten months or a year is considered, he has made less than the foreman or cook who remained at a grade camp on railway construction.

For, at best, prospecting is an adventurous occupation – full of chances and hazards, hopes, surprises and thrills, disappointments and satisfactions. As the Romans would say, it requires a heart of oak and triple brass. All this has an attraction, however, for the red-blooded impelled by the zest of seeking rather than the joy of having. The deterrent force of risks is less than the attractive bait of sudden gain. Incentive and pay work up to the margin at which probable returns would in the long run reward the outlays involved in time, experience and actual manual work. The very nature of the work, however, unsettles a man for a steady job. He will not get up at the sound of the whistle, eat at an hour fixed by the cook and do a set task each day, but he will cheerfully undergo hardships that would discourage others with less optimism. For he sails in the ships of Tarshish, dealing only in purple. Compared with the navvy, the one plays for stakes, the other seeks the reasonable and sure return on his day's labour – not the possibility of sudden gain but the assurance of a fair competence.

While the mines in the Temiskaming country directly attracted the virile and aggressive navvies, they did not, previous to 1911, divert a great proportion of the foreign-born. Until then the mines had seemingly but little attraction for them. Only when systematic mining was well under way and when much heavy manual work was thus afforded, did the mining camps provide an alternative field of labour for the Slav workers on railway construction.

ON RAILWAY EXTRA-GANGS
The navvy in the grade camp had, also, a third alternative, and in a similar occupation – work with the large railway gangs employed in track maintenance and repair.

The backbone of a railway is its roadbed. Safety of travel as well as operating efficiency depend in a large measure upon the care exercised, all along the line, to keep track and ties and ballast in first-class condition. Work of this nature is performed by the extra-gangs.

Scores of extra-gangs are employed each year by the railways of Canada. A few operate throughout the whole year, but the busy season for most gangs extends from April until the freeze-up in December. These extra-gangs are employed in necessary repair work: track renewal, ballasting and needed improvements for switches, abutments and other structures. Each gang engaged in such work requires a capable head and a few experienced assistants, but the routine work of the men calls chiefly for heavy manual outlay.

The work of the many hundreds of local section crews may also be grouped with that of extra-gangs. These crews, however, are usually composed of men who have had more experience than those who comprise the large work-groups.

The railway extra-gang consists of from sixty to one hundred men. The foreman will have among his assistants two to six straw-bosses. Some of these will be of foreign extraction. They serve as a link between the men and the officials of the work. Quite commonly an extra-gang will be comprised largely of men of one particular nationality – Italian, Polish, or Ukrainian. Better results are obtained from a homogeneous force of this kind.

The men of the railway extra-gang live in box-cars. These are grouped according to the number of men so employed. From ten to fifteen cars accommodate the usual gang. The string of cars consists of an office-car, carrying also a small stock of needed goods, such as would be bought by the men; the stores car, with its supplies for the cook; the tool car, with its heavy jacks, shovels, chains and spares; the diners; and several bunk-cars for the men.

The extra-gang appeals to the foreign-born worker. Housed at a siding or in a yard, the men of the extra-gang live under more orderly conditions than do the inmates of the bunkhouses on construction. The men in a bunk-car have some incentive to keep clean. The chore-boy on an extra-gang is less rushed and more attention is paid to the upkeep of the sleeping quarters than is the rule in camps ahead of the steel. There is less crowding. Sixteen men can comfortably occupy a jumbo or sleep-car. The bunks, double-decked, are lined down each side of a centre aisle. Such cars, too, are well heated, for coal is always at hand.

Bunk-cars are usually dry and airy, but like most camp buildings they are also poorly lighted. While apparently cleaner and more attractive than the bunkhouse, they are, not infrequently, infested with bed-bugs. This is particularly the case when the same car is used continuously to house men on both winter and summer works. Being on wheels, the average bunk-cars, unless specially re-lined, are subject in extreme weather to winds that would not easily penetrate the walls and well-banked buildings of a bush camp.

While, too, an office van with supplies in charge of a clerk is maintained on every large railway extra-gang, there is not the same necessity to buy from one source. Being close to towns and seldom far removed from a village or settlement, the individual workers have opportunity to make their necessary purchases at outside stores and at prices freely prevailing in the district. These are more reasonable than at a distant grade camp where no competition exists.

The food on the average railway extra-gang is often inferior to that provided the workers in other camps. With every facility to procure the needed supplies for the cookery car and at fair market prices, the table there shows to disadvantage with the board provided men for a similar rate at the mill or the mine. The cooks, too, except on the very large gangs have had less experience. In fact that ethical admonition contained in the Utopia for man to cultivate a disdain of desire and seek to grow culturally at meals would thrive but little in the crowded eating-cars of a maintenance gang. This may partly be accounted for by the fact that the feeding of men on railway extra-gangs is often sublet. It is ominous for the well-being of a frontier worker when more than one has an interest in the paring of his meals for profits. Even the most illiterate among the foreign-born are not slow to discern the fact when once meals are doled by measurement to various gangs on a contract. Neither is the visit of the local food comptroller under such a system unnoted. These labourers may not always be able to express their opinions of him in English but meaning nods at the mealtime disclose observations which imply: 'All the time, lots of bosses watch cook – few raisins in the pie.'

There is still a marked discrepancy on all railway lines between the provision made for the care and comfort of trainmen at the several divisional points and the housing in cars of men who do seasonal works. Regular employees of the road, drivers, conductors, brakemen, and other members of the train crews are amply accommodated, even on remote divisions, at well-equipped hostels. And this is well, but navvies on the extra-gangs receive but a scant portion of such recognition. While some cars used on temporary works, occupied by small staffs of engineers, bridge crews, and men on telegraph upkeep, are comfortably equipped, the ordinary box-cars which are the domicile of the large extra-gangs still leave much to be desired. In referring to this it is well to keep in mind, also, that the employees who receive material considerations are usually English-speaking and well-organized, while the occupants of the box-cars, too often improperly equipped, are commonly foreign-born, their work temporary, and themselves largely migratory in their habits.

There are, too, on the extra-gang the usual deductions for the doctor and the medical fees, yet more is given the men in return for such dues; the professional visits are regular and, in case of need, efficient hospitals for treatment are often near at hand. The railways, too, have always co-operated with their men on the extra-gangs by providing transportation both ways if satisfaction is given. This may mean sometimes the moving of men for considerable distances, even from one province to another.

The extra-gangs shift frequently. Seldom do they remain more than a month at any one place. They are utilized wherever an emergency exists. Their work, however, corresponds more to that of the activities which mark the secondary stage of railway construction. Its different employments may best be compared with work in the finishing stages rather than with early developments ahead of the steel. The work of the pit-crew, the lift-gang, and the ballast trains are all duplicated in the different occupations which vary the pursuits of the railway extra-gang. There is, in consequence, a frequent interchange of the foreign-born in such works.

The work of the extra-gangs beckons to the foreign-born navvy in another way. The tools in use there are the same as those to which he has already become accustomed on construction. The grub-hoe, the picaroon and the crow-bar need not be replaced in his hands with new and untried implements such as the peavy or the hook. The work, too, while heavy, is not entirely new. There is less custom to combat, and the daily associations of the extra-gangs promise the continued companionship of kin and tongue.

During the building of the National Transcontinental the pay for men on railway extra-gangs was lower than that promised in camps on new construction. The prevailing rate for a ten-hour day on the former was $1.35, whereas construction camps offered $1.75 ahead of the steel.

Formerly, the railway extra-gangs were composed largely of English and French-speaking workers. But, during the third period of railway expansion, these gangs, too, underwent a change. Gradually the foreign-born drifted to these works. Few English-speaking men were found in extra-gangs during the later years of this period other than the officials or bosses. In this work the newcomers made good, and during the final ten years of the period they usurped the whole field. Eighty per cent of the work of the railway extra-gang to-day is performed by those classes designated foreigners.

Much of this is due to the fact that during these years the alternative employments for the English-speaking navvy had rapidly enlarged. The bush camps and the extra-gangs were given little consideration in the face of bigger inducements in other fields. Western Canada was opening up and mining had received a sudden impetus.

But no form of alternative frontier employment offered any avenue of real competition to the foreign-born. Narrowed in opportunity by his limited capacities, confronted in other works by rooted customs, and handicapped by language, he was forced by actual circumstances to continue under the hire of the railway contractor, at least until such time as his meagre savings permitted him to make his way westward to the prairie lands of Saskatchewan or to live in nationalist groups in the larger industrial centres.

Chapter 9

What constitutes real wages for the bunkhouse man?

LET US turn aside, for a time, from the more or less beaten paths of
the detailed activities of the navvy and other campmen to consider
some of the elements which properly enter into any discussion of
what is implied in a fair remuneration for work done in frontier
camps.

What constitutes real wages under such conditions and how are
they determined? Can a worker, endowed with the rugged qualities
which such tasks demand, be assured of fair pay in return? Does
consistent service given for hire in some camp on railway construction result in a corresponding personal gain? These and kindred
queries arise when one seeks to answer the question: Are the
earnings of the campman too frequently diverted to others?

The man who follows the camps year after year acquires definite
personal qualities, many of which contribute to the efficiency of his
work. He learns early to fit in to whatever the circumstances
demand. He has to master team-play. His work days are marked by
the regularity of barrack life. The hours at a grade camp are utilized
in mass movements, all pulling together under the guidance of the
foreman, whose orders are usually obeyed promptly.

A rigid obedience, too, to accepted customs, is required of
campmen. They retire about the same hour, rise early with the
sound of the horn or the clang of the gong, for punctuality is a habit
soon acquired in all camps. No self-respecting cook will encourage
delinquents at the meal hour; nor is it well to incur his displeasure.

Many intangible qualities, also, are required of workers in camps;
self-control and good-nature are not their least profitable assets. Men
herded close for weeks in bunkhouses, with all that that implies in
little daily frictions, cannot afford to be short-grained. That gets one
nowhere, particularly in the face of the other annoyances – the
interminable pests of flies, the vermin frequently, and the fickleness
of the weather in its varying moods during the short hot summer of
the northern parts. Neither will any large force of men at an isolated
camp work smoothly without a good measure of confidence in one
another. Bunkhouses on the grade soon sift the personal worth of
the inmates, no matter what their pretensions, for the interchange of
badinage from bunk to bunk begets a knowledge of human values,
and an understanding of the camaraderie of life. And the majority of
the campmen measure up; they are not found wanting when the

common man-qualities so much required under such circumstances are weighed in the balance.

Despite appearances sometimes, sobriety is also a characteristic of the bunkhouse man. He should not be judged entirely by his conduct when, between jobs, he visits a frontier town or some city at the front. The test of his industry is the long months of patient service in some camp on construction. He is dependable through many weeks; he works contentedly in isolation, foregoing the recreations, the sports and the amusements of a more orderly life.

For the bunkhouse man, exultant in his physical exuberance, will endure the many discommodities ahead of the steel buoyed up by the hope of ultimate gain, which, in his case, is usually measured by a stake. It may be the small stake which is his goal, since, with many, the acquired appetite or the abnormal propensity cannot go long unheeded. Some seek the seasonal stake, in with the spring, out with the freeze-up. But others will be content only with the big stake. This may call for months of isolation and many privations, with heavy tasks in distant camps, but a reward is anticipated which will put behind for good any further need of navvying on the grade. The big stake is the try-out for any campman. To make and hold gives added confidence; to slowly acquire and squander heedlessly begets the grouch, and the casual, with the manners of a beast at bay.

Nor need it be implied that the camp worker is of one common type. Any hundred-mile stretch of busy construction soon makes apparent that the human capacity for rendering service varies among the navvies as elsewhere. There is evidence of unending differences in experience and natural ability; a special training is even demanded of the worker at times, and there are particular undertakings in all camps in which only a few among the men can excel. Rockwork and blasting call for keen mental qualities, for judgment, alertness, and quick perception; all men who are proficient in such work are properly experts, possessing the trained skill often of stone-cutters, plasterers, and other highly-paid artisans. Even the station-man at his obscure tasks combines, also, those physical qualities which fit him to face hardships with equanimity, and to deal effectively with emergencies when nature moves with sudden shift.

While the work in an isolated construction camp can hardly be defined as seasonal, yet it is irregular. The farther out on the grade,

the more numerous are the hindrances and the less it takes to tie
things up. The result is an insecurity in the work of the campman.
There are many causes for interruptions on railway construction; the
idle weeks during the break-up, the prolonged wet spell, a forest fire
which endangers the camp for days, all serve to make precarious the
actual working time of the navvy ahead of the steel.

The campman, thus, is restricted in a way to a particular work.
For, while in such employment, he is personally free, many circumstances arise which interfere with the fluidity of his labour. His pay
under such circumstances should not only compensate for physical
expenditure but should, in some measure, serve as a retaining fee to
reimburse him for the many unavoidable delays and the consequent
wastage in his pay cheque.

The station-man, for example, taken as a type of jobber on a
camp work, has a crude efficiency. This, in turn, is capitalized in the
allotting of such work. Pass through some muskeg where a
station-group, with barrows and shovels, have been busy for months;
there stretches the finished portion, lined on either side by the
blackened tamaracs, beautiful in its contour, shapely as the
stone-hewed quay which confronts the sea. Could such portions of
the grade have been built or the mud cuts excavated as well by the
sub-contractor and a force of men at day labour? Could that bed of
rock, blasted from the hillside by a bunch of Finns and built into a
stone causeway at the narrows there in the lake, have been so
effectively removed by the camp boss and his men? If so, the work
would have been done by day labour. The local sub-contractor
knows which way means little worry to him, less oversight and
probably bigger gains, so he lets out to jobbers. In this way he gets
out from under some of his obligations. It provides a means by
which he may escape the losses, but does he share likewise the
profits he so often makes?

Station-work is undertaken from choice. Each work-group
voluntarily assumes the uncertainties of any actual gain. Yet, such
service gives inspiration, in having an intelligent part in the progress
of the road-bed. Efforts so expended, drab as they appear, are not
the mere repetitive work of the machine tender. These men work
somewhat under the conditions of the handicrafts, where each
worker is owner of what he creates. It should return a pleasure
measured in terms of suitable compensation.

Camp work in many forms means eager and willing service. It brings into play latent resources, all of which appeal to the manual worker imbued with confidence and enterprise. On paper, at least, it offers inducements. The pay, too, may be satisfactory, under normal surroundings, but there are times when the earnings are subordinated whether by weather or undue motives of personal gain on the part of the employer. Wages in the end are then very different from the rate of pay promised. There are rights more sacred than safety. There can be no liberty of labour when men are bound by agreements which fetter rather than assure a reasonable return! Such is the menace of a peculiar privilege. Camp workers under these conditions pay dearly in tonnage and poundage to their masters.

One form of remuneration which workers in camps receive, at least indirectly, should not be overlooked. Many employers of labour in frontier places deserve every credit in that they feed their men well. Perhaps it is a necessity due to the competition in the labour market, for other things being equal, campmen will go where chuck is best; in any event, food in camps has been good ever since the turn of the century. The company usually supplies more bacon, ham, cheese, meats, coffee, vegetables, dried fruits, canned goods, and staples of all kinds than may ordinarily be found in a city boarding house. In fact, the average home, not excluding that of the lower-paid professor, could not begin to provide food for the family as do these employers of men in camps. The supplies are there, and while cooks may vary, even the poorest among them considers himself a tin god in the camp. Before the loaded table in the cookery the newcomer from Europe seats himself in wonderment and feeds with alacrity. There he may abandon himself to the simple joy of eating, for here even the lowly are at home. Nor need the newcomer be regulated in his course, pastry and soup, puddings and meat are not infrequently interspersed. A teamster of the camp at the sound of the gong swaggers to his meal with the airs of one who has dignity to conserve.

But wages under frontier conditions should afford not merely food and bare maintenance, but also some comforts and the promise of ultimate gain to those campmen who practise thrift. Why leave their pay to chance? It represents not only a fair payment for efforts made but further a consideration of the results achieved. If wages come ultimately from the product, what measures their contribution? Do men in such works get what they produce either relatively or absolutely?

Not that it is affirmed the sub-contractor makes no contribution to construction; he has his place, and it is a needed one, too. The navvy, with his barrow alone, cannot build the grade; other factors are requisite. Admittedly the sub-contractor encounters many difficulties. The cost of his supplies mounts rapidly with every additional mile of haul. His handicaps increase proportionately for every ten miles ahead of the steel. But on the other hand, if he is capable in bargaining he receives minor compensations when dealing with the head-contractor, which help atone for such obstacles. Only rarely is a corresponding provision made for the man employed by the sub-contractor. His work is not so essential, and as an individual he is usually more dependent. For, in far-out camps, both the sub-contractor and his men are face to face with nature and new elements enter into the conditions of pay. Primitive laws benefit the overlord; the waste and penalty imposed upon the campman under such conditions are greater than the cost of removing them.

The general conditions of labour in any camp lead to great wear and tear on the human body and result, eventually, in lower standards of life. Even the dirtiness of an occupation may tend to lower wages. Efficient production should at no time trespass on the opportunity not only to maintain health but to develop intelligence and morale. To ignore the need of the bunkhouse worker to recoup himself culturally is to reduce the enterprising on any work to the level of the worst.

For as has already been indicated, there is a tendency, even under the best of conditions, for the heavy monotonous labour of the campman to become merely routine drudgery endured for a time in the hope of a subsequent release, marked by a period of license. But, where his tasks are but scantily rewarded, there is a further loss to the frugal worker who has other aspirations for his savings and leisure time. Rebuffs of this kind react on his character. It is the plastic relation of the bunkhouse man to his environment. One result is the gaming spirit; he turns his back on the long bitter effort that consumes the weeks, and courts instead the luring smile of chance. A shiftlessness results, and it is not long before another recruit has entered the ranks of the semi-nomad and casual workers. This tendency, too, may account partly for the frequency with which men, who nominally have been earning good wages in camps, will be found in the off-periods of seasonal works standing in a city bread-line or soliciting a dime to supplement the price of a meal.

Many campmen in their efforts are not unlike the legendary Sisyphus: Slowly they acquire their stake, to have it suddenly disappear. The never-ending, still-beginning process goes on, but gradually and surely it tells even upon the strong. The firmly-knit frame gradually gives away, a chronic tiredness succeeds the buoyant energy of other years, and the man of fifty-five in a camp is old. To riches few of these men attain and to the Fortunate Isles – never!

Then, how account for the fact that, even in the face of conditions so unfavourable for real wages, large numbers of men continued to flock to the camps during years of railway expansion? Other factors entered into the whole question of demand and supply. Because of these the wage system on the National Transcontinental was worsened.

The years 1903-14, inclusive, marked a period of great material development throughout the Dominion. Not only was Canada passing through its third period of railway expansion, but there was correspondingly great industrial development in the older cities of the country. It has been estimated that during those twelve years three billions of dollars, much of it British money, was invested in Canadian municipal and other undertakings.

This prosperity, in turn, was accompanied by a heavy immigration to Canada from the British Isles, from portions of the United States, and from Continental Europe. This peaceful invasion increased annually, until before the close of the period, as many as four hundred thousand new arrivals entered the Dominion in one year. Previous to 1914, almost three million newcomers had in this way been added to the country (see Appendix D).

To the people of the provinces, still numbering even with these large accessions less than eight millions, this movement constituted a serious problem in adjustments. True, one-third or more of the immigrants were lost again to the Dominion, either by the return to Europe of many who had been temporarily attracted across the Atlantic by opportunities of work, or by the never-ceasing drift to the Great Republic, whose vast wealth and diverse employments have ever proved a lure to the virile men from North of the Lakes.

But this influx had another phase, and one that pertained more directly to frontier camps. While the major portion of the immigrants – approximately two million – had come from the British Isles and the United States, and presumably were thus fitted to resume their respective occupations and trades, unhampered by barriers of language and changed environments, more than seven hundred thousand on the other hand were foreign-born nationals largely from the continent or the Mediterranean lands. These latter were less adaptable to Canadian pursuits, other than manual employments.

It may be inferred, too, from the results of investigations made a decade later (See *Census of Canada*, 1921, vol. II, pp. 474-83) that this body of foreign-born was supplemented in turn by a considerable number of kindred nationals, who entered the Dominion during that same period from various states of the Union, classed as Americans. Many of these, too, if not directly employed on the land, fitted in readily as labourers on seasonal works.

But from whatever source, there was a surplus of labour to be utilized. A solid proportion of the man-power represented in the migrations of that period proved a ready source of supply, a reservoir of unskilled workers, among the unplaced but newly arrived, which was freely tapped to provide men for camps on the hinterland.

This condition of abnormal supply did not benefit the foreign-born navvy, while it was a palpable deterrent to the English-speaking navvy who, ordinarily, would have gone on railway construction as in Australia, where great trunk railways were pioneered at times over vast stretches of sparsely-settled and forbidding lands. That such resources were there to be utilized, and that there was a willingness on the part of the new arrivals to work in railway camps under whatever conditions of pay, does not palliate the wages paid the navvy. May it not be questioned, if even a willingness to take what is offered, to meet a temporary requirement, is itself a sufficient cause to override the necessity of a minimum wage to the campman for stated work?

The intricacies of work and pay under bunkhouse conditions arouse conflicting thoughts. Certain human qualities so marked in campmen – thrift and hard work alternating with weeks of seasonal idleness – leave the men in the off periods in a state of veritable dependence. In all camps it is quite commonly the custom to pay once a month, or perhaps only when the man is quitting. True, if paid fortnightly, the wages might be lost in games of chance, but it is equally true that money in hand gives rise to forms of thrift even among those prone to waste.

Then, too, men of the bunkhouse are usually paid by check. Along railway construction a man leaving a camp must pay cash for his meals. His pay-check, good only at the company's headquarters, perhaps sixty miles away, must be discounted and often at a considerable charge. The system of paying once a month may have advantages to the company concerned, but it has irritating drawbacks to the campmen.

Thus the wage bargain of many camp workers is leaded. This is due to the peculiar circumstances of their employment. The very conditions of their work, in isolated camps, are a barrier to their quitting and going elsewhere. They are often in a ring fence, and it is in the interest of some to keep them there. Seldom is there mutuality in the bargain which gives them employment. It is the relation of boss and hireling. The obverse side of the whole wage bargain for many frontier workers shows the cash nexus as the only bond, and that unduly distorted.

'Oh!,' it is said, 'it is the way of life – the strong and the spoils. If the railway contractor had not profited from this inflow of labour, during the period of railway expansion, the industrialist would.' That may be true while human nature is still the control lever in all of us, but let us arrange that the worker in camps, is not without security.

Is it not possible to give to all workers in camps a monthly wage – a basic rate to insure a reasonable return when competent services have been duly rendered? While pay by the day may appear larger in the aggregate, it fails to meet requirements when the peculiar aspects of the situation are considered. To the basic wage might be added a surplus, based upon a careful adjustment and depending on the nature of the particular work done. This could be considered always from the standpoint of the individual concerned, for much of the labour expended by the campman is a personal activity measured by human outlay which also determines the specific contribution to the product.

The reason for a basic monthly wage is apparent. The preceding pages have shown how the camp system works when a navvy is paid by the day. Certainly the only satisfied men on railway construction are those paid a monthly wage. Upon what principle is a choreboy, a cookee, an axeman at a residency, paid by the month while their fellow navvies, muckers, surface-men, dump builders – just as efficient, and generally more so – lose all time due to interruptions in the work? Is it reasonable for a man to lose much time during the inclement weather of a changing climate and, meanwhile, have his board pile up at seventy-five cents to a dollar a day? He is there at the disposal of his employers, their interests brought him in; he should be paid, rain or shine. It is next to impossible to make real wages in any other way.

It may not be logical that a basic wage can be assured on all forms of work. The moment that wages are more than the undertaking can pay, the result is unemployed campmen. But, if a clerk, a teamster, a barn-boss, a sawyer can be paid monthly, the station-man, the driller, the cement mixer and the many other workers are also surely eligible. For they are equally productive; in the face of their efforts and their manual outlay they, too, should be assured reasonable sustenance, fit housing and fair charges on all purchases made in camp.

Nor is the fact overlooked that wages cannot be set arbitrarily. World-wide conditions, due to the many intricate relationships of present-day services, determine locally not only the price of cotton and wheat, but also the pay of a worker in some isolated camp. But does it not appear that somewhere there is an interference with the natural economic reactions, such as pertain to wages in camps? If so, is the country the gainer when the pay of the bunkhouse man is scamped?

And further, it may be suggested that the pay of workers in camps start from the time they sign up for work. In the case of a navvy who engaged with a contractor for work at what proves to be a distant camp, his meals and a reasonable amount of transportation might also be allowed for coming and going.

Campmen will work as hard tramping for days to reach their place of work, as they do at any other time. They are already in service when thus en route. Distance, in this respect, co-operates with the employing firm in that it helps to hold men. The same rule can be made to work both ways. Nor need any unnecessary time be lost in transit; a scout from the agency shipping the men can conduct the party directly and with but few delays.

As has been indicated, wages along railway construction can be increased in one of two ways – by reducing the profits of the different contractors overhead, or by increasing the amount of production of each man on the grade. But, in the case of the station-men, it has been shown that usually theirs is a very real production, that their hours of labour are extra long, and yet their living is almost at a subsistence margin. But, if high wages depend on good workers, if skill and high productivity count, such workers earn real wages and should receive them.

The country is best served by the widest distribution of money expended on big undertakings. And this applies particularly to the earnings of men employed on frontier works. The bunkhouse man should not merely exist. In view of his unique contributions he is entitled to a wage surplus which will land him back, unhampered, in the regularly organized life of the Dominion.

To do otherwise puts life on a very material basis. The bunkhouse man possesses, in a marked degree, independence; self-sufficiency and self-reliance, at least, to adapt himself to frontier conditions. Let the resultant pay compensate fully for the unusual environments. He will become more efficient if he secures a just share of the final product of his labour. Should any worker in camps, particularly on construction being built by the public of Canada, labour under the conditions of quasi-serfdom such as existed along whole stretches of the National Transcontinental? The earth does not rest, as the ancients depicted, upon a giant or a tortoise. There are, too, intangible forces of volitional control.

To estimate properly the true earnings of bunkhouse men in Canada, do not ask merely: What money wages are being paid; but, what deductions will be made?

A definite advance toward real wages for the navvy and all workers in frontier camps of Canada will have been made:

1 When the time of a campman employed on an isolated work starts from the day he signs up with a company.
2 When all workers in camps, who so desire it, are paid their wages at least fortnightly, and in cash or paper negotiable locally and at par.
3 When all workers in frontier camps are assisted in their transportation, if necessary, at least for a reasonable distance, any having rendered three months' service satisfactory to the company.

4 When all campmen are paid at a monthly rate, with no deductions on account of unfavourable weather. (It may be questioned if, having the whole year in mind, a married campman can afford to work, even under present conditions, for less than $60.00 per month and board.)

5 When the officials of the nearest government Labour Bureau are given wider powers to deal directly, when necessary, with cases of local maladjustment in camp employments and pay.

Chapter 10

What's wrong with the contract system?

FROM A PERUSAL of the contents of the foregoing sections the reader should now be in a more favourable position to estimate in a practical way how the contract system affects the labourer in a construction camp. At least two things have been indicated: that the head-contractor in some phases of his work possesses a monopoly power, and that the tendency to sub-let is, in the end, a detriment to the navvy in the matter of his pay.

The question naturally arises: What's wrong with the contract system? and further, if wrongs are inherent in the whole practice, what suggestions, if any, can be made toward undoing some of its more mischievous aspects? In seeking answers to these queries, let us reconsider briefly the actual relations between the head-contractor and his different sub-contractors.

It has already been pointed out that the supplies intended for the camps on the grade must be purchased from the warehouses at the headquarters camp. The head-contractor purchases in big quantities from the wholesalers, and in turn retails to his sub-contractors at a safe profit, charging them as well for the freighting over twenty, thirty or fifty miles. When the supplies are landed at the grade camp they have cost the sub-contractor dear. But the latter in turn, must make a profit, and the campman ultimately foots the whole bill for the accumulated costs of the supplies.

Take, for example, the usual camp stores — the flour, the beans, the meats, the sauer-kraut — any one of the many essentials, each of these after being landed, at wholesale prices, in the warehouses of the head-contractor will have to bear the following extra charges before they are sold from the warehouse of the sub-contractor at a grade camp:

1 The profits of the head-contractor.
2 The heavy charges for freighting.
3 The added profits, also, of the sub-contractor.

There will be a further charge, too, if unfortunately for the navvy, the head-contractor has to haul his supplies by train over the line of a rival. Friction is sometimes in evidence in this respect between head-contractors. Invariably where one company is dependent on the rail haul over the private line of another company his disadvantage of location will cost him a high freight rate.

'And what,' we may ask here, 'would be a fair basis for all charges made the men on goods purchased in isolated camps?' This of course is not readily determined. Many disturbing factors arise in any such quest on frontier works, due alone to varying circumstances of time and place.

But reverting once more to railway construction along the National Transcontinental, we may at least start with the probable costs of supplies when first delivered at the warehouse of the head-contractor. Take the case of several camp staples and note the upward trend in the charges made for such supplies when landed ultimately in camps on the grade.

The wholesale prices given in the following table were quoted by reliable firms in Toronto and North Bay for delivery at the town of Cochrane in Northern Ontario. This was then the nearest regular railway point to portions of construction here under consideration.

From that little distributing town, where head-contractor No. I had his headquarters, was a rail haul of one hundred and thirty miles, with track in pretty fair condition, to the headquarters camp of contractor No. II. All the supplies for No. III had to come over this piece of road.

From the warehouses of contractor No. II the goods were distributed during the sleigh-haul to the warehouses of the sub-contractors, twenty, thirty, sixty, and even seventy miles up the line. This was expensive, but there was, in the case of this contract, nothing exceptional in the haul. The country was flat, there were few natural obstacles, and the ice on lakes gave unimpeded tote-roads for big stretches. An average load during the best weeks of the sleigh-haul would be three thousand five hundred to four thousand five hundred pounds.

The table on the following page shows approximately how prices will work out.

Column one contains wholesale prices for representative items when laid down in the warehouses of the head-contractor. Having in mind that large orders would be placed by a head-contractor, these prices would doubtless be materially reduced.

Column two is an assumed fair price for these articles when toted by sleigh forty miles and landed in the warehouse of the sub-contractor. Such a price allows the head-contractor twenty-five per cent profit on his purchases, and twenty-five per cent in addition to

PRICES OF STAPLE SUPPLIES

	Price paid by head-contractor	Assumed fair price (made up as above stated)	Price actually charged
Sugar (per bag)	$5.84	$10.80	$12.00
Lard (in pails of 50 lbs., per lb.)	.13	.22	.30
Pork (long clear salted, by the side, per lb.)	.12	.20½	.23
Flour (per bag)	2.65	5.74	6.50
Stoves (2-hole)	1.75	3.25	5.50
Stoves (4-hole)	4.20	7.00	12.00
Prunes (in boxes, per lb.)	.10	.17	.25
Beans (per lb.)	.02¼	.05	.10
Syrup (in ½ barrels, per lb.)	.03½	.07¼	.11
Raisins (in boxes, per lb)	.09	.15	.18
Tomatoes (box of 2 doz.)	3.40	6.20	8.56
Condensed milk (case—4 doz. tins)	3.80	7.08	8.20
Rice (per lb.)	.03¾	.07¾	.10
Wheelbarrow	.90	1.90	4.50
Shovels	.60	1.10	2.00
Straw hats	.10	.18	.75
Cheesecloth (for mosquitoes, per yd.)	.02½	.04½	.35

the sub-contractor for his handling. It also includes $30.00 a ton for cost of teaming, with a further allowance of ten per cent to cover overhead expenses and costs resulting from unavoidable delays.

Column three shows the prices actually charged station-men by sub-contractors.

These figures are restricted to a few staple supplies, but they present the contractor in the best light. If dry goods, tobacco, and numerous small purchases which are lighter to freight are traced, the percentage of profits procured show considerably larger. This is reflected at once in the wider spread in prices charged for wearing material at different camps. The goods sold under such conditions from a van, are not usually of a fine grade, but they are invariably strong and capable of giving good service.

The nine items listed below indicate the range of prices charged for wearing apparel in camps along a stretch of the National Transcontinental in 1911-12-13. The first price column shows the prices – high and low, charged at the same period, for similar purchases, made under regular conditions of trade and competition in the busy towns of the Temiskaming country. The second price column shows the charges made for the same class of goods by contractors and sub-contractors at various camps along construction.

PRICES OF ARTICLES OF CLOTHING

	I Price at front	II Price at camp
Overalls (cheaper quality)	$ .50–$ .75	$1.25–$ 2.00
Overalls (better grade)	1.00– 1.25	2.00– 2.75
Socks (good woollen, pr.)	.25– .40	.60– .75
A cheap sock	.12– .20	.35– .40
Heavy boots, half length, per pair	2.75– 4.50	6.50– 12.00
Heavy coats	3.50– 4.25	5.00– 7.00
Towels (per pair)	.25– .35	.60– .75
Work shirts	.60– 2.00	1.50– 3.50
Shoepacks (half length)	2.25– 4.50	4.25– 9.00
Heavy underwear (per garment)	.60– 1.50	2.00– 3.50

Any one who has even a meagre knowledge of all that it means to tote supplies for a work, will readily admit that sub-contractors are often at immense expense in forwarding their necessary stores. It is no uncommon thing for freighting to cost twenty dollars and thirty dollars per ton; it is not improbable that expenses so incurred will under some conditions amount to sixty dollars a ton, but the whole brunt of such costs should not be borne by the worker in the far-out camp without a corresponding compensation in his remuneration. There is still less reason for the exorbitant prices charged on dry goods and wearing material which are easier to transport.

Nor is the campman in such position that he can refuse to buy when prices become unreasonable. Owing to the nature of his work certain foods are practically essentials on the grade: among many such may be mentioned flour, syrup, sugar, pork, tea and various canned goods. The demand for these is constant. It will shrink but little even with enhanced prices.

And prices for supplies sold the men from the local warehouses of the sub-contractors, mount frequently with unsteadying alacrity. Staples, purchased periodically, increase in price every few weeks. This cannot always be attributed to tote charges. It has been known to occur even where charges for freighting have been lessened by one-half, due to the steady approach of the steel.

Naturally it is to be expected that the more distant the camp and the longer the haul, the higher the prices, yet such is not always borne out by the prices charged for similar requisites at different camps. Goods are sometimes cheaper farther out. Does the distance alone, over which supplies are freighted, account for such differences, or do they vary in places according to the whim of the seller?

For what is to regulate the prices that a local sub-contractor may, upon occasion, charge for the goods sold from his camp warehouse? Certain it is there can be no competition – whatever be the cause, many articles of common wear and food will vary in prices even on adjoining contracts, and where there should be but little difference in original costs.

Figures become wearisome, but the following table shows the variation in prices charged in 1911-12, for similar commodities, on sub-contracts covering adjoining pieces of work.

No. I Work located 25-36 miles ahead of the steel. Several groups of Swedes were employed at station-work in this vicinity.

No. II Work located 36-44 miles beyond the end of the steel. While some Slavs were employed, the station groups were chiefly Swedes and Finns.

No. III Work located 44-60 miles beyond the steel. Much of this work was done by Slavs. There were also some Spaniards employed.

VARIATIONS IN PRICES

Staples	Original wholesale price	No. I	No. II	No. III
Rice (per lb. in bulk)	$ .04	$ .10	$ .25	$ .15
Sugar (per bag–100 lb.)	5.75	9.50	12.00	13.00
Flour (per sack, 90–100 lbs.)	2.70	6.50	8.00	7.40
Tomatoes (per case of 24)	3.40	6.00	5.50	7.00
Beans (per lb. in bulk)	.04½	.08	.10	.12½
Pork (long clear in cases, per lb.)	.13	.23	.28	.24
Coffee (per lb.–40 lb. tins)	.21	.55	.40	.50
Wheelbarrow (ordinary make)	1.25	4.50	5.00	5.00
Stove (4-hole camp stove)	4.20	10.00	12.00	9.00
Cheesecloth (per yd.)	.03	.35	–	.25

The writer wishes to point out, in fairness to the sub-contractors, that there were probably many different reasons for local variations of this nature. There may be scarcity due to prolongation of a work,

forest fires often destroy much needed supplies in spite of all precautions, while rains and frosts militate against the keeping qualities
of many foods – but the fact remains, and this is what it is intended
to show, that, in view of increased charges for supplies there is too
seldom a corresponding consideration in the wages paid the men.

In these particular recitals there lies the root of the matter
pertaining to the wage of the navvy. Men in isolated camps
employed at station-work are crippled by the high prices charged for
supplies. The undue increases in this respect start, as have been
indicated, once the goods have been delivered to the head-
contractor. They cost the men in the camps dearly, but the local rate
is based directly on the prices charged by the head-contractor. It is
safe to say that on a sixty-mile piece of work a head company will
clear $75,000 a year on the supplies forwarded its sub-contractors.
Selling goods pays the company as well as building trestles.

The pressure which enacts toll of the labourer on the line,
emanates from the head-contractor. He holds the strings and milks
dry every source of income, wringing tribute from his subs in a
dozen different ways. They in turn must needs recompense
themselves from their station-men and the workers in shacks. Is it
hard to find where the pinch will come under such methods?

While we are considering the practical effects of the contract
system along construction, let us here make a brief digression for
purposes of a comparison.

In its extent of close on two thousand miles, the National
Transcontinental, passed, for great portions of the road, through
stretches of land that previous to the advent of the railway had been
largely dominated by some of the more southerly posts of the
Hudson's Bay Company. Contiguity had bred a slight acquaintance.
But somehow the very mention by name of the ancient body of
traders, served but to engender remarks, disparaging usually, of that
particular company. In the current gossip of the camps, they were
frequently associated with all that is selfish and predatory. The
remark was commonly heard among officials and their various
foremen on the line that the Fur Company stood condemned
becuase it had exercised for generations an undue monopoly in trade
and jurisdiction over the whole north country. The Indian, it was
maintained, had as the result of long continued dealings with them,
been robbed, stock, lock and barrel.

But in this connection the question may legitimately be asked: How did the remuneration of the Indian domiciled in the country tributary to the nearby post of the Fur Company correspond with the pay of the navvy at an adjacent railway camp?

In answer it may be pointed out, that while the great trading company took every advantage of its position, and may at times in their long years of trading have shown avarice and even aggression, yet its officials invariably displayed, even in remote places, a keen sense of their deeper responsibilities. For wherever did rise a frontier post, there already were those intangible qualities of government and associations of law and order in the hinterland. Through two long centuries and more, agents of the company exercised wide powers but usually with due consideration for the needs and the permanent welfare of the native race, so dependent upon them. What other great companies, and throughout long periods when commercial responsibility was but tenuous, have cared for the sick, sought for the lost and housed the homeless as has invariably been the rule among these distant factors?

It is in the interests of the local factor to encourage the Indian. The industrious among them is grubbed and clothed. He is outfitted for the season's hunt. When necessary he is sustained during the lean years of the chase. These hunters receive real wages from the Company, at least, in that they have been able during the long decades spent under such tutelage to thrive and perpetuate themselves in their family groups.

Given corresponding powers of trade, and an unlimited sway, would the several railway contractors and their different agents – and these, too, largely our own Canadian and American born – have treated the Indians as well? With no brief for any fur company, the writer would rather trust his labour to the nearest factor than to the working out of a contract as a station-man, under a sub-contractor, particularly if the latter is having poor results. Extended observation among camps leaves only one inference, namely, that had the Indian been treated by the Hudson's Bay Company as was, too commonly, the foreign-born navvy in grade camps and on station groups along the National Transcontinental, they would have been reduced to veritable want, if they had not been exterminated as a race, in fifty years.

And here may it be added further, that, when increasing wealth has given more opportunity for research in the Canadian universities, greater tribute will yet be rendered the memory of the exceptional men, who in the different companies laid the foundations of the fur trade. How often their deeds antedated the beginnings of things historical in our national life, not only in the North and West but in many portions of the American States.

So far, in this chapter, we have been dealing largely with the matter of charges for the supplies sold the men on the grade. That is one direct consequence of the contract system. We may now examine further the relations between the head-contractor and his sub-contractors in the matter of sub-letting.

For sub-letting is the direct corollary of the contract system. To understand the skillful method of allotting various portions of the contract is to be in a position to understand the effect on the wages of the campman.

The figures following set forth approximately the sum allowed the head-contractors, by the Railway Commission of Canada, for certain classes of work on the National Transcontinental. They show also the average price in turn allowed the final sub-contractor for the same class of work after it had been let and re-sublet down through different grades of intermediaries. A portion of this final amount would go as wages to recoup the navvy at the camp.

While these prices are not official, for they varied on different contracts, yet they are not far astray for contracts granted on the National Transcontinental Railway. They bear, also, a true relation to the figures quoted hitherto, showing prices charged the navvy for his store supplies.

	Price allowed head-contractor	Price paid final sub-contractor
Cutting right-of-way (per acre)	$100 to $125	$56 to $70
Concrete	5.00 cu. yd.	3.50 cu. yd.
Tie-making	.60 a tie	.45 a tie
Trestle and pile driving	.65 a ft.	.40 a ft.
Grading and ditching:		
Rock work	2.00 to 2.25 per yd.	.90 to 1.05 per yd.
Loose rock	.60	.45
Muskeg	.40	.33
	.33	.27
Clay	.55	.40
	.40	.32

But there is one part of the work in railway construction which is not sub-let, that is the laying of the steel and the ballasting of the new track. This is done by the head-contractor. There are many reasons why this is so. The secondary stage of railway building begins with the track-laying. The permanent work — completing the 'lifts,' replacing temporary trestles with steel bridges, has all awaited the coming of the steel. The grade camps of the sub-contractor disappear, but the large, active, noisy ballast pits take their place. All this requires heavy outlay for locomotives, hundreds of ballast cars, steam shovels, pumps and other expensive equipment.

The head-contractor, however, has a compensation in two ways: first, that the grade, already constructed by the station-men and at sub-contractor's camps during the primary stage of construction, has given him substantial credits with the Railway Commission: secondly, that his outlay for locomotives and ballast cars in this stage of the work brings him immediate returns by advances from the Railway Commission on every 10,000 yards of ballast distributed. Then, too, there is an increased amount allowed for yardage if the train haul is unduly extended in distributing ballast. The operation of several ballast-pits is at once the most serious outlay for the head-contractor, and yet, at the same time, the biggest revenue producer. Continuous operation at a pit means gain. A tie-up, for whatever reason, of engines and plant is costly.

There is a revenue also from another source. The usual railway contract lasts six years. No head-contractor surrenders his rights prematurely, for, the last two years, as already indicated, mean added profits from his passenger service. The steel on new construction is laid only gradually. At the end of the second year the work on any new railway contract will begin to shape up about like this: sixty miles of steel laid, with twenty miles in pretty fair condition, the other forty having but little attention; then for about eighty miles beyond where the rails end will be active camp activities, under various sub-contractors, building the grade and preparing for the continued advance of the steel.

At the end of the third year, one hundred miles of steel will doubtless have been laid, the first thirty miles in good shape, the second forty with only one lift, and the remainder, skeleton track, laid on the ties; beyond this, again, would be another eighty-mile section of the grade under primary construction. The different

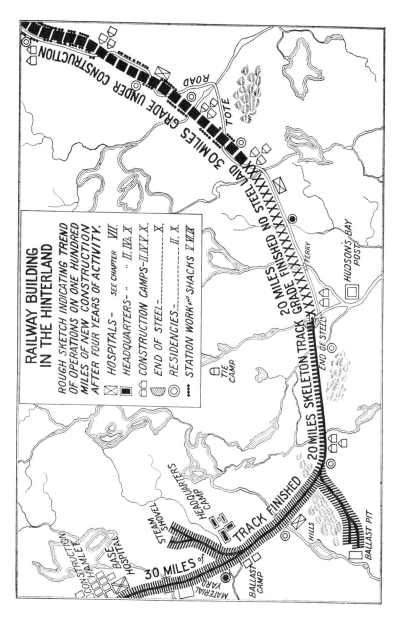

RAILWAY BUILDING
IN THE HINTERLAND

ROUGH SKETCH INDICATING TREND
OF OPERATIONS ON ONE HUNDRED
MILES OF NEW CONSTRUCTION
AFTER FOUR YEARS OF ACTIVITY.

HOSPITALS–   SEE CHAPTER VII.
HEADQUARTERS– "   II. III. X.
CONSTRUCTION CAMPS–II.IV.V. X.
END OF STEEL–   X.
RESIDENCIES–   II. X.
STATION WORK AND SHACKS I.VII

The steel advances

works on the contract progress about in this proportion until, finally, after five years or more, the steel is laid along the whole grade of a three-hundred-mile contract.

Many thousands of workers during the period of construction travel over these finished and semi-finished portions of the road. This gives the head-contractor a lever to charge his own rates for freight and for the passengers who are forced by circumstances to use his line. The opening up of a whole section of new country, following the advent of the rails, may be made tributary to the contractor's private system. The supplies for all the camps and the oats for the settler's horse as well, are alike charged what is deemed most profitable. Passengers on a flat car pay a rate of ten cents per mile return. If an ambitious young merchant wishes to start a store up the line which may offer some competition to the wares of the head-contractor, he is quickly nipped in the bud by extreme charges for freight or his prospects are blighted by the wilful carelessness with which his goods are delayed or handled in transit. The head-contractor desires no competition anywhere near the line and his clerks know well how to thwart it. For the small dealer to try to combat it, particularly if he is foreign born, is like attempting to do that traditionally impossible thing of making velvet purses out of sows' ears.

There may be no law east of Suez, but there is still less on the far-out construction. Rights fade at the last frontier town; they disappear entirely when the end of the steel is passed. Along the grade the head-contractor is supreme. Where would you get a meal, or a bed, hundreds of miles from a town or sixty miles from the steel, if the company, through its agents, closed down on you? They are masters of the situation. They hold the trump cards and can enforce their bidding in a dozen ways. Only those so favoured may trespass on the company's domain. For, not unlike the Tartar chieftain, the large contractor on the Canadian hinterland bestrides his realm; he is as the templar, plumed and mounted, in the land of the paynims.

The head-contractor on the National Transcontinental had another source of income: it was in re-classification. Work let as clay, according to the specifications of the engineers, may, under actual working conditions, prove to be hardpan, even requiring dynamite; portions of the contract listed as loose rock may better have been classed as solid rock. All this means added expense. There are always unforeseen contingencies for which a reasonable return can fairly be made to the contractor. An Ottawa report in 1916, however, states that $3,740,000 was granted a group of contractors in this way on the score of re-classification for work on the National Transcontinental Railway. One may ask: What proportion of this went to reimburse the station-men who in 1910-11-12, had asked for this same consideration in the settlements for their work with local contractors? Be it affirmed too that this same bonus was granted largely upon the product of work previously completed by station-men.

A railway contract once obtained is not unlike a valuable franchise; it may be dickered, sold and re-sold. Not only on the National Transcontinental Railway, but on other railway construction in Canada, contractors have undertaken three hundred to four hundred miles of a new line, then sub-let a half of it, or a third, to another contracting company, making clear profits without touching the work.

It is well known that one three-hundred-mile section of the National Transcontinental was let and sub-let three times. 'A' Company was the successful tenderer. It was allowed much higher prices because of the inaccessibility of the section and the desire on the part of the Government to have the work on that particular section completed as soon as possible. 'A' Company, however, sat tight, doing little for two years. Meanwhile other sections were being rapidly opened up immediately east and west of their contract, which obviated many of the difficulties of transportation for which they had been allowed special rates. Finally, 'A' Company, with little done, sub-let to 'B' Company, receiving $700,000 for their 'rights,' 'B' Company, in turn, sublet to 'C' Company, at a substantial profit. The third Company finally completed the section. This much-handled section, too, was a pivotal loop in the whole road.

Now let us continue this further. When 'C' Company sub-lets to fifteen or twenty sub-contractors, when these smaller portions again, are divided and re-divided into stations with foreign-born men in shacks doing so much of the actual work, and when the many heavy charges for hauling, owing to the distance and inaccessibility are taken into account, what portion will remain as pay for the campman? Simply the crumbs fallen from the table.

Take one example from that same stretch of work: the tie-makers who finally cut and landed the ties on the right-of-way got fifteen cents apiece for them. The difference between the sixty cents first allotted for a railway tie and the fifteen cents which actually landed it at the grade went to the intermediaries of one kind and another who, in their turn, had shared in the various sub-lettings since the contract was first granted.

It is on just such a piece of railway work, much transferred, where oppression arises, and skilful book-work 'figures' the navvy out of his bit of pay. Down through the hands of men who sub-let and re-sub-let, the contract system passes, the pressure varying directly as the distance from the head-contractor increases. Is it any wonder that the weight of the whole system lands ultimately, with an impact, on the backs of the manual workers and the unskilled foreigners of the camps? They are the pawns in the game.

There were men in Ottawa and other Canadian cities who were partners in the contracting and sub-contracting companies on the National Transcontinental, yet they were seldom near the line. The main asset under such conditions was the fact of being an interested partner in a railway contract. It was an unholy sort of absentee business which put the screws on the men lowest down. By continuing in this way to allot contracts along the National Transcontinental, the Railway Commission apparently acquiesced in the methods which so flagrantly reacted on the pay of the navvy.

Just where is the necessity that the head-contractor needs be given such control over labour? Is station-work a veritable sweating system? Do men engaged on railway construction live in unsanitary bunkhouses and noisome shacks along the grade? Is the present medical system associated with such contracts a farce? It is because of pressure exerted directly from the office of the head-contractor. No other large businesses in the country during those ten years could surely have enjoyed such immunity from restraint and supervision as did the big railway contractors and their sub-contractors. On them, apparently, the country had bestowed unlimited powers for greed: For what reason?

Nor does it make matters better to defend the contract system by such remarks as, 'Well, whom shall we get to build these railways if these large contractors are not treated generously? Who else can do it?' Let us see again. Where is the million-dollar plant that must receive adequate returns? Where is the hundred thousand of ready cash required? It would be hard to find. Not uncommonly a railway work of this nature, undertaken with but an indifferent outfit, has been finished with a splendid equipment. The contract may carry itself, for advances are warranted as the work progresses.

As a matter of fact, what does the construction of a three hundred mile stretch of railway mean, when completed, in the matter of remuneration? About as follows:

1 That the head-contractor has made very substantial gains.
2 That of twenty sub-contractors, three out of five would also do well, a small proportion might fail entirely.
3 That salaried men – office officials, foremen, residency staffs, have been fairly paid, and by yearly salaries.
4 That hundreds of train-men, mechanics and skilled workmen, getting union rates and working extremely long hours, have made big pay for short seasons.
5 That a small percentage of station-men have made good money.
6 But that thousands of unskilled workers, including many foreign born, have made little or nothing as real wages, and too often have been housed like brutes.

The whole contract system is top-heavy and lop-sided; it fattens the purses of the fortunate head-contractors – it gives good pickings to the sub-contractors, but it begrudges living conditions and a human wage to the navvy who handles the barrow and shovel. For when we come down to the nub of the matter, how can it be otherwise? Is such a system possessed of nine lives that it cannot be banished? Let us be reproached as a people that these malign practices in railway building have so long continued without any effective regulation.

The National Transcontinental cost the people of Canada $168,000,000: something over $92,000 per mile. This work, some 1,800 miles in length, was let originally to twenty-one contractors. The amount thus expended on this portion of a great national undertaking shows that the Dominion Government was not niggardly in its outlay. But after making due allowance for necessary and heavy expenditures in so many directions, other than for labour, the total shows that the road cost enough, even after the head-contractors and their friends were liberally rewarded, to provide the navvy also with a fair wage. Why did they not always receive it? If railway building in the face of difficulties has been Canada's glory, her chief material contribution toward world progress, the treatment accorded some of the foreign-born navvies, throughout the Dominion, should be our shame.

The outlay on the Grand Trunk Pacific, a piece of work employing men under similar conditions during this same period, has been put at $190,000,000. These two roads comprised about one third of the total outlay on railways in Canada during the third period of railway construction.

But while defects are readily apparent, it is not so easy to point to the remedy. Nor has that been wholly intended by the writer. But in view of the foregoing, two suggestions may be offered here as a part solution for the untoward tendencies inherent in the contract system: a modified form of building by Force Account; replacing the functions of the sub-contractor by enlarging the duties of the men at the different residencies.

1 Force Account system puts the contractors on a percentage basis. Their profits are based on the actual outlay. There is thus no particular incentive for any repression of fair wages.

This method, too, is not without its weakness. It may prove costly if outlays are not carefully guarded, but capable agents can assure proper accounting of all expenditures, and a check be made upon any undue extravagance.

2 Similarly, the sub-contractors themselves might often be replaced by engineers from the residencies. Particularly is this true where station-work is much in vogue. The needed supplies for a ten-mile piece of work could be placed in warehouses at the nearest residency, and the station-man could then deal directly with the engineers. Being assured of their monthly pay the men of the residency will not have the same incentive to squeeze the station-man. The profits of the sub-contractor, at least those made from selling supplies to the men, would thus go largely into increased wages.

Then, too, if the head-contractor is to be curbed locally on the work, it must come from giving increased powers to the resident and district engineers. They are most conversant with actual conditions and should act for the men when exactions are imminent. The able staffs of the head-contractor and his subs, will then encounter men of equal or superior ability, and can recognize in them, men, who under their appointment, are actuated by no desire to harass the campman in his pay.

It is the system not the man that is at fault. The individual contractors, carefree and well-met, while hardly fitted to serve as models for Theban judges, have not personally the desire to coerce; they seem oftener to be actuated by the sheer joy of accomplishment. But the undue control of labour in any form, now as down through the centuries, may lead to callousness. The possession of any field unchallenged has a baneful influence, as brutalizing as the delights of Capua on the soldiers of Hannibal.

The contract system on railway construction may originally have had some distinct advantages. There is still much to be said in its favour, but as pursued in the building of our most recent transcontinentals, it over-reached itself. The substance of this chapter is voiced as an orderly protest against the continuance of the system, at least in unamended form. The basic conditions of work and pay, inherent in the whole method and particularly as exemplified on the National Transcontinental, are not in keeping with the wholesome aspirations of recognized labour in Canada. To perpetuate them is to produce wastes and tundras in our social life.

Chapter 11

Ottawa and the camps

SO FAR, an effort has been made to limn the contract system in its varying aspects. Doubtless before this the reader has asked himself more than once: Is not the railway contractor, in turn, confronted by regulations designed to protect the labour of the navvy?

It is true that the Federal Department of Labour at Ottawa enact fair-wage provisions which prevail on all government undertakings throughout the Dominion. And such clauses were duly embodied in all contracts for the pursuance of work along the National Transcontinental. The usual stipulation was as follows:

All mechanics, labourers or other persons who perform labour for the purpose of the construction of the works hereby contracted for shall be paid such wages as are generally accepted as current for competent workmen in the district in which the work is being per- formed, and, if there is no current rate in such district, then a fair and reasonable rate, and, in the event of a dispute arising as to what is the current or a fair and reasonable rate, it shall be determined by the Commissioners, whose decision shall be final.

Any contractor obtaining a portion of the new road subscribed to this. It was broad and, at the time, a step in advance which betokened a real desire on the part of the Dominion Government to ensure fair consideration for the navvy, a credit to the foresight and thought of the Labour Department at Ottawa. But opportunity has already been afforded, in the foregoing chapters, properly to estimate the probable effect of such a fair-wage clause. So far as it affected manual workers in distant camps, it was circumscribed in operation and frequently valueless.

Fine words will not butter parsnips. Under actual conditions of camp life there is little in common between a two-dollar wage for manual labour paid at the front and an equal amount credited for similar work at an isolated camp. The two modes of work are hardly comparable; when the heavy charges for van goods are met, when time is lost through wet weather, and when all the usual camp set-backs are provided for, it is an impossibility for even one man in five, working by the day, to make a fair monthly wage. Further, there are few men who engage in station-work that make much beyond a fair wage.

During the building of the later transcontinentals, representatives of the Department of Labour at Ottawa were occasionally deputed to investigate wage conditions in the camps of Canada. How then does one account for the findings which these officers so frequently made? In part answer, the following paragraphs may not be out of place.

The information which reaches the authorities at Ottawa comes too much from men connected with the residencies, as well as from the head-company and the sub-contractors themselves. The Labour Department has not kept its ear to the ground, at least so far as the inmates of the camp bunkhouses are concerned. Too much information is obtained from favoured sources. Able and thinking men are in the residencies, but there is as little contact between the group of buildings there on the hill and the bunkhouses down on the works as between the master of a plantation and his people of the slave quarters in ante-bellum days. Between the two there is a great gulf fixed. Campmen have suffered too frequently from the aloofness of fair-wage officers.

A company having a large federal contract has always a representative close to Ottawa. This ensures a hearing, and is a local advantage with the Department of Labour. When information is desired on some disputed wage matter the company's side can always be ably presented, but on the other hand, what of the bunkhouse inmates on the distant work? Many of these may feel they are not receiving justice in the matter of their pay, they may suffer from misrepresentation and overcharges but they are seldom heard directly. It is also true that in most cases their accounts may be small and to fight means time and individual loss. The game is not worth the candle — instead of making a fuss over a few dollars, they let the matter drop. Drink, procured locally, and a few days of carousal in the frontier town soon leaves such men penniless and fit for nothing but construction again at some other camp on the line. Of such small happenings, which in the aggregate are vital, the Department of Labour hears little.

Let us look now, from the point of view of the navvy, at the methods sometimes adopted by the Department of Labour, when investigating wage conditions in isolated camps on railway construction during the building of the transcontinentals.

A report is made to Ottawa of unfair conditions of pay on a distant piece of construction, and a fair-wage officer is sent to look into the matter. He travels the line ahead of the steel by the office route and the relays of comfortable residencies. Finally he reaches camp and due investigation is made.

The books of the company at the head office and at the different grade camps are frankly and freely thrown open to inspection. Five things are always plain:

(a) That the men are being paid at the rate of $1.75 a day and up.
(b) That board is reasonable.
(c) That there is a mail service.
(d) That big prices for 'van' goods seem justified by the freight haul.
(e) That a medical system is provided.

Many other things which on paper look well are pointed out. The pay, in proportion to current rates, is seemingly reasonable and even a little higher than the usual pay at the front. Yet with all these allowances the figures misrepresent the actual working of the system in its various details. Such investigatios may be honest, thorough, even painstaking, but they are formal and not practical. They are potent only at short range. When a fair-wage officer wants to learn the working-out of construction wages for unskilled workers he will not obtain it living with the contractor's officials, traveling from residency to residency, and only occasionally dropping in on the men in the bunkhouse to ask them to register with him any protests they may desire.

Let a fair-wage officer, say in a camp thirty-eight miles from the end of the steel, go to the bunkhouses at noon and ask the inmates if they have any complaints to make. You say: 'This is the time for the men to act.' Well, it is, and it is not!

There may be a dozen men in that camp short in their last pay-check for varying amounts. One may claim dollars still due according to the representations made to him by the employment agent of the company, and yet this same man may register no complaint with the fair-wage officer. That does not mean, however, that no wrong exists. There are several reasons why no formal protest will be made. Here are a few:

(a) Many in that bunkhouse will be foreigners, mistrustful or afraid of any official. They little understand the purpose of the visit of the fair-wage officer. Further, they get the tip from the "straw-boss," usually one of their own tongue, that the man who squeals goes out, and goes quickly, too. They know what that means.

(b) There are English-speaking men who, while confident they have been outfigured, will not compalin; the individual amount may not be large, and there is little gained by grouching in camp.

(c) The company always holds the trump cards. Let a man kick, they know it at once. That man is let out. All the suspended charges are raked up. He will be charged fifty or seventy-five cents for meals, and fifty cents to a dollar for every night he sleeps in the company's bunkhouse. Just then may be a rainy week. Where else is there shelter within a hundred miles, other than in the company's camps? There is little warmth on inland lakes! Why court the chill of the muskeg? A bird in the hand is worth two in the bush! He'll stay where he is, till he gets ready to come out.

Then, too, if the man 'takes his time' at the office he is not yet clear of the company. The man going out under such circumstances is not favoured in any way. His reputation will precede him down the grade, from camp to camp, by tree-phone or the quicker method of moccasin-news. In the two days which it takes him to reach the steel he will suffer pressure from the company at every turn. He may be forbidden the company's ferry to cross the river, or at least charged a dollar for the favour. His meals will be served him in passing only at enhanced rates. Before he reaches the frontier hamlet much of his stake is gone. To quit a camp on a distant piece of work is not like walking out of a factory door with work at hand in the next block. It is much better to have the goodwill of the company, and the campman knows it. Conditions of pay must be judged from actual circumstances, not by comparison.

But is it fair, because men so placed make no ready complaint to the fair-wage officer, to report that such causes do not exist? Not on the back of some navvy or foreign-born illiterate should be placed the onus of showing up the wrongs so well-entrenched. Strong-armed and firm-purposed they may be, but to essay such a task under the particular circumstances of their work is not always easy.

If a fair-wage officer from Ottawa wishes to know how the wage system really works for the navvy there is only one trustworthy way: go to a distant grade camp in April before the tote roads break up, don overalls and a heavy shirt, engage as an unskilled labourer at $1.75 a day with board at $4.60 per week; be isolated there by impassable grades for two months following the break-up, lose whole

days and pay board through the wet weather, house in camps the
tar-paper roofs of which drip wet, and sleep under blankets so lousy
it is impossible to keep clean; work on through the fly season with
its heats, dig in long rubber boots the moving gumbo, or shovel
concrete on the sweat-board; meanwhile purchasing the needed
supplies of wearing apparel at camp prices, getting the mail whenever
the convenience of the service warrants it and the company permits
it, and, then, find that the resulting pay-checks, when all deductions
have been made, run like this:

April	$ 7.10
May	16.40
June (much wet weather)	12.20
July (worked overtime)	26.00

The experience of four months so spent will hang upon his mind
like the mist upon the waters. It will impress on him as long as he
lives the injustice of the statement that men are being paid $1.75 a
day, with but a moderate charge being made for board. Only then is
it fully realized that there is a discrepancy somewhere between the
rate of pay reported to Ottawa and the actual wage received by the
navvy. Such a fair-wage officer will be glad sometime in early
September to cash his last time-check at a good discount and shake
the dust of the camp from off his feet; his stake further depleted for
meals en route, ferrying across rivers, waits, maybe of days, for a
supply train, until he reaches the nearest frontier town some two
hundred miles away. How much will he have left, think you, for his
summer's work? Will he be in a position to report to his department
fuller details concerning the pay of the navvy? Yes, and that same
fair-wage officer will be blessed of the gods if, during his months at
camp, he did not meet with an accident, or lose time in sickness. Will
he call the pittance which is finally salvaged from the conditions of
his hire a fair wage? Would you like to give your industry for it?
Marry, kind sir, and one must be over-stupid to suppose it!

It is small wonder that at times three-quarters of all unskilled
workers on whole stretches of the National Transcontinental were
foreigners and largely of Slav origin. So-called white labourers were
scared off the grade; they had burned their fingers once, that was
enough!

There was talk in 1912 of bringing five thousand Scotchmen to navvy on an uncompleted section of the new transcontinental. What a pity they had not come! Inside of three months there would have been such an outcry as to the nature of conditions on construction that the Labour Department at Ottawa would have been roused from its continued lethargy in the matter.

There is but little danger that Scotsmen would fill the bill. Even as manual workers they will not become serfs to any set of sub-contractors. As for the Englishman, he is not wanted at all. He is such a stickler, always, on his personal rights, even far out in a grade camp, that he worries the life out of the old-time foreman, who designates him a 'cockney' and is glad to let him go. The Scandinavians gravitate to the heavier rock work. The native-born Canadians in grade camps man the posts at clerical work. So that the heavy mucking and digging falls largely on the foreign-born, variously designated as Poles, Magyars, Bulgarians, Russians, Croatians, Serbs and Lithuanians. Even Turks and Spaniards may be brought to Canada as navvies. The contractors find from experience that there is less friction in employing the non-English-speaking workers. They are easier to handle.

It is on just this polyglot mass of foreign-born navvies that the pressure is most exerted. In their ignorance of the country they are least able to resist. Usually they are under the influence of some wily leader amongst them who, while curvetting with the contractors, jockeys the men of his own race. Such men complain little. They are used to the iron heel in other forms, and have not yet become mistrustful of conditions in a new land.

Ottawa concerned itself too little with the wage conditions of the bunkhouse man. During a ten-year period marked by huge Federal undertakings in railway building, not enough thought was given to the earnings of the individual navvy. Incidents already mentioned herein have indicated clearly enough that there was need.

The irony of it! Once in a while, from camps on the National Transcontinental, or its associated work, the Grand Trunk Pacific, murmurs were heard as far as Ottawa. There was a shuffling for a moment from one foot to the other, an official inquiry was formally announced, but the findings did not much disturb conditions as they were. A report was made, not unduly harsh on the company, and quietness again settled down on a system which with its sub-letting and petty charges remained unhampered, secure in the possession of one whole field of labour in Canada.

One who says otherwise does not know the facts, at least as they pertain to the occupant in the bunkhouse. Men, forced by necessity to go to the camps as day-labourers, who have undergone the system and who know the working of it in all its exacting force, are the best able to judge. Other investigations will be superficial and misleading, even though published as official findings in the columns of the Labour Gazette.

During this third period of railway building men, as individuals, complained to local magistrates of wage conditions, whole station-groups at times stated their grievances, even the Consular Agents of two foreign governments more than once drew the attention of the Labour Department at Ottawa to injustices reported to them by their countrymen.

And the men of a foreign consulate do not usually act in haste. One such official, however, in 1912 expressed himself to the present writer as follows: 'With experience as a Consul for my government covering many years, in Europe, and in South America, as well as in this Dominion, I know of no other country where the rights of workmen have been so flagrantly abused as on railway construction in Canada.' Surely we as a people boastful of material results, have overlooked the existing conditions of work and pay for the navvy, and other workers in the isolated camps throughout the Dominion.

As the wage system actually worked out for the navvy on the National Transcontinental, apart from losing his personal liberty, a man would have been more comfortable, less molested with flies and mosquitoes, would have had a real bed and much better sanitary surroundings if, instead of going for six months to railway camps, he had gone to Kingston Penitentiary. He would have had, too, nearly as much money at the end of the term. Certain it is, he would not have wrought as hard as did some of the navvies on construction. The prisoners who comprised the convict gangs then maintained by the province of Ontario, on the Porcupine Road between Matheson and Night Hawk Lake, were better housed, had shorter hours, and were as well fed as were the navvies who builded the grade in the Abitibi country.

During these many years the Province of Ontario has pointed with pride to her prison reform. Her newly-constructed jail farms have buildings which are models in their arrangements. Nor is the welfare of the inmate overlooked in the matter of lighting, heating, running water, and with space allotted for a table and a mattressed cot. The hours of labour are not excessive, and deep-toned bells toll out across the fields the call to meals. Time has only accentuated these tendencies until music and movies, baseball and even drama, may be had in well-appointed prisons. The parole system of the Dominion exteds a helping hand to those who have erred; so much is done that such men may go out strong to confront anew the world – and all this need not be disparaged. But what care, apparently, is exercised to make good citizens of men, not always mentally deficient, but oftener miscreants, who in their inordinate desire for sudden gain and the hope for an indolent life have lightly tossed asisde their obligations to society! What provision is made to protect the health of men in mind and body who least deserve it!

Yet for years a much more numerous class, not criminals but industrious workers, in the grade camps and shacks on construction, were treated precariously and herded unhealthily in filthy shacks. They, too, were the making of citizens, foreign-born though they were in many cases. Their industry deserved better of any people – protect and hedge and guard the footsteps of some who should receive the lash and ignore the others, leaving them to suffer from the mercenary practices of the line! The treatment accorded to the campman through many years shadowed the whole construction of our latest transcontinentals.

Meanwhile during this same period there had emanated from Ottawa labour legislation for the settling of industrial disputes that had commanded the attention of leaders in other lands. Then how explain that toward the work of the navvy along the National Transcontinental and its due remuneration, the Federal Department of Labour continued strangely inattentive. In this matter it slept the sleep of Vergor there at the Foulon – sloth, and the post unguarded, while the wage returns due to seasonal workers were flagrantly purloined.

Chapter 12

The bunkhouse man and public opinion

WHAT, then, are the reasons for the general apathy which prevails toward these conditions of work? Why is not more heard of the circumstances which surround the employment of campmen? Many probable explanations can be given. Here are a few of them.

It is always in the distant camps, thirty, forty and sixty miles from the steel, that things are worst for the campman and accommodation is crudest. The isolation, combined with the fact that the average grade camp is often temporary, tends to render futile any complaints which may arise as to local camp conditions of work and pay.

The English-speaking men who, under more normal circumstances, would soon make known the conditions which in certain cases are tantamount almost to oppression, are usually themselves a part of the system. They are the foremen, the straw-bosses and other minor officials of the head-company or the sub-contractor. Such men are well paid and are generally hired by the month, with board included; they lose no time for wet weather or other delays and are satisfied. Their positions usually align them with the company rather than with the men they are handling; consequently, no complaint will come from them.

Those campmen most insistent of their rights, in fact, the most aggressive in every way among the frontier workers, are the English-speaking men of the gravel pits – the train-men and the employees of the machine shops. These men are paid by the hour; as firemen, conductors, steam-shovel men and gasoline operators, they invariably draw the highest union rates paid. By working very long hours, seldom under sixteen, and with increased rates for overtime, these men usually make good pay, even though their season lasts but a few months.

The conditions of living with them, too, are fairly comfortable. Their bunkhouses are better built and of lumber; they insist on a good cook and the chuck is the best, being varied with green vegetables and even fruits in season. There is, also, a regular mail service and the married men among them are never entirely without news from home. So they, too, considering frontier conditions, are well satisfied, at least for the time being. But, transfer the seventy or a hundred English-speaking men of a gravel pit to some grade camp fifty miles beyond, where, for five months, they will be forced to undergo the conditions usually prevailing there; would they long remain passive?

It is the frontier town at the end of the steel which has the best chance of judging the conditions of things out on the line, for it is in daily contact with some phase of its working. A construction town has many of the impulses of older places – a school, some rival and struggling churches, a police force of one or two, occasionally a weekly paper, and an embryo community life of merchants, bankers and professional men, with perhaps a score of resident families. Surely, here one would expect that some action would be taken toward seeing uniform justice to men on the line. But it is seldom so: the frontier town is practically muzzled. Too often it owes its very existence to the money being spent by some big company in its midst.

The greater number of small merchants who make up the business life of a frontier town have gone in with health, hope and confidence as their chief assets. They usually start with small stocks and grow up with the town. They are a compliant class. Business is their first aim. There is seldom any farming community to rely on as yet. So, directly or indirectly, the merchant, too, is dependent on the money spent on the line. It is not in his interests to ostracize trade by criticizing any methods of the contractors or their subs. His business sense requires no prod.

The weekly paper in new towns is similarly circumstanced. It has but a meagre circulation and struggles hard to get on its feet. The printery depends largely on job work, much of which comes from the offices of the builders of the road. How, then, can it speak out? Why kill the goose that lays the golden egg?

The lawyer found in a small construction hamlet has two alternatives: he can work with the big interests, or he can, in turn, handle the petty cases of complaint for the workers against the company. The former is the more lucrative course and is generally adopted. Workers with claims for wages are often compelled to enter action through a lawyer at a city hundreds of miles distant, for the local lawyer finds it impossible to handle them and retain, at the same time, the more remunerative local business of the company.

Nor need too much be expected from the local police. They seldom show any initiative in such matters. In new towns whether near mines, on railway construction, or in other frontier places, the local police do not rise higher than the public life about them. They are not eager to interfere in any way with the big company upon whom in the end the very existence of the place depends.

Most new towns, in the exuberance of their rapid growth, will have a pretentious Board of Trade. Such bodies, however, are staunch allies of the existing conditions. It is only when a frontier town attains considerable size, and where the people are not so dependent, that the Board of Trade will speak out unequivocally as to conditions of work and pay in nearby camps. In the smaller places such bodies are moribund.

Magistrates themselves become calloused. There are magistrates and near-magistrates; the class of men who act as magistrates in new towns and in districts pervaded with camp activities do not always receive their appointments because of fitness or particular capacity for the work. Many pliant men have been made magistrates in frontier towns – men so broad that they are 'good heads' with all that that implies in dereliction of duty. Some have received appointments in hamlets on construction who, but a few weeks previously, had openly been accounted law-breakers. What, then, can be their attitude in appraising other delinquents?

But there have been magistrates in construction towns not made of just such stuff. They have endeavoured to deal fairly not only with the company but with the campman as well, whether foreign-born or English-speaking. But does it pay? In due time the word is passed that such an official is no good for the town; that he is a knocker; that business will go elsewhere – and soon he has the ill-will of every blind-pigger and blackguard in the place. That, usually, such a man can face; but when his wife is insulted and his children are molested – it takes more to stand that! Gradually the capable and conscientious magistrate is weeded out and replaced by a man of another type who does not look too closely, so long as there is plenty of activity and the quick-budding hamlet continues to boom.

After counting up eight or ten new towns which sprang to life in different parts of the Dominion along construction during the third period of railway activity, and, having in mind the magistrate in each, during the formative period, in how many cases could such an appointee be counted on to insure aggressive action when needful to protect the bunkhouse man in the matter of his pay? Probably not in two cases!

Invariably the attitude is this: the company means more to the town than the individual disgruntled over his wages, so any action is discouraged. If a man has a grievance, he is advised to wait around a day or two; meanwhile the company will be sounded unofficially. Finally the campman, tired of losing time and with the uncertainty of further delay, will accept a settlement, and there the matter drops. The contest is too unequal. As the bunkhouse man puts it: 'You might as well sue the devil and hold the court in hell.'

The question naturally arises in this place: How do the Churches minister to the needs of men on frontier works? It should be pointed out in answer, that the Church in all such places is confronted with problems peculiar to the hinterland. Foremost among these are the isolation and the transitory nature of most camps, coupled with the migratory habits of the men themselves. Yet, in the face of these obstacles, the Churches have been slow to display any adaptiveness to meet the peculiar needs. Methods and organization effective enough in a settled community do not best meet the needs of men socially segregated by the very nature of their employment.

The Church has never properly appraised the campman. Even until very recent years a whole hinterland is placed under one superintendent. He is expected to cover an area bigger than France and Germany put together. While the leaders so chosen are zealous men, they can reach each point of their immense field only once in many months, perhaps a year and longer. At that, they stop at the fringe of things, somewhere near the rail-head. Extended duties seldom permit the higher church officials to visit isolated camps. If they go at all, they are well received and comfortably housed at the well-appointed residencies. They see little of the campman at work, and know still less of his actual living conditions; they do not dwell with the men in the bunkhouse.

But there are always younger assistants located by the Church among camps on railway construction. Clean, eager, hopeful, they are persevering in their tasks. They mingle frequently with the navvy at his work and short services are held, often in the cookery, or occasionally in the bunkhouse. These ministrants lack, however, continuous contact with the worker in the bunkhouse.

Then, too, the Churches continue to send each year among frontier workers, young and immature students. While they may be brilliant in the class-room, they lack qualities which win men in camps. Men who have rubbed up against the raw realities, whose judgments have slowly matured under obstacles often encountered and frequent reverses, who, with the passing of years, have grubbed unaided for the fundamentals of life are not easily reached by boy-students. Send no ignoramus to men on the frontier. The men in such places call to the Church for a picked man, professor it may be, or leader with popular gifts, but first and foremost he must measure to full stature as a man; for the sturdy inmate of the bunkhouse will pay obeisance in his soul only to equals.

There is surely another oversight on the part of the Church in its efforts to reach campmen. Seldom is the successful student missionary returned to the same field. It is implied that by varying his summer activities he will acquire a broader knowledge of men and their needs. One result is a succession each year of new and untried students as missioners for the Church among the camps. The season for any one of these, all too short as it is, draws to a close just when he is beginning to grasp some of the real needs of the frontier workers. It is possible, too, at times, that in his enthusiasm the young student himself is more concerned about his future work which he deems to be somewhere in Cathay rather than with the men among whom he dwells: Though when did yet a saint arise who was not first a patriot. Too often he appears to be in leash and only bides the time for his return to the city and to college life. This the worker is not slow to discern. He will adhere to the churchman whose interest in him does not vanish with the passing of the few short months of a vacation.

But the Church is not laggard. It desires to reach the campman as well as other workers. Real co-operation with the former, however, seems to be lacking. There is need of more genuine accord between its representatives and the bunkhouse. Are its leaders properly cognizant of the importance of camps in Canada? If the Church would escape the mistrust and dislike current among such seasonal workers, let it show a new and deeper concern for the conditions which environ their living and places of work.

The press of Canada, including also the magazines and the weeklies, has always been liberal in giving publicity to frontier activities. For a whole generation the Canadian Northland has been made the protegé of the big dailies domiciled in the larger centres of the Dominion. Prolific in possibilities, the development of the new lands has always been encouraged, and, at times, special writers, alert and colorful, are employed to detail in column the various undertakings which bespeak material progress in those parts.

Along with the other frontier activities, railway building during a decade received a pre-eminent place among the specially illustrated articles. But the different writers invariably set forth to their readers the material side of the accomplishments, and in language which responded to the thrill of the whole undertaking. They made but little mention of the actual conditions of work and pay among the dwellers in the bunkhouse. This oversight can be accounted for in the fact that writers, for whatever journal, in search of material on a big work are always themselves the guests of the company, or are housed conveniently at residencies. And where else under the circumstances would one expect them to reside?

That the press of Canada did not scan closely the camp conditions along the National Transcontinental Railway may be accounted for in another way. As has already been indicated, all eastern Canada was for a decade obsessed with the sudden mineral development. The news of remarkable silver finds at Cobalt were further accentuated for years by the tidings of successive discoveries in the different gold fields in adjacent regions. The mining fever found a reciprocal chord in the hearts of the people. Within a few years the capitalization of new mining companies exceeded one billion and a half of dollars. The whole country was flooded with stock, all of it implying a cross-trail to sudden wealth. The press of the country followed the lure. The columns of the papers reflected the glimmer of gilded certificates, and the camps which in the meantime had largely been manned with foreign-born workers, lagged perceptibly in the background.

To sum up: the new town on the frontier work is preoccupied and dependent; the local business men are jealous of losing any advantage of trade; the public-spirited professional men are few in number while the minor officials of all such new places are too often indifferent; the church is out of touch in any real way with the inmate of the bunkhouse, while the outside press, enamoured of the bigger things, remains uninformed, all of which lulls the public and serves to tether the labourers in such places to the existing conditions of work and pay. Being, too, but a relatively small part of the whole field of labour, the work of men in isolated camps does not loom large in the public eye, and it is apt to be overlooked. The fact, also, that such a large proportion of the men engaged on frontier works are of foreign-born extraction plays no inconsiderable part in the apparent neglect of the bunkhouse man in Canada.

Chapter 13

The challenge of the migratory workers

TO ORGANIZED LABOUR

Having in mind some impressions gleaned from the preceding chapters, may we not ask: What have organized labour and its leaders been doing for the navvy and those men employed on seasonal works? And further: Why were the recognized leaders of union labour in Canada so long indifferent to the wage conditions of the navvy on the National Transcontinental? Only in the closing years of the period, so far, at least, as the writer has been able to discover, was any official action taken by them in an effort to protect the interests of the workers in the camps.

It may be recalled, too, that organized labour in Canada, during those same years, was by no means inactive in other fields. Men among them were vocable enough in the cities and larger industrial centres. They interested themselves in education and other measures for the betterment of the workers: evening classes were multiplied, technical schools were inaugurated that have since increased in mighty strides, compensation laws were enacted in the different provinces, and other practical results achieved, which in themselves were a direct recognition of the demands of organized labour, and most of these have since proven their worth.

But, meanwhile, organized labour has never convinced the man in the bunkhouse that it is so valiant in its fight for the consideration of the labourer on frontier works. The bushman has had some gesture of sympathy but the navvy is overlooked entirely. Is Labour not concerned about camps, wherein men engage in tasks that require of each strong personal assets? Is this apparent neglect a penalty for broadbacked men, who, in their toil strive largely as individualists? This oversight is serious. It lets down the bars for more radical movements which secure a foothold among the unorganized workers in the isolated work-groups of the frontier.

While in cities organized labour can man its walls with plenty of sentinels, in camps and frontier works the opposite prevails. There, the rights of workers may frequently be infringed. On all stretches of new railway construction, the building of culverts and the draining of muskegs are closely scrutinized; the piles that enter into the building of trestles are carefully inspected by officials on the job, but on the human side the conditions of work and wage may be overlooked.

Solitude fosters the independence of a man's nature, but to be continually ignored and deprived of healthy leadership is but to add dignity to the more virulent. The migratory workers of the camps and the frontier, shifting, homeless and womanless, come in contact with the ugliest features of human hire and pay. It is not desired simply that all such men be assured fair pay, but that they have more wisdom to govern the use of their wages. In this they claim the guidance and intelligent sympathy of the leaders of the better organized and more successful labour. Given this, and with fair conditions of employment, they would become a bulwark rather than an enemy of ordered government.

It is uncanny how men at work in distant camps seem to sense accurately the prevailing business conditions of the world outside. It is an anomaly that when times are good there is restlessness among campmen and a bold response to anything that disturbs. They grumble at all and sundry things, their petulance most displayed in matters of petty detail. But, on the other hand, when times are bad they passively sit tight, seeking only to hold the ground already occupied. The demagogue gets little encouragement then. The birds of the air pick the seeds from beaten paths. The agitator can save his talk. The wise man, even of the camp, is not swayed by every wind that blows across the Areopagus.

The efforts of extremists to fashion into dependable shape the seasonal workers in camps have been but partially successful. Any results so far attained have flourished largely on promises. Nevertheless, the ensuing state of mind, attendant upon disappointment, following a settlement for work as a station-man, to mention only one possible source of irritation, makes fallow ground for discontent. True, the result may not at once be apparent, but the aftermath is cumulative.

While I.W.W. was little in evidence in work-groups along the National Transcontinental, yet its counterpart, the One Big Union, which a few years later reared its head in the mines and logging camps of Western Canada, and hissed its venom in the streets of Winnipeg, in June, 1919, was a direct product in part of the neglect of the navvy and other workers in the camps of Canada. It was an echo in the lives of men whose hearts were first made bitter by the slipshod methods of pay meted out to them for work in frontier places. Men, galled under such servitude, had shown through years much patience.

Too often the workers in camps are themselves to blame. Casuals by the very nature of their tasks, they remain untethered. Frequent

shifting is their bane. The small-sized railway extra gangs on the
North Shore, even at the present time, will frequently show a
turnover of one hundred and sixty men in three months, to maintain
a working average of twenty-five. While even large gangs, located in
settled parts of the country, have shown eighteen hundred workers
on the roll during a season lasting five months, to hold a working
force of less than two hundred men. And here a more extreme case
may be mentioned, one perhaps unusual, where in little over a
month in the mid-summer of 1922, on a branch piece of railway
construction located in the hinterland, seven hundred and eighty
men went in on the work and six hundred and thirty came out — the
gangs employed being decimated every few succeeding days.

Nor should the bunkhouse man be wholly blamed for the
migratory tendencies that infect his pursuits. There are, too,
frequently work conditions that unprop, while the fluctuating
nature of much frontier work makes of the campman a transient at
his tasks. Neither are such men prone to rely on somebody
else — self-reliance with all such is a prime asset.

Thus the cohesion which permits united action is hard to obtain.
There is consequent disintegration and weakened lines, when rigid
ranks would better hold what had been won. All of which makes
towardly these workers of the camps.

These very qualities, however, of shifting and unrest so inherent
in seasonal workers, need not prove a permanent barrier to
recognition by labour in some form. The right of the navvy and
other frontier workers to organize is fundamental. It is even
necessary. To be able to negotiate with the employer in an effective
manner is just as essential to the campman at some isolated work as
it is to the machine man in the mill of a factory town. If conditions
of work and pay in camps do preclude effective organization, all the
greater is the need for a tangible recognition from organized labour
in some other form.

This is a challenge to leaders whose concern is for the protection
of workers. Has organized labour in respect to men in camps lived up
to its opportunities? Or is its chiefest concern bounded largely by
the horizon of the local unions? To the occupant of the bunkhouse,
it lends the impression that its efforts are confined wholly to the
sacred groves in urban places where it rears its many temples.

Leaders of organized labour could be better informed of work
conditions in isolated places. To many of them the frontier camp,

employing often a large force of men, is a closed book. Representatives of labour, duly accredited, should require freer access to all isolated works, for at times a whole plant may be forbidden one whom the company mistrusts. This is a detriment to the campman. He is unvoiced. Strange things happen to labour under such conditions. More is not heard of them, because the man of the bunkhouse is not naturally querulous. He will grin and bear, but inwardly resolve at the same time that there will be two moons in the sky when he is caught in such meshes again. But, with the coming out and the relaxation, his modest stake is spent before he leaves the frontier town, so he drifts back again to the camps. That class of worker looms large on all seasonal works. They are fit material for the supervision and counsel of a reliable representative of organized labour.

The interests of any large company operating camps are usually well protected. Take the case even of a railway sub-contractor: when deemed expedient, he hires an engineer, duly qualified and at a good salary, to protect him in the matter of measurements or other possible disagreements arising with the residency staff.

But what in turn is there to check the same sub-contractor in his dealings with the men on his work? They are few, if any. With the exceptions of the Scandinavians and some of the English-speaking groups, few of the campmen are capable of measuring competently their own work.

All frontier works give rise to exceptional placements in labour. Such camps frequently are situated beyond the effective jurisdiction of regularly appointed law-officials. Disputes regarding phases of work and pay often arise in far-out places, which require immediate decisions. Any delay with perhaps a subsequent tramp back over the trail, or down the lake by canoe to the nearest magistrate, is always at the expense of the worker himself. This simply means that disputes of any kind are a disadvantage to the campman. Neither, on the other hand, does the bunkhouse man consider the battle fairly drawn when he must remain on the work and confront lone-handed the decision of the company or its agents.

Give to organized labour a representative or 'observer' on all undertakings that employ large numbers of men in isolated or unorganized parts; a man of tact, capable as a district engineer and paid equally as well. His remuneration could be shared by the Central Trades and Labour Congress, the province in which the work is located, and the Dominion. Such a man would be in place wherever one thousand men are employed or on every hundred miles of railway construction. There need be no friction with the company when the right man is appointed, and in this way a measure of security would be provided for labour, even among men who are calloused as to the necessity for being organized in the regular way.

These observers could, upon request, give their services toward settling locally a dispute pertaining to some aspect of work and pay. Organized labour represented in this way by a competent man who is resident on the works will do more to protect the pay of the navvy on a hundred-mile piece of work than the occasional visit of a fair-wage officer, who, capable as he may be, makes a casual visit to investigate and then hastens out again.

There is another way in which organized labour can protect the interests of campmen: a company employing bunkhouse men may fail on one piece of work, but later undertake another contract, with the further opportunity to recoup themselves. This is sometimes accomplished in spite of the fact that the men who wrought for them on the former work were unfairly remunerated. The second contract should carry with it the wage obligations of the former. In view of this, leaders of labour, with their larger facilities to appraise a situation, might properly countenance a rating of employers of camp labour – Good, Fair, or Indifferent, according to the proved worth of a firm in handling men in frontier places.

Similarly, if a company, or a contractor – and they are many – has earned a good reputation by honourable dealings with its men in camps, it can receive at the hand of organized labour a favourable rating. Thus, not only would the financial standing of a company be listed with Bradstreets, but the proved capacity of the same firm for handling men on frontier works would also be known at the official employment bureaux.

Nor need this be a black list. It is a yardstick by which the bunkhouse worker may measure employment value in particular camps.

One other phase of employment in camps may be mentioned here. On a piece of construction such as the National Trans-continental, extending over great stretches of sparsely-settled land, frontier operations frequently become extra-provincial. The navvy, then, at his tasks, presents a problem that may be wide as the whole country. On all such undertakings the campmen might well be placed directly under the supervision of the Federal Department of Labour. When oversight is limited to action which varies respectively with the different provincial governments, the bunkhouse man will suffer in consequence.

For the challenge of the migratory worker is direct. It is an appeal to the best in organized labour. It has increased, also, with the enlarged activities that mark the present period of frontier development in Canada.

TO THE UNIVERSITY

The challenge of the camps comes also to the universities of Canada. What direct benefits do the men in the bunkhouses derive from public funds bestowed in generous sums on large centralized colleges? Does the campman enthuse as he reads of the donation of a noble building devoted to art and to recreation, facing some university campus, or the erection in stone of well-appointed dormitories for favoured students, who in their lives have already been nursed for years in preparatory schools, while he, performing a much-needed and essential work, is housed within the walls of a camp often under conditions of squalour and filth. By the average campman the name university is disliked almost as much as the word capitalist; too long it has designated a thing apart.

Each year an increasing proportion of the public revenues of the different provinces of Canada is expended on outlays in education which in the end benefit most the commercial and highly-paid professional classes. While it is well that we have splendid faculties of medicine, science, and commerce, are ceramics, helium gas, or West Indian trade, important as they are, to be of sole concern while the workers of the camps, employed in the primal occupations of the hinterland, are denied at their tasks the opportunity to acquire even the barest essentials of an education. Between these two extremes a gap exists which has never been adequately bridged.

Unfortunately, for the good of the student himself and the Dominion at large, our systems of education in some phases have still a mediaeval tinge – obsolete as the culverin. We educate for the so-called learned professions. The product of the university still draws away at a tangent from direct contact with the worker as such. Can we make education more realizable by closer association with the common experiences of life? The class-room is but the ante-hall of the wider and more strenuous world. Give the man of books more frequent contact with manual labour other than by the gloved hand.

Education in the Canadian universities has been distorted. It was started in the first place end-ways-to. Throughout a whole century, opportunity was had in this land to fashion an unique system of higher education, one best fitted to the needs of a peculiar situation. Here was a people with a sparse and poor population confronted with the task of subduing half a continent, a domain at once rough and forbidding, bald and austere, and yet withal rich in potentialities. What other young country similarly circumstanced had such a heritage of rocks and woods and seas? But guarded meanwhile by a climate of stern untempered moods; great rains, and summer heats alternating with months of passing cold. Here were the secrets of a vast silent land to be unraveled. To combat successfully these obstacles of whatever kind was, from the first, the real duty of advanced education in the Dominion.

Yet, in face of this unusual opportunity for original and constructive methods, higher learning during the formative period of educational life throughout the provinces was shaped and fashioned on what had gone before. Canada but continued here in the Dominion the higher schooling of old France, of Scotland, and even of world-famed centres such as Oxford. A new land with problems of education immediate and pressing, its polestar unsighted, became in such matters but an imitator of the past; a young giant, uncouth perhaps, but with pristine strength and powers, seeking to duplicate the age-old habits and cloistered knowledge of Pavia and Louvain.

Higher education in Canada has long been in leash. The universities based on such foundations are exotic and but ill-adjusted to meet the needs at hand. They may even render disservice to the pioneer. For, chained to the fear of want of success in untried paths, they have failed to acknowledge the horizon of the Dominion.

The practice, also, early begun, of looking to the home countries for academic leaders has been but accentuated with later generations. Scholarship as such means much, but it may prove costly to a young country if it be accompanied by a lack of concern for the varying needs of Canada as a people. Can we expect a Principal Grant, purposeful in his patriotism, and imbued with a knowledge of

Canada directly acquired in the outer places, among the men of learning, coming to us from abroad, who had as lief serve in Natal, or Australia, if not in a state university of the neighbouring republic? Continuing numbers of these men do not broaden the outlook of universities in the Dominion with the deeper interest in problems, distinctly Canadian.

Higher education, as at present pursued in Canada, is out of proportion to the material progress of the Dominion. It lacks as a sustaining factor the necessary material development that should pervade the people as a whole. The universities of the New England States, while of slow growth, were the natural accompaniment of a period marked by hard-fisted efforts among the great body of the people themselves. For one hundred years and more when the opening-up of a vast interior domain provided business adventure for generations of traders, shipping, too, whether to the North Pacific, to the Indies, or Ceylon was at a premium. The result was the gradual accumulation of great wealth and social conditions in which the college did not get ahead of the requirements.

The Canadian seats of learning have endeavoured to bridge this very necessary interval in a young land's growth by the steady accretion of college buildings in favoured places, built largely by governmental assistance. The result is a university system that, while flattering perhaps in several aspects, is disproportionate to our needs and is injurious, also, as a real factor in denuding the under-developed towns and villages and country-sides to place youths in professional careers.

One marked tendency, in consequence, is to evolve graduates whose professional training best fits them for service elsewhere. Many, specially trained, and often at public expense, eschew, for one reason or another, the obligations thus incurred, and follow eagerly the runway that ends somewhere at the border. Thus the postern is opened as an exit for the educated among the native-born, their places taken often by new arrivals of foreign extraction. The Dominion suffers from this unceasing exodus of men educated at its universities. Should one, under the circumstances, even for professional success, make of himself an alien to his own land? In the face of our resources undeveloped, any university man with a four-year period of service in the Dominion unperformed, or a cash remuneration made for special training obtained, should be ashamed to leave

Canada until there are thirty million people north of the Lakes. Let us not boast of the great men we send out of Canada, but of the useful men we retain.

But, 'tis heard: 'Larger opportunities, and greater service for our graduates!'

And a land still gaunt in its nakedness?

What mummery! Canada is bigger than the world all else!!

Education procured in the provincial universities of the Dominion should give a man primarily a feeling of responsibility toward his fellow-countrymen. Special training thus bestowed is not intended simply to guerdon, with a well-considered income, a professional career. Equipped largely at public expense, the graduate is a protegé of the people. Nor should it be overlooked that in a land like Canada, a very considerable portion of the funds that build and maintain costly laboratories is rooted in its ultimate sources, back in some form of frontier activity. Dormitories, too, have been erected at chosen centres, to forfend in comfort the college youth, that are in part the product of bunkhouse labour where, meanwhile, the housing of campmen had seemingly been ignored.

The universities, not the tariff, nor the climate, have retarded natural development in Canada. With half-averted looks, they have turned their backs on the problems of the Canadian people. With the exception of the younger institutions of the West, they stand with eyes turned outward on the world. They continue to scan the horizon eastward beyond the Atlantic and in the Orient, but ignore the tasks of the great, bare, and unoccupied heritage at our threshold. Undue concern for other-world adjustments, while neglecting greater deeds at hand. Canada can make no bigger contribution to the world than to subdue the natural forces of her own domain. With these tasks still unattempted, the more pretentious efforts of her universities seeking world recognition in chosen fields are weird and hollow – chilling as the sounds of night when the wolf gives tongue 'mid the tumbled logs of a disused camp.

For, after one hundred years, Canada still finds itself unbuilded, and until very recent years in a state of underdevelopment. Here is lack of vision the guilt for which the college must assume. Confronted throughout its domain with a huge hinterland, much of it workable and livable, that in its gigantic proportions extends over four-fifths of the whole country, the greater is the need that seats of learning in the Dominion give much thought toward the solution of problems pertaining to the frontier. This should be constantly displayed in a continued and rigorous endeavour to dissever the thongs that fetter development. There are problems innate to the conditions: transportation; assisted homesteads; extension north-ward of the wheat-line; sweets from muskeg wastes; harnessed waterways and transmitted power; fuel at a minimum with heating for the old, and wool at hand to clothe in comfort children of the homestead and the settlement; these and kindred quests are of more immediate concern to any university in Canada than some vain attempt to compete in a field of accomplishment with older schools, long situate in populous lands and already safely ensconced in funded wealth and merited traditions.

The schoolman in a land such as Canada may well dwell close to the processes of the frontier. The campus of a university is as broad as the confines of the country itself. The camp on the frontier, not the class room, is the pulse of this Dominion. Then let the colleges make known the empty places of the Dominion, so startling in their magnitudes. Put a map of the Dominion, with the northland heritage set forth in true proportions, on the walls of every lecture room in Canada. Not so potent perhaps as the lion and the unicorn above the judge's seat, but useful nevertheless, and an incentive to students. With the Hudson Bay the great dominating physical feature of the land, give every matriculant an increasing and very real knowledge of the many large lakes and mighty rivers, with all that they import found north of the divides.

It is a national necessity, also, that no body of illiterate adults whether on the frontier or crowded in the city, be left without reasonable means to improve themselves. A well-instructed campman is as much an asset to the country as an educated farmer or a graduate in business subjects from a school of commerce. For in the long run the educated navvy also wins out. His work, when full-fruited, adds to the material wealth of the country. One needs but a slender social philosophy to think this way.

While it is true these days that the universities are eagerly hastening to extend the advantages of higher education to many classes hitherto deprived, yet the efforts, so far, in extension favour those fortunately situated; men and women already partially equipped along academic lines are particularly benefited. The farm, also, is aided directly by short courses prepared for the rural communities. Industrial workers, too, in the large towns and urban centres profit much from their enlarged opportunities. But the sturdy men of the bunkhouse continue largely to be mere dwellers beyond the pale of all university influence.

Better that the universities keep in the lead among the unskilled workers in camps and frontier places. Sober truth may often enough strain hard to catch up with fallacies once given rapid headway. Economic half-truths slip along easily when aided by the impulse from glittering promises of much for nothing. Nowhere is this more evident than among the ranks of the navvy. It was not the fear of absolute want that in 1920 produced such unrest in railway extra-gangs. Wages, then, had reached the highest point ever paid the navvy; most of the men were half a generation removed from the fear of old age. It was but a phase of the unrest that had, in those tense June days, at Winnipeg, shown itself in resentment and violence – a dynamic force among the ill-led which, under proper leadership, would better be expressed in prudence and saving and healthy desire for orderly progression.

Here lies food for thought. The demagogue, actuated by personal spleen or ambition, or, as is sometimes the case, lacking any real understanding of causes and their inevitable effects, comes to the fore. Such leaders are not steadied by knowledge, nor disciplined by hard thought. Zealous and imaginative, they advocate rapid advances along untried paths. The more vociferous their talk the greater is the influence among foreign-born campmen, otherwise sober-minded, but whose hindsight has been untrued by abnormal mental environment. Too long we have denied to the navvy and the bunkhouse man even the barest chance to learn at his work that human institutions grow out of a man's needs and frailties, grooved along the way of compromise; not out of ideals which, as a magic force, will by a turn of the hand alter the animal so latent in us all. The days of manna are passed; there is no longer the never-failing cruse.

There is need. Will graduates of the universities stand aside and allow work-groups in construction camps to be dominated by the agitator and the breeder of unrest? Where is more required the mental stimulus of the trained mind than among the scores of men in a bunkhouse, or with the inmates of a string of cars in an extra-gang on the siding? Men sit nightly in such groups reading with avidity, by the glimmer of a candle stuck in a bottle, or from the light of a borrowed lantern whose cracked globe has been patched with flour and paper, pamphlets and circulars cooked to inflame, not tempered with saneness. Only the influences closest at hand most determine whether there is evolved a Lincoln or a Lenin. Education reared in such a dress may present as hideous a front as religion chiseled solely in the charm of cathedral stones.

The campman will respond to enlarged opportunities. Betterment will result which will be registered in the character and capacity of the frontier worker. Economic salvation is personal, too. Help him shun the bypaths of sudden change and traverse the highway of saner progress. Education is still the sheet anchor of any peaceful commonwealth. Let beaten paths in Canada lead from the chapter houses to the camps.

This the Frontier College has attempted. It brings the man of the university shoulder-up in the ranks with workers on isolated works. It has thus become the clearing-house for students from Canadian and American universities, willing to serve in obscurity as instructors, employed meanwhile at stiff manual work.

In educational effort of this nature much, too, will depend upon the instructor himself. But any student who can handle an axe or other tools of the work-group where he is located soon finds himself on the right side of his foreman, no matter what may be the opinion of the latter as to the need for holding classes. The ability and willingness to partake in the heavy tasks, day in and day out, is sufficient passport also to win the esteem of fellow-workers at any camp.

To be successful such a man must not be clothed in cloistered virtues which droop at the first breath of an unfriendly air. He is not a hothouse plant but an all-weather growth; up in the morning, using basin and soap, he is with the men at luncheon and at work. A particular opportunity is given to him: he starts right in where he is, and does with what he has. He works alongside men who in their outlook on life may not be within one hundred years of his vantage point. His human experience serves to groove the life about him. Can he exploit for general good those differing powers? He is a steadying factor, a rush-light in an obscure corner of the common society to which we all belong. Such work is a common-sense appraisal of human nature. It should be undertaken by one who appreciates the decalogue as well as understands the differential calculus. This is one direct form of challenge from the man of the bunkhouse. It is worthy of fitting response.

And how much even an old land owes to its preceptors. Life in Scotland has long been buttressed by the village dominie – a man, often with honoured attainments at the university, he turns aside from the more lucrative posts to share in a humble way the fuller benefits of his culture with the youth about him in some obscure hamlet. The leavening of such a life who can measure? A counterpart in Canada is he who, similarly prepared for life, shares his knowledge freely with his fellow labourers in an isolated bunkhouse.

Ture, one instructor thus engaged has seemingly little influence. But very definite results are reasonably to be expected from a hundred and more such men, located systematically in the larger camps of the Dominion. It is a reaching-out from the secluded glens of learning to the barren lands of a country's confines, and this means much in the development of a nascent people.

Bursaries, studentships and fellowships are awarded annually by the Federal Government for definite periods of research work. Why are these encouragements to university students restricted so largely to the physical sciences? Violet rays or atomic energy are not the sole concern of the people. Genius can well take care of itself: let there be more concern to dispel the fogs that obscure the nearby lamp-posts. Does not the student at manual work with a railway extra-gang perform, in his practical study of labour, just as real service as a fellow-student of his class, and perhaps with lesser attainments, who, at the same time, fingers a test-tube at Ottawa watching some precipitate in its changing hues?

One uses a pick and shovel from May till October – there is nothing congenial in it, but purpose is there and a sense of duty. About him through the weeks is the chatter of nationals, and his bunk shares space in the car with the workers of the group. The whole atmosphere is that of the environs of Cracow. A strong back is not the only essential required for such experiments. They call for exceptional qualities of both mind and body. Is not an intelligent cross section of a work-group, procured in this way, as important to the whole life of the country as a graph indicating the fluctuations in the steel industry, or a curve showing the development of the export trade? Why not a post course in the back country, bursaries in the study of labour on an isolated work as in the utilization of straw or the forging of metals? Should Commerce and Finance entirely eclipse the Humanities?

Nor need this be any new thing. Let us recall that in the period eighty years since and more, when English navvies first wrought in France, provision was then made by the large employers to have the schoolmaster and the parson accompany the labourers. But this phase, as originally adopted, was allowed to lapse in America, particularly through the half-century of rapid expansion in the frontier places of the United States and Canada.

The campman claims fuller recognition from organized labour in the Dominion. He looks to university men for trained leadership; this constitutes his challenge. Withhold no opportunities for education from the man in the bunkhouse. Unrest is rooted in continued neglect. It is not merely the welfare of the campman that is desired, nor solely the making of a citizen, but the saving of Canada from being stunted in its growth.

Conclusion

The bunkhouse man: his place in the life of the Dominion

CANADA for another hundred years will march by way of the camps. We must look to the frontiers to shape and fashion the life of the Dominion. The hinterland, in an unique way, affords opportunity to display resolution, determination and an unconquerable faith in the national heritage. The continued advance of settlement, combined with the measured development of physical resources, reflects not only a spirit of reliance in the individual, but becomes a permanent element in the life of a people. Material progress in any young nation is proportionate to the size and extent of its frontiers.

It is hard to visualize with a good-sized map just what the word distance means throughout the Dominion when applied to unexplored lands. Whole areas, their treasures in some respects the heritage of the future, and many of them larger than a European kingdom, still remain practically unknown, forbidding often in outward appearance, desolate as Avernus. Yet consider the possibilities when the increasing skill and ingenuity of man have made profitable and even pleasureful habitation in these remoter confines. For climatic conditions will some day be overcome, the barren lands will yield of their resources, and camps and mills creep still northward to the further shores of great inland seas.

'And what,' we ask, 'is Canada?' Is it solely the wooded banks and farms of the mighty St. Lawrence, the fishing ports and fertile valleys of the Maritimes, well sheltered slopes and fruitful portions of the Pacific, or that minor area of favoured land which, like an arrowhead, is thrust downward between the Lakes? If so, then are we but a pent-up Utica, cabined and cribbed in circumference? These portions combined mark but the holdings of a lesser Hapsburg. The Canada that will command recognition lies northward! The resourceful Franklin as he toyed with Oswald to shape in course a nation's bounds, perceived not, that the Laurentian rocks and glacial lakes beyond the Ottawa, stretching by interminable waterways, northward for one thousand miles, would some day prove, with all their latent powers, as productive of wealth as the fertile lands of the Ohio Valley he so jealously guarded. But as yet with the possible exception of some mining districts, and the wheat lands of the prairies, we have not actively entered into the northern heritage. Do we believe in the value of Canada? Is it worth the investment of a life? If so, as well could a grave slab thwart the growth of an oak.

Canada will do things, but they will be rough-handed, due to the spirit of the frontier. Such is her nativity, her tasks inherited of the rocks and woods challenge the weakling, but strengthen the strong. Opportunity is here, but it is cruel to the unfit. Her very climate as a flaming sword guards from softened lives. Whole portions of the Dominion will never have the problems of the long governed and over-crowded lands with castleated towns and leaguered cities where stress and strife are ever present, lurking in social unrest as the wolf that shadows the traps of the hunter.

If sternness confronts us as a people we should glory in the tasks. There is an uniqueness which deserves recognition in frontier activities. Such works are not to be viewed with disfavour. They serve as a relief to man's estate. Our system of free enterprise places a premium upon initiative in these undertakings. Campworks of whatever kind stand on rock bottom. The bunkhouse will still continue to house the intrepid among the workers. Then let the yardstick of our endeavours fail not to encompass their activities.

The camp site on the frontier still delimits material advance in Canada. The man of the bunkhouse is ever found in the vanguard, he occupies the outposts. Trench by trench he assays the ramparts in nature's fastnesses. For the domain of the North rears hardihood, an iron dauntlessness that makes for manhood. It encourages the type of man who matches life in the struggles of the years. Such places have nursed the best in the life of the world.

Few men physically are so splendidly endowed as the workers in frontier camps. They have not only the masculinity that can endure privation, but the courage to confront physical dangers. There is evident, too, an undercurrent, that vital reserve, which in its terseness bears witness to the silent struggles of firm-knit men. Abounding health is theirs with something heaven-sent in their laughter and the freedom of untrammelled ways. But, while massive thighs give pride, let us salvage and join to ourselves as a people, by a fitting display of more real human interest, this mighty resource of sinew and strength – men undaunted, and fitted to bear the grapes of Eshcol.

The labour of the campman is very real. He does not write epics on sheets of paper, nor are his personal achievements recorded in the archives, but he makes of the winds and the snows a playfellow. With his hands he has transformed the woods and the mines. There

be those among them, who by sheer rugged strength and native
hardihood acquit themselves in emergency. The fortitude of men in
arms, dragging of old the cannon, in hollowed trunks of trees, up icy
slopes does not surpass in deed the campman's ability to cope
successfully with sudden obstacle, whether in the long transport of
supplies over broken roads, or the handling of timber on gullied
steeps. Nor is the worker of the camps, employed often in weather
of great severity, rationed on rum, as were the men entrenched
through winter months before Sevastopol.

More than formerly, we need to be acutely alive to the great
company of manly men who toil on frontier works. Spare of speech,
as men who live much to themselves, they have nevertheless that
invincible culture that accompanies primitiveness. Such may not be
phylacteried in comely virtues, nor are they always delicate of
speech, but they dwell close to the verities: these are not beaten men
of a beaten race. A knowledge of this causes one to enter a
bunkhouse humbly.

Not enough study has hitherto been made of life and work in
frontier places. Too long the great hinterland has been but an inset
on the maps. The tasks there performed are for the enhancement of
the whole people. Good camps are most essential. The bunkhouse is
as necessary to Canada as the bungalow. Indeed the building of
camps should be an art throughout the Dominion, a prideful point in
our history as when some centuries removed cathedral building in
Western Europe was the mark of the age.

Canada is indebted to the men of frontier works for the one
distinctive attire of the people. The garb of the campman is
appropriate for the needs of life and work throughout the greater
part of the country. In mackinaw well-clad, with heavy shirt hung
loose, his muscled limbs begirt with socks and pliant packs, the
bunkhouse man with easy stride confronts the sun. Here is clothing
adaptable to a land of seasonal works, indigenous, too, more so than
the professor's hood or the churchman's gown.

Yet these men scarce have claimed their own. Rugged of face, and
big of heart yet sensitive to hurt, furtively they lurk about the
shipping points and railway depots. Half reclined on bench or
platform, idling in groups, they seem intruders in the very towns
they have helped to shape; as though ignored by those whose lives
and labours are but an aftermath of the physical exertions of the
campmen.

Thus far the seasonal workers of the camps have failed to assert themselves. With even but a limited unit allowed for family life, they represent a constituency of half a million – a not inconsiderable factor in the whole life of the Dominion. Meanwhile, there are provinces in the Confederation considerably smaller in population, that are clamorous always in their demands for recognition. But the bunkhouse man, helping to produce, as he does, such a large proportion of the country's wealth, is still unheard and practically ignored.

The handminded, he has been called in derision. But his very restlessness has stirred the imagination: his works give freedom to the mind. Shanty songs again are heard, sung with gusto in well appointed hostelries, but lacking there the crowded bunkhouse in the background, unrelated as the Court of Antoinette to the hovels of the Korponne. In a popular book or a film play, hastily constructed, the campman is depicted as one whose undersense is not without discernment, but whether as a navvy, a bushman, a mine worker or a river driver, it is seldom that the actual worth of his tasks to the country at large is adequately implied. Just as surely as trade in Canada, moving from West and East, follows in fixed channels the routes of those daring spirits of former days, who by canoe and paddle were wont to storm at the gates of adventure, so the very foundations for enlarged material development in the Dominion rest largely upon the work of men in frontier camps. We can point as a people to thousands of miles of railways, to busy mines, and mills and kindred development, all in frontier places. We are proud of these achievements. But what of the human investment – those qualities of endurance, courage, resourcefulness, and even heroism – which are embodied in all such undertakings: Has not humanity the final word in human relations? If we are to maintain ideals of a national character, we can ill afford to subvert the workers of the camps. If the final test of our civilization in Canada be the point below which the weakest and most unfortunate is allowed to fall, it must apply equally to the bunkhouse men. What is the real value of their contributions unless justice and human consideration duly influence their conditions of work and pay?

The campman is a national asset. The very nature of his tasks stamps manhood on his frame. Given as good housing conditions and equal opportunities for social improvement, he would naturally constitute a stable and contented class among the workers of the

Dominion. And in emergency he has demonstrated his worth to the Country. In those immortal days, when in October, 1914, there sailed from Valcartier the first armada from this Western world to engage in the conflicts of Europe, the bunkhouse men, in more than proportionate numbers, thronged among the bronzed faces on the decks.

For Canada still thrills to the romance of the pioneer. Endowed with prodigal gifts, her natural resources, in spite of adverse isothermic lines, are unsurpassed except in coal and tillable land even by those of the United States; while her habitable area is one-third that of her neighbour. Canada with but ten million people, stands to-day in proportionate development where was the Great Republic in the years of readjustment following the Civil War. The people of the Dominion have never failed in optimism. They build on the last great frontier in America; than this land there is no farther West. Not in vulgar figures do we estimate the future. The mines and open spaces will call her sons to the great joy of conquest. Will Opportunity find us a puny people?

Then let the Dominion scan carefully conditions of work and pay, in every avenue of its life. Thus in the activities of the hinterland the employer and the man of the bunkhouse are alike considered. For even apparent progress may be obtained by the surrender of elements which make for truer solidarity.

Appendices

APPENDIX A

Tonnage passing through the Erie and the Welland canals, 1840-49

Year	Total tonnage Erie Canal	Total tonnage Welland Canal	Per cent of total
1840	830,000		
1841	905,000	277,144	30.6
1842	710,000	304,983	42.9
1843	820,000	224,408	27.3
1844	945,000	327,570	34.5
1847	1,660,000	255,836	15.4
1848	1,600,000	246,328	15.3
1849	1,620,000	265,326	16.3

APPENDIX B

Immigration to the Dominion, 1903-14

Year	From U.K.	From U.S.	From other countries	Total
1903	41,792	49,473	37,099	128,364
1904	50,374	45,171	34,786	130,331
1905	65,359	43,543	37,364	146,266
1906	86,796	57,796	44,472	189,064
1907	55,791	34,659	34,217	124,667
1908	120,182	58,312	83,975	262,469
1909	52,901	59,832	34,175	146,908
1910	59,790	103,798	45,206	208,794
1911	123,013	121,451	66,620	311,084
1912	138,121	133,710	82,406	354,237
1913	150,542	139,009	112,881	402,432
1914	142,622	107,530	134,726	384,878
Total for 12 years	1,087,283	954,284	747,927	2,789,494

From *Canada Year Book, 1914*, p. 85.

APPENDIX C

Nature and total amount of outside investments in Canada, 1926

A Nature of investment	U.S.A. Capital	U.K. Capital	Other outside capital
Public securities	$879,000,000	$437,000,000	$ 5,000,000
Railways	435,000,000	951,000,000	35,000,000
Industries:			
Forestry	425,000,000	70,000,000	25,000,000
Mining	300,000,000	110,000,000	25,000,000
Fisheries	7,000,000	30,000,000	10,000,000
Public services	200,000,000	125,000,000	30,000,000
Other industries	625,000,000	160,000,000	10,000,000
Land and mortgages	100,000,000	165,000,000	50,000,000
Banking and insurance	45,000,000	90,000,000	12,000,000
Total	$3,016,000,000	$2,138,000,000	$202,000,000
Grand total	$5,356,000,000		

(Meanwhile, Canadian investments abroad are estimated at $714,651,000)

Comparative statement showing the increase in loans since 1913

B Source of loans	1913	1923	1926
Great Britain	$1,860,000,000	$1,995,000,000	$2,111,000,000
United States	417,143,220	2,475,500,000	3,016,000,000
Other outside sources	139,589,650	323,000,000	183,000,000
Total	$2,416,732,870	$4,796,500,000	$5,310,000,000

Reference: *Monetary Times of Canada,* Year Book, 1927.

A 'In 1924-25-26 half a billion dollars of American, British, and other outside capital has come to Canada to be invested in the development of our natural resources, and in the extension of the economic superstructure of the country – its railways, public services, etc. This has brought the total investment of outside capital in the Dominion to over five billion dollars, a large amount, but not to be regarded as dangerously out of proportion to our total national wealth, estimated and probably exceeding twenty-five billions at the present time.' *Financial Post,* Survey 1927, p. 247.

B 'According to our records there has been invested since 1915 in the hydro-electric industry of Canada approximately $450,000,000. In the mining industry there has been invested about $420,000,000, and in pulp and paper and other forestry industry about $325,000,000.

'There is no exact information to indicate how much of this was American capital, how much British and how much Canadian capital, but from our studies of the trend of capital flow in these industries, we would assume that about 50 per cent of these sums have represented Canadian capital, about 35 per cent American capital and about 15 per cent British capital.' Editor, *Financial Post,* March 4th, 1927.

APPENDIX D

The bar-diagram subjoined shows the various nationals commonly found on frontier works in Canada. This information, based on different seasonal works and relating to approximately 18,600 bunkhouse men, was obtained at 81 points during the years 1923-26, inclusive. While the proportions vary in different localities, the general picture shown is accurate.

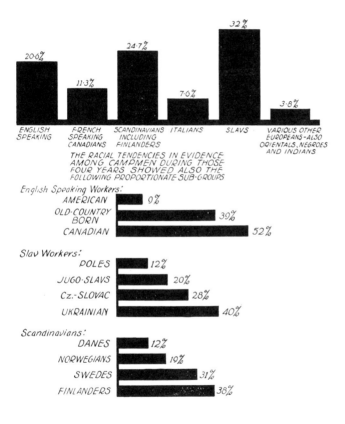